OPEN SPACES

OPEN SPACES

VOICES FROM THE NORTHWEST

Edited by Penny Harrison

UNIVERSITY OF WASHINGTON PRESS

Seattle and London

UNIVERSITY OF WASHINGTON PRESS
PO Box 50096, Seattle, WA 98145, USA
www.washington.edu/uwpress

"What Is This Thing Called Love" from *Wake Up and Dream*.
Words and music by Cole Porter. Spanish version by Johnnie
Comacho. ©1929 (renewed) WB Music Corp. All Rights Reserved.

"Fire and Water," *The Pine Island Paradox*, Kathleen Dean Moore, 2004.
Reprinted with permission from Milkweed editions.

"A Slight Sound at Evening" © 1954, reprinted with permission
from ICM and Martha White.

LIBRARY OF CONGRESS CATALOGING-IN-PUBLICATION DATA
Open spaces : voices from the Northwest / edited by Penny Harrison.
    p. cm.
Includes bibliographical references and index.
ISBN 978-0-295-99107-8 (pbk. : acid-free paper)
1. American literature—Northwest, Pacific.
2. Northwest, Pacific—Literary collections.
I. Harrison, Penny
PS570.O64 2011
810.8'036—dc22   2011004810

COVER ILLUSTRATION: Michael Brophy, *The Sunset Photographed*, 2005.
Oil on canvas, 56 × 44 in. Courtesy of the artist and G. Gibson Gallery, Seattle

Frontispiece and scattered illustrations by Kurt D. Hollomon

To my husband, Marvin, and to our children,

John and Rebecca, without whose ideas and inspiration

this project would not have been possible.

Contents

PART IV: HOW DO WE USE WHAT WE KNOW?

FOREWORD

Denis Hayes

WAVES of human migration have been spurred by agriculture, gold, furs, wood, a lust for freedom, or simply a search for safety and stability. All of these have played a role in populating Cascadia—the green, progressive, well-educated northwest corner of the United States and the southwest corner of Canada. However, the most important migration in today's globalized, mobile, wired world is arguably the movement of smart people to wherever they want to live. That is the most important growth factor in Cascadia today. Washington, Oregon, and British Columbia are at or near the top of every list of places where creative, ambitious, world-changing people want to live.

Why?

Whether climbing Mount Rainier, rafting the Snake through Hells Canyon, hiking the Olympic Peninsula, skiing Whistler, windsurfing at Hood River, sailing the San Juan Islands, or scuba diving with the giant but timid octopi in Puget Sound, people who want experiences to remember will find them in Cascadia. The author of Microsoft Excel, for example, can be found most summer weekends at his paragliding school on the dry side of the central Cascades, and a world-renowned pioneer in systems biology spends every leisure moment scaling difficult peaks and exploring remote realms.

With less then one-eighth of one percent of the global population, Seattle and Portland are home to Microsoft, Nike, Amazon, Boeing, Starbucks, and Costco. Most residents might not even recognize the name Paccar, but the $15 billion company makes Kenworth and Peterbilt trucks—possibly the most efficient "smart trucks" in the world. Less surprisingly, Cascadia hosts REI, Columbia Sportswear, K2, many of the nation's most distinguished green architecture firms, "smart grid" pioneers, and America's largest marine and fisheries sector. In fact, Washington's fish exports are larger, by weight and value, than those of the other forty-nine states combined. And, of course, the nation's largest forestry firms are located here.

With nearly two dozen live theaters, Seattle has the most creative environment for drama in the United States outside of New York. The paintings of Jacob Lawrence, the photography of Art Wolfe, and the glass works of Dale Chihuly have all enriched the region and the world.

In 1937, seventeen-year-old Ray Charles traveled to Seattle to launch his solo musical career, and he soon met and befriended fourteen-year-old Quincy Jones. Popular music was changed forever. Bing Crosby, Jimi Hendrix, Ernestine Anderson, Kurt Cobain, and Eddie Vedder all hailed from Cascadia. Paul Revere & the Raiders and the Kingsmen recorded their dueling versions of "Louie Louie" in the same Portland studio (across the street from Powell's Bookstore) at almost the same time.

Powell's and Elliott Bay are probably the most highly regarded independent bookstores in the nation, and Amazon is the leading electronic book purveyor in the world. Seattle has the largest percentage of library cardholders in America, and its residents spend twice the national average on books each year.

Cascadia is home to six world-class research universities and numerous superb colleges. Its crown jewel—the University of Washington—draws more federal research dollars than any other public university in the country. The region has also become an unrivaled global hub for health sciences. The Fred Hutchinson Cancer Research Center, the Institute for Systems Biology, the Infectious Disease Research Center, the Allen Brain Research Center, and Amgen's Helix Campus are all working at the very frontiers of knowledge.

Oregon and Washington have a tradition of bold legislation. They have led the nation in establishing urban growth boundaries, keeping ocean beaches open to the public, implementing America's first compulsory curbside recycling laws, being the first to rationally prioritize health care benefits, and granting people the right to compassionate end-of-life options.

Cascadia has always had an abundance of colorful characters, from idealistic Wobbly activist Joe Hill to Teamster thug Dave Beck to business titans like Bill Gates and Bill Boeing to the state's first female governor, Dixy Lee Ray. The region boasts the world's largest charitable foundation and a wide array of innovative philanthropies. It also contains three of the greenest cities in the world and some of the most enchanting islands.

When artists, entrepreneurs, and agents of social change cluster, they look for forums where they can interact and be challenged and provoked. In Cascadia, *Open Spaces* magazine plays this role. It is where thoughtful people publish essays that push readers to think outside their comfort zones.

Open Spaces is edited for critical thinkers, and this volume contains articles culled and updated from some of the magazine's best and most provocative authors. This collection will almost certainly provide you with facts and reasoning you haven't encountered before, but *Open Spaces* is not ideologically right or left. The object of this collection is not necessarily to convince you of any particular agenda, but to make you think.

Enjoy! ◙

Acknowledgments

THE articles and essays collected in this anthology have been selected from *Open Spaces* magazine, a collaborative project benefiting greatly from the active participation of many people. Working with these talented and thoughtful artists, writers, editors, board members and advisors—all good friends who have made contributions to the community far beyond this project—has been inspiring and the greatest pleasure of this endeavor.

Open Spaces magazine began with an enthusiastic response to the concept that became the magazine from Barbara Walker, Ronald S. Grossmann, Lynn Spruill, and Julie Mancini. Their encouragement and advice set us on our way. The energy, ideas, insights, and intelligence of the *Open Spaces* editors have kept the project going, maintained its quality, and made it fun. I can never sufficiently thank them for their many contributions—from the essays and articles they have discovered, written, and edited to Jo Grossmann's selection of the magazine's striking covers, which express its spirit so well.

OPEN SPACES EDITORS

Gretchen Brevig
Susan Bucharest
Marlys Chapman
Elizabeth Cosgriff

Jo Grossmann
Rebecca Harrison
Maura O'Scannlain
Ellen Teicher

Special thanks are due to the *Open Spaces* board for contributing the richness of their life experiences to developing much of the substantive content in *Open Spaces* magazine. With exceptional achievements in their various pursuits, their contributions to the quality of the publication are immeasurable.

OPEN SPACES BOARD

Tom Allison
Emory Bundy
Tom Corddry
Suzanne Hartman
Dale Hess
Michael Huston
Harry Kingston
James Knoll
Kathleen Murphy
Maura O'Scannlain
Robert Sack
David Savage
Edward Sheets
Pat Soden
Bob Williams

For making *Open Spaces* beautiful by integrating art with the writing and for making my work immeasurably easier, I am especially appreciative of the magazine's art director, Amy Chan. For generously sharing their expertise and educating us all in the process, I thank David Moldal, Brian Gard, David Brewster, Clyde Van Cleve, Stimson Bullitt, and John Harrison, Special Agent. For their friendship and encouragement, I thank Carole Alexander and Sonja Connor.

For contributing significantly to the spirit and content of *Open Spaces* through their art and writing—work that would have been included in this anthology had its subject matter not been beyond the theme pursued in this collection—I sincerely thank artists Deborah DeWit, Michael Durham, Sarah Jane Lapp, Matt Wuerker, Larry N. Olson, Gary Buhler, Alice Wanke Stephens, and Terry Toedtemeier and writers Rick Bass, Steve Blakeslee, David Brewster, Maria Cantwell, Daniel Jack Chasan, Tracy Daugherty, Steve Davis, Bob Dietsche, John Esler, William Faries, Charles Goodrich, Debra Gwartney, Melissa Hart, Lyanda Haupt, Mike Houck, Jay Inslee, Clay S. Jenkinson, Daniel Kemmis, Michael Kiparsky, John A. Kitzhaber, Judith Kleinfeld, Amy Kober, Jim Lichatowich, Lydia Pallas Loren, David B. Marshall, Bruce Mate, Tom McAllister, John C. McAnulty, Stephen S. McConnel, Robert S. McKelvey, Richard J. Mullins, Theodore Roosevelt IV, Gerry Stroh O'Scannlain, Betsy Otto, George R. Packard, John Santa, Jeffrey D. Sachs, David Sarasohn, Shelby Scates, Robin Schauffler, Ethan Seltzer, Floyd Skloot, Ana Maria Spagna, Ted Strong, Robert Sullivan, Ronald Turker, Rich Wandschneider, Mary Wood, Christopher Zinn, and puzzle maker Matt Jones.

Finally, I am deeply grateful for the enthusiastic encouragement and commitment of Executive Director Pat Soden, for the professional judgment and guidance of Editor Marianne Keddington-Lang, and for the talented and dedicated staff of the University of Washington Press for publishing the *Open Spaces Anthology* so that the history, insights, and creative solutions of the included works will continue to inform and inspire. ◙

GROUNDTRUTHING

AN INTRODUCTION

Penny Harrison

A CHILD standing on the shore of Spirit Lake in southern Washington scooped up a handful of grayish white pebbles and held it out to her mother with a question. "Pumice," her mother answered. "A very long time ago . . ."

A few months later, Mount St. Helens, the volcano that stands above Spirit Lake and has been known to native peoples for millennia as the maiden Loo-wit, exploded. Rivers flooded, homes were destroyed; people too close to get away perished. Spirit Lake was filled with debris. Northwesterners watched in awe and with concern as huge clouds of ash billowed forth, dusting the ground from the rhododendrons of the Willamette Valley to the aspens of Billings, Montana, before continuing on air currents around the world. They worried about the effect on the soil. Some put on surgical masks to protect themselves and their children from pollution. Then, almost as quickly as it had begun, the mountain quieted, the sky cleared, and volcanic ash was eventually found to enrich the soil.

We who make our homes in the Pacific Northwest on the edge of faults feel our susceptibility to the forces of nature just as we are stirred by the beauty those forces create. We only half smile at historian Will Durant's observation that "Civilization exists by geologic consent, subject to change without notice."

While acknowledging these uncertainties, *Open Spaces* magazine focuses on the significant impacts we can have on our environment and the quality of our lives. The magazine attracts accomplished authors who contribute to *Open Spaces* because it provides a place to present their thoughts in depth and in context, unhindered by preconceived agendas. They know that their work is read by an educated, active, and productive audience whose influence extends across many disciplines.

Sharing expertise is particularly crucial at this time, when it is becoming difficult for us to determine what it is we really know. Information is fragmented into headlines and online news bites where we have traded depth of understanding for speed of transmission. As a nation our neglect of history provides little context to help us distinguish between insight and the bluster of self-promoters who obscure events and fabricate scenarios. Meanwhile, niche concerns and identity politics polarize discussions so that problem solving becomes impossible. Conflict is good entertainment, and entertainment sells. Serious people, however, know that all positions are not equally valid. *Open Spaces* offers a forum for these people who seek credible information and educated opinion.

The editorial board of *Open Spaces* meets around a dining room table with cups of full-bodied coffee close at hand. Bookshelves share the walls with images of owls and bears depicted in the strong red and black strokes of Native American artists and a painting of the sunlit fields of the Willamette Valley by Robert Weller. While we are far in time and place from the Algonquin Round Table in Manhattan, where Harold Ross, founder of *The New Yorker*, met with the literary luminaries of his day, we feel a kinship with his belief that a magazine should "assume a reasonable degree of enlightenment on the part of its readers. It will hate bunk."

Before coming together around our table, each of us on the editorial board of *Open Spaces* spent years in our respective specialties of medicine, law, politics, art, business, education, scientific research, community volunteerism, academia, and international affairs. Our purpose was twofold: provide readers with in-depth, contextualized discussions of current issues by experts in various fields and reflect the unique vision provided by our sense of place. As home ground and inspiration for *Open Spaces*, the Pacific Northwest is a source of independence and initiative. By creating a voice outside of the echo chamber filling the airways, we put forth fresh perspectives and insights that contribute to a broader vision and encourage an activist energy leading to innovations in a wide array of fields, from computer technology to land use planning, from health care to music, from salmon management to storytelling, from mountaineering to marine reserves. Although the issues it explores are national and international in scope, *Open Spaces* is a creation of the Pacific Northwest. It reflects a state of mind as well as a geographic entity, a place where one can live a full and meaningful life within the larger framework of the natural world.

Here in the Northwest our habitat extends from the rocky cliffs of the Pacific Ocean to patches of the cedar, alder, and Douglas fir of the Cascades, through farmland spread over rolling hills, down carved gorges of inland waterways, past old-growth forests and glaciated peaks on mountain passes built over black, hardened lava, through the wheat fields of the Palouse in eastern Washington, and to the expanses of sagebrush and juniper of Oregon's high desert. Outside of the bustling cities of Seattle and Portland, population is sparse; wilderness and isolation, solace and a sense of awe are never far away. More than fleeces and lattes, the open spaces of the Pacific Northwest define us, inspire us, comfort us, and bring us together. We are of this place where we choose to spend our lives.

Coming to the West has long been a matter of choice and inspiration. It has given people one more chance to do things right. In his essay "Walking," published in the *Atlantic Monthly* in 1862, Henry David Thoreau wrote that in choosing a direction for his daily saunters, he invariably ended up traveling toward the West:

> The future lies that way to me, and the earth seems more unexhausted
> and richer on that side. Eastward I go only by force; but westward I
> go free. . . . I believe that the forest which I see in the western horizon
> stretches uninterruptedly toward the setting sun, and there are no towns
> nor cities in it of enough consequence to disturb me. Let me live where I
> will, on this side is the city, on that the wilderness, and ever I am leaving
> the city more and more, and withdrawing into the wilderness. I should
> not lay so much stress on this fact, if I did not believe that something like
> this is the prevailing tendency of my countrymen. I must walk toward
> Oregon, and not toward Europe. And that way the nation is moving, and
> I may say that mankind progress from east to west.

There is a distinct advantage in being at the western edge of North America. Travelers learn lessons as they move from east to west. As they pass through miles of suburban sprawl, abandoned mines, and the devastated habitats of species in decline, they vow not to repeat mistakes. They set to work trying to think things through, to look to the long-term results of short-term schemes, to gather all information available, and to plan so that they can create communities that fit within the realities of the natural world.

In the Pacific Northwest, nature is ever present. Stand in the middle of downtown Seattle, and Puget Sound is at your feet. Look up, and Mount Rainier and the Olympics spread out across the horizon. Head south of Seattle to Portland where the Columbia and Willamette rivers, Mount Hood and Mount St. Helens all keep the city in its place, reminding the inhabitants of the smell of pine, the crunch of snow, and the respite of solitude.

In his book, *Of Men and Mountains,* U.S. Supreme Court Justice William O. Douglas wrote that his memory of the mountains sustained him during his long tenure in the East. In dull moments in the courtroom, he would take himself back in his mind to the Northwest. One day after court, a friend asked Douglas what he was thinking, having noted a far-off look in his eyes. Douglas told him he "had been after trout in the Big Klickitat of the Cascade Mountains in eastern Washington," not far from his hometown of Yakima, and he assured him that he had had "wonderful luck." Justice Douglas worried for those who had not experienced the wilderness in which he had grown up:

> Perhaps man was losing his freedom in a subtle manner. He was becoming more and more dependent on other men . . . for his entertainment and for his ideas. He looked to people rather than to himself and to the earth for his salvation. He fixed his expectations on the frowns or smiles or words of men, not on the strength of his own soul, or the sunrise, or the warming south wind, or the song of the warbler.

In earth science, the term "ground truthing" is used as a shorthand for the process of ensuring the accuracy of data collected at a distance (e.g., by remote sensing, aerial photography, satellite imagery, etc.) and the tentative conclusions based on that data by gathering actual data from the ground that may confirm, complement, or dispute those conclusions. In the vernacular, ground truthing has come to mean a process by which we observe things up close and test objectively what we call reality. As such, it not only applies to science, but can also be used to test our assumptions, beliefs, judgments, and the trajectories of our lives.

The writers in this collection have spent their lives "ground truthing" through both scientific inquiry and personal experience. Such an approach is an absolute necessity in planning realistically for the future. As historian William Cronon tells us in his essay on "The Uses of Environmental History," there is ample evidence that "the natural world exists quite apart from what we believe about it, that it powerfully affects the course of human history, and that if our beliefs diverge too far from its realities, we will eventually suffer as much as it will."

History is replete with examples. Particularly apt to issues covered in this anthology is the story told by Wallace Stegner in *Beyond the Hundredth Meridian*. Stegner's book chronicles the life and work of Major John Wesley Powell (1834–1902), soldier, explorer, second director of the U.S. Geological Survey, and author of the *Report on the Lands of the Arid Regions of the United States*. Among his many roles, Powell was a "dust-on-the-boots" field geologist who conducted surveys of the West in the 1870s. After evaluating conditions, he proposed policies for developing the arid West that would preserve the waters and irrigable lands. Powell's observations led him to believe that only the approximately 2 percent of land near water sources was suitable for agricultural development. As for the rest, he proposed conservation and low-density grazing. He also proposed irrigation systems and state boundaries based on watersheds to reduce conflict.

But boosters for growing settlements, local business interests, and railroad companies with vast tracts of land lobbied Congress hard to encourage farmers to develop those lands. Horace Greeley, publisher of the *New York Herald Tribune*, roused people with his exhortation to "Go west, young man" and spread the popular but mistaken theory that "the rain follows the plow." Powell's observations were largely ignored until insufficient water produced the Dust Bowl of the 1930s, bringing suffering and failure to pioneer subsistence farms. The settlers understood what Powell had seen and reported half a century before: land is of no value without water, and rainfall in the arid West is either seasonal or nonexistent. It was tragic, but it was predictable.

Stegner illustrates what can result when ground truthing observations are overrun by rhetoric, and expertise goes unheeded. Today we have our own stories and face our own dangers. We can spare ourselves some of the hard lessons of the past by heeding those who have done their own ground truthing, such as the contributing authors of this book.

It is late August in the Wallowa Mountains of northeastern Oregon. The car door slams as each member of the family shoulders a pack and steps into the dark, cool forest. It takes but a moment for the group to find its pace. As they walk along, a mountain stream rushes by, filled with run-off from an evening thunderstorm. Farther up the trail the water is gray with glacial melt. It is late afternoon when they reach their campsite in the cirque at the top of the trail; they are alone amidst the ring of mountains surrounding a sparkling alpine lake.

All their senses are awakened now, attuned to the natural world into which they have entered. Deer, elk, or even a bear may wander through. The weather may change and fill the air with thunder and lightening. But tonight the stars spread out across the sky. Peace descends.

Living amidst both unpredictability and grandeur fosters a keen awareness of our place in a long continuum. It pushes us to transcend the insularity of our individual histories and prejudices. We reach out to a larger world, both natural and human, and are moved to preserve the beauty and harmony we find there as best we can.

As the content of this anthology reveals, this reaching out is no small thing. It requires energy and insight. It requires thought and work to move beyond ourselves, to define the issues of our time in the context of history, geography, and community, and to plan for the future. It requires us to test assumptions and values and to keep in check the excesses of our egos. But in so doing we will discover pathways to those parts of our human nature and our habitat that bind us together and help us turn old problems into new opportunities.

The authors of this anthology, whether creators of art or policy or both, clear pathways that facilitate reaching out. *Open Spaces: Voices from the Northwest* is a collection of nonfiction, fiction, and poetry by just a few of the magazine's many skilled and knowledgeable writers and thinkers. Collectively, these authors have special currency today, when fresh energy and imminent need provide opportunities to move in new directions. Individually, their work touches our deepest sense of human experience and continuity in an exceptionally beautiful and challenging world.

The articles, essays, stories, and poems in this anthology were selected to evoke multiple aspects of the special character of life in the Pacific Northwest seen through the eyes of some of our finest writers. As William Kittredge observes in his essay on the Klamath Basin, "Other visions will no doubt be presented in other ways. Over time, built stone by stone like a rock fence, we hope, a more complete and socially useful vision will accumulate." We don't know precisely what that vision will be, but we do have a hint as to its character. As John Daniel writes, "Northwestern landscapes, weathers, and wild communities involve themselves in what we write not merely as backdrop or setting but as imaginal matrix, the very stuff of human life and longing. . . . How could we live among Pacific salmon and old-growth forests and fail to be hopeful? We aren't much given to irony or alienation. We're given to the possibility of redemption."

We in the Northwest are inspired in our perceptions and actions by the majesty that surrounds us. The writing collected in this anthology celebrates that majesty and at the same time reveals the attempts of many thoughtful and energetic people to get to work and take up Wallace Stegner's challenge to "create a society to match the scenery." It is my hope that these articles and stories can provide generations to come with a context for current and future concerns so that they can see the importance of their own contributions to moving forward with knowledge, understanding, and inspiration.

It is summer in the Pacific Northwest. The blackberry bushes have shed their spring flowers, leaving in their stead the fragrant fruit that calls a three-year-old boy down the path his father has cleared. But he hesitates a moment before diving in, and surveys the pattern of the branches covered in thorns, searching, as his mother taught him, for an opening. Then, ever so carefully, he twists his hand through the thicket and plucks two fat, shiny blackberries. The sweetness of the berries fills his mouth, and he smiles as the juice runs down his chin. He has overcome the perils to grasp the possibilities; he is learning to use what he knows. ▣

OPEN SPACES

I

WHAT IS IT ABOUT
THE PACIFIC NORTHWEST?

Others . . . can of course also be responsive to where they find themselves:—
artists have to be. That's the ground for their art, the place where they live.
—William Stafford, *My Name Is William Tell*

Writing West

John Daniel

A R E there characteristics that distinguish Northwestern writing from the literature of other regions? To answer is to generalize, and to generalize is to overcook the soup, but I would respond with a qualified yes. The roster of Northwest writers is long and varied, but many of us within that variety tend to invite the influence of natural places and processes into our work. Northwestern landscapes, weathers, and wild communities involve themselves in what we write not merely as backdrop or setting but as imaginal matrix, the very stuff of human life and longing. As a consequence, despite the environmental damage in which all of us are implicated, I'd say we are hopeful writers. How could we live among Pacific salmon and old-growth forests and fail to be hopeful? We aren't much given to irony or alienation. We're given to the possibility of redemption.

These qualities are of course not strictly Northwestern or even Western, but—at present, at least—I would argue that they are more Western than Eastern, and it is partly because wild nature infuses our work that Western writing is sometimes deprecated in the East as "regional" in a euphemistic sense, meaning local color, work of limited value and influence. Norman Maclean had a world of trouble trying to publish *A River Runs through It*, because, in the words of one editor, "These stories have trees in them." Our great nature poet, Theodore Roethke, though a more interesting artist, remains in the shadow of his confessional Eastern contemporary, Robert Lowell. Even a writer of Wallace Stegner's stature suffered slights both great and small from the literary brokers of New York. Reviewers and critics reflexively called him "the dean of Western writers"; they never announced who held the deanship of Eastern writers.

East-West regionalism, though, is only one dimension of the dispute. Avatars of high culture have long disparaged writers whose work is bound up with *any* locality. It was this snobbery in T.S. Eliot that dismissed William Carlos Williams as a poet "of some local interest, perhaps." Eliot thought art must seek the universal by sterilizing itself of the personal, the particular, the immediate. Williams believed that it was only through an intense imagining of the ordinary particulars of his town and countryside, and his life as part of them, that he could approach the universal.

Williams's poems persist, tenacious as dandelions. So will the work of William Stafford, who endured some of the same condescension from the muckamucks of high art. Stafford was open to anything a natural place or human encounter could teach him, and so his two principal landscapes, the Great Plains and the Pacific Northwest, are persistently evident in his work. His imagination naturalized both and made of them a world in which any reader was welcome. Alertness was all he asked, and maybe it's a kind of transpersonal alertness that characterizes our literature at its best. We try to attend not to our personal pains and ecstasies alone but also to the greater memberships we belong to, memberships that William Stafford had in mind as he weighed what to do with a dead doe on a mountain roadside, the body warm with an unborn fawn and a danger to human motorists. "Around our group I could hear the wilderness listen," he wrote. "I thought hard for us all. . . . "

One hazard of this orientation is piousness about the natural world, and some of us do fall too frequently into a default tone that Kim Stafford has aptly tagged "the first-person rhapsodic." A second hazard, to which anyone who writes of his own region is prone, is defensiveness. Many Western writers carry a chip on the shoulder (you may have sensed one in this essay) about the attention or inattention paid us by the greater literary culture. This attitude, sadly, is itself more injurious than any slings or silence from New York. Defensiveness is never fertile. Stegner and Stafford and Roethke and Maclean showed us the answer. The only reply to regional bias, finally, is to write well enough and long enough to overcome it.

And besides, the greater culture is coming to us. More and more western writers are winning at least a modest national audience, some of them through East Coast publishers, others with one or another of the vigorous small and mid-size presses—for-profit, nonprofit, and university—that have established themselves on the West Coast and in the interior West as well. The number of agents headquartered in western cities has probably quadrupled in the last twenty years. And new or resurgent literary and general-readership magazines, some of them regionally based, seem to be blossoming all the time.

J. Hector St. John de Crèvecoeur, a Frenchman farmer in the newly born United States, asked two hundred years ago, "Who is the American, this new man?" Wallace Stegner, in his "Wilderness Letter," offered an answer: "A civilized man who has renewed himself in the wild." By "wild" he meant both wilderness and the quality of wildness, the presence in our lives of Nature's original energy. Henry David Thoreau, in one of his most famous utterances, gave a directional definition to that presence: "The West of which I speak is but another name for the Wild; and what I have been preparing to say is, that in Wildness is the preservation of the world."

Thoreau's Wild West is a state of spirit more than geography, native to all the American land. For some of us it flourishes best in the mountains, rivers, and lonesome reaches of the West, but readers everywhere are hungry for the wild, hungry for imaginings in language of how we belong or could belong to the living land. "There was need of America," Thoreau wrote, referring to the tame listlessness of European literatures, and just as the cultures of Europe renewed themselves in the American East, the East is now looking west for its own renewal. It may remain the home of our cultural capitals, but more and more the East is turning in our direction to drink from the wild perennial springs of vitality and hope. ◙

Otey Island

William Kittredge

PINTAILS and mallards and teal, in their quick undulating vee-shaped flights, were everywhere in the twilight, wheeling and calling, setting their wings, settling. I was with Tupper Blake, at the little property he calls March Island Ranch, looking out over the Lower Klamath Wildlife Refuge, and I was happy like a child.

Only a week or so before, Jim Hainline, the head biologist at the Klamath National Wildlife Refuges, had flown the wetlands in the basin, and counted about 3.7 million waterbirds, some 525,000 mallards, slightly over 700,000 green-winged teals, and 772,000 pintail ducks.

Those were big numbers, way up from the annual fall count in recent years. But in 1955 some 7 million birds had been counted. Maybe the seemingly irreversible decline in the numbers of waterfowl using the refuges had stopped. Maybe the efforts of preservationists like Jim Hainline were beginning to pay off. Maybe the flyway was coming back.

The actual birds, some small portion of them, flying in the sky before us, were like confronting a sight of infinity, the earth, our only habitation, thronging with life.

Not long ago I heard a man point out that the lives of most citizens in the partway mechanical world we've invented for ourselves in recent centuries can be thought of as semi-denuded. Only in the last one hundred years has it been uncommon for people to witness great wildlife spectacles.

My great grandfather saw millions of passenger pigeons darken the sun over the forests of Kentucky. The last passenger pigeon died in 1912 in the Cincinnati Zoo. My great grandfather also traveled the Great Plains in the 1850s and saw buffalo in thousands moving over the sand hills of Nebraska. The great herds flowed over the grasslands like the wind or waves on the sea. They were ordinary. Now they are gone.

Salmon thronged in rivers like the Klamath. We're a hunting creature, evolved to revere such sights. The sight of so much life lights up our minds with visions of luck, and possibility, success.

But there's more to it. Sacred, to me, means that which I will not consent to do without. Those birds in their multitudes, there in the twilight sky over Lower Klamath, are to me sacred. The sight of them convinces me that I participate in a flow of meaningful energies, that I am thus meaningful. It's a solacing notion, derived from witnessing life. It's about as religious as I get.

Tupper Ansel Blake is a professional wildlife photographer, and I am a writer. We had parked at the foot of Otey Butte, a volcanic extrusion on his property, just on the California side of State Line Road, and climbed the couple of hundred feet to the top. We were there to begin work on a joint book about watershed problems in the Klamath Basin. It was our job, as I understand the social responsibilities of writers and other artists, to see as accurately as we could, and to pass on what we'd seen to others in ways that might lead them to see as we saw. I was obliged to depict the flying waterbirds in ways which would lead others to not simply understand but to participate in my feelings about them.

On Otey Island, in turn-of-the-century homestead days, there had been an artesian well on the little flat at the top, and a small orchard. We stepped over the remains of old rockwork fences, laid up when the butte was an island in a sea of tule marshes, reachable only by boat. Life for the men and women who settled there must have been defined by hard work, and by sweat, and more work. And by dreams.

Northeast of the marshlands preserved by the Waterfowl Refuge are thousands of acres of ordered, irrigated, and drained farmlands. Beyond the agricultural lands are dry hills, which look much as they have for millennia. Beyond them lie a thousand miles of mostly unbroken Great Basin deserts.

Tupper came up from California, and spent time and effort and money in order to turn his property around Otey Butte, second-rate farmland when he bought it, back into swamps, for the waterbirds.

When local farmers saw equipment cutting imitation sloughs through the fields which had once been laboriously drained, Tupper told them to think of him as the first local "Duckaroo." A lame joke, but the independent spirit that went with it seems to have won them over. Tupper's neighbors treat him with respect.

Maybe he's crazy, the thinking sort of went, but he loves the birds, and he's lucky, and able to indulge his passion. Anybody would love the birds. "It's like looking out over the ocean," Tupper said, as we stood at the top of Otey Butte. Thousands of birds were flying.

"More animal hearts," he said, "than human hearts." Maybe he's not so crazy. But, then, he's not trying to make a living off farmland in the basin.

Tupper Blake and I make our livings as witnesses. Out there on Otey Butte, feeding on the natural glories, we were like tourists. We could, if we were not careful, allow ourselves to honor only our private inclination to regard the birds as sacred. But there are many versions of what's most useful.

So we'll try to honor and respect other versions of what's going on in the Klamath Basin. But we're only ultimately responsible for presenting our own vision. Other visions will no doubt be presented in other ways. Over time, built stone by stone like a rock fence, we hope, a more complete and socially useful vision will accumulate.

Tupper and I will have tried to do what we can, as artists; we will have honored our responsibility; society in its ways will come to an evolving notion of how to proceed. If we're true to ourselves we will have attempted being useful in the only way, as citizens trying to be artists, that we can be useful. ◙

Rhapsody for Blackberries

Sandra Dorr

I MUST make jam. Every time the refrigerator opens, I see the berries, as black as bears, their eyes shining. They have voices: a low crescendo that climbs higher every day. They tell me what it's like to lie hidden under the green fingers of leaves, listening to cars chuff by. To grow darker and darker in the light. When I grow old I'll be one of them, a blackberry wizened into a bobbled tooth of sweet, hot sun.

What pulls me to drive off roads whenever I see them? Is it because they're free? And everywhere, like swallows, in an Oregon summer? The very last berries are dropping off bushes right this minute under the eaves of the Wave Crest Hotel, in the air of salt brine and fog, bushes that grow like big men with bristling hands. I passed their white flowers that rippled like butterflies, and their light perfume in June, when my legs had begun to turn a nut brown and my walk had slowed with the beginning of summer. The road along the old, yellow hotel was filled with blackberry bushes, gathering force. The tide was the lowest of the year, and people were walking out the beach to the volcanic rocks that stand in the waves like far-off castles. It seemed that I could walk forever, breathing in the bushes and the soft, ocean air; I would not get tired, and the waves would keep returning. This is how the berries grow, and grow.

On Sauvie Island, it's said, an almost unthinkable mass of blackberry bushes once flourished on a knoll fifty feet above sea level, one of the highest points of the island. A group of explorers poked through it one morning and discovered a wall. The historical society dug out a nine-room house, built in the 1850s and preserved in blackberries.

In July I found blackberries springing out from the cliffs on the Wind River, in the forests of Mount Hood, in shallow gullies along highways, even in supermarket parking lots. They fell apart in our fingers, and we ate them in the car until our chins dripped. Warm, and sweeter than sugar. Then we scrubbed the purple juice from the seats, and I promised everyone the best jam this side of the Rockies.

So I line up the lids, the honey, leftover pectin, and the pots of boiling water—oh, lord, they're hot! The blackberry voices trill and crescendo. My husband hollers up from the basement, "Sandy?" and I stop to see his project.

He turns fine-grained cherry, alder, and oak over in his hands, considering them the way I consider the berries. The saw has screamed; there's been a thwacking of paint, and now a lean set of shelves—perfect for jars of jam—stand, under the basement stairs. "Gosh." I mutter, "they're great. You did it so fast."

I want to be a woman of purpose, to mash the bowl of berries and to fill the solid glass jars with the wildness and the sweetness, months of eating that can trickle down my kids' chins, just the way the milk once did. Food is love, my mother said.

Now these berries will last only another day or two. But blackberries are ancient. The first waves that rubbed bits of sediment from rock must have glimmered with specks of pleasure that ripened into seeds that floated on air, were stroked by light, and were sucked back and forth by waves until they began singing. And in that great singing of the green world, a spontaneous joy flowed from the heart of the plants, and remembering the dust of stars they flowered and gave birth to the effulgent, black fruit. As black as cormorants. As deep as space. What could be more wild than the very reaches of what we do not know, that somehow reaches us, when we snake our hands past the stinging thorns and find the fruit, softer than our own skin? And we stand on the tops of mountains or on serene roads or in a parking lot, watching the red sun drop.

I turn off the kitchen light. It's too hot in here. The bowl comes out of the refrigerator and onto the porch.

"Julian," I call. "Lilly! Come on out here. Let's be bears." We are going to sit on the porch and eat blackberries until it's night. Until our chins are purple and our tongues are black, and we've swallowed summer. ◙

II

WHAT IS THIS THING
CALLED FULFILLMENT?

Meaning is not something you stumble across, like the answer to a riddle
or the prize in a treasure hunt. Meaning is something you build into your
life. You build it out of your own past, out of your affections and loyalties,
out of the experience of humankind as it is passed on to you, out of your
own talent and understanding, out of the things you believe in, out of the
things and people you love, out of the values for which you are willing
to sacrifice something. The ingredients are there. You are the only one
who can put them together into that unique pattern that will be your life.
Let it be a life that has dignity and meaning for you. If it does, then the
particular balance of success or failure is of less account.

—John Gardner, *Personal Renewal*

Ballet in Bifocals

Linda Besant

The one thing which we seek with insatiable desire is to forget ourselves, to be surprised out of our propriety . . . and to do something without knowing how or why. . . . The way of life is wonderful: it is by abandonment.

—Circles, *Ralph Waldo Emerson*

THE night before my first ballet class, I pace up and down the stairs in my house, living room to bedroom and back again. Now and then I whimper with fear, like a pressure cooker letting off steam to keep from exploding. Inside me, voices shrill relentlessly: "Who are you kidding—even stairs make your knees hurt." I'm 55 years old, 35 pounds heavier than the weight I used to say I'd never exceed, and terrified of being ridiculous, or of truly injuring my knees, already worn down by decades of backpacking and skiing, or of finding it's too late to experience even a whisper of the lilt and symmetry of ballet in my own body. Ballet—the shining joy and passion, some even say the obsession, of my middle age.

It's been seven and a half years since my conversion from regular person to balletomane. I'd been a relatively normal ballet fan for about a year, after a friend overcame my stubborn misconceptions and persuaded me to attend a performance of Oregon Ballet Theatre. One moment dancers swirled across the stage like ocean currents, the next they sprang beyond the bounds of gravity, arms outstretched like wings. Ballet wasn't stuffy and old-fashioned after all.

How did those people train to become such artist-athletes? When OBT set up an outdoor studio, called OBT Exposed, in a tent in Portland's South Park Blocks, I rode my bike downtown to see what a dancer's workday was like and pedaled into an improbable epiphany.

The morning was cool, so the dancers were swathed in warm-up clothes as they began their daily company class with a combination of *pliés*. There was no hint of the glamour and excitement of performance; rather there were 27 supremely skilled young people, a master teacher, and an accompanist as focused as monks in meditation. They flowed in unison, like the flocks of birds which sometimes pulsed past the tent, their concentration unfazed by the crowd of kids from the day care center up the street who mimicked *pliés* in front of the stage.

Who can explain why a human heart sparks to a certain art, as mine caught fire that day? I warmed to ballet's fusion of movement and melody, to its stretching, yearning symmetry. And to the dancers' unadorned beauty; their loyalty, sustaining work this hard year after year; their togetherness, lucky pilgrims, to labor in community. As a writer used to struggling in silence and in solitude, I wanted company class. I wanted this beauty to imprint the air forever, the way words stay still upon the page. But it was more ephemeral than frost.

So I did my grocery shopping and laundry in the middle of the night, rearranged appointments, and made it to the tent every morning for the rest of OBT Exposed. Like a tourist discovering a new culture, I was hungry to decipher each mysterious detail. What's going on when the dancers listen to the instructor's words, twitch and flap their hands in response, then burst forth with glorious jumps and turns? By the end of the two weeks, I had new purpose in life: I would become the Sister Wendy of dance, the Bill Nye the Science Guy of ballet.

My ignorance demanded a total-immersion course of study:

Observe and listen. At birthdays, Christmas, and anniversaries, ask for money for a ticket fund to attend ballet performances wherever you travel. Go to all pre-performances wherever you travel. Go to all pre-performance talks and all dance lectures you encounter. Volunteer so many hours at OBT that you can see each program several times, to the extent that the dancers begin to ask, "Whose mother are you, anyway?" Shamelessly copy dance videos from rental stores and libraries. When necessary, buy new videos outright.

Read. Begin to work your way through the county library's excellent collection of dance books. Build your own library, making dance your focus in used book stores.

With each new tidbit of information—dancers are "marking" when they flap their hands like that, beginning to grasp a combination of movement, saving their energy for the real thing—I felt 15 again, often clueless and confused, always excited and boundlessly hopeful.

In 1997, when OBT's dance historian retired, they invited me to write an "auditions" piece about *The Nutcracker.* I've been writing feature articles for their playbills and newsletters ever since. By January of 2002, when OBT decided to offer an adult ballet class for absolute beginners as part of their ongoing adult outreach program, I had observed hundreds of classes, rehearsals, and performances. Seven years of total immersion had made it clear I would never really understand ballet unless I tried it, and James Canfield had agreed to teach OBT's beginner class. Where would I ever have a better opportunity? Yet I felt far too worn at the joints. How could jumps and pirouettes be possible?

Still. Almost every day I see OBT's dancers. In the part of company class devoted to strengthening their balance and control, they sometimes do *développé.* Standing on one leg, they slowly draw the other leg up and extend it into the air. Seemingly without effort they reach equipoise. They are as beautiful as shooting stars, and I am filled with longing.

At 9:30 on the morning of January 16, in sweatpants and a baggy sweatshirt, I overpower the force of resistance and drag myself to OBT. The studio is packed with people and quiet as a church when I arrive. One man and one woman have grayer hair than mine. One woman is thicker of waist and thigh by quite a lot, and I think she is the bravest person I have ever seen.

James Canfield strides in promptly at 10 a.m. and asks us to lie on the floor, feet toward the mirrored front wall, and make a T with our arms straight out from our shoulders. He passes among us, squaring our alignment. Soon we are flexing our feet, then pointing with careful articulation through the arch, the ball of the foot, the toes. Flex and point. We turn our legs out at the hips like Charlie Chaplin. James directs us to visualize little tornados spinning in our muscles to help produce turn-out. We flex and point, turn in, turn out, raise and lower one leg, then the other. Though it looks about as strenuous as nap time at day care, I'm sweating hard inside ten minutes. Cramps shoot through my feet. My shins burn.

After "floor *barre*" we stand with left hands on the real *barres* and right hands over our hearts like patriots. Standing is more complicated than I thought, with the muscles of our buttocks, backs, and abdomens engaged in ways I never before imagined. We try *demi-pliés*, half bending our knees, keeping our heels on the floor. James is all over the room, correcting nearly all of us as our butts mistakenly tilt out behind us. In *grand plié*, bending our knees until our heels come off the floor a bit, bright pain jabs my left knee and I must settle for *demi*. At the end of class James gives us a simple-looking exercise consisting of an up and down pattern for one arm, with the other arm repeating the same pattern a beat behind, like singing a round with our hands. "Dancing is all about coordination," he says, "so practice this while walking."

For days, muscles in my calves and deep inside my buttocks are sore in places a lifetime of biking, skiing, and mountaineering has never touched. An OBT staff member who took pictures of our class brings me a photo. I look stout and sweaty and as happy as an enchanted nine-year-old. All week I walk around my neighborhood attempting turn out, arms flailing.

By summer, four instructors from the School of Oregon Ballet Theatre rotate teaching the adult beginners. Slowly, we are progressing. I'm losing weight; I can hike steep trails again. I can even do *grands pliés*, though I often have to ice my knees after class.

Today, with Anne Mueller teaching, we'll try *chaîné* turns for the first time. To prepare, Anne has us stand with our hands on our shoulders as if ready for calisthenics. Standing in place on our tiptoes, we rotate round and round like tops, each keeping our eyes on our own image in the mirrored front wall of the studio as long as possible, when whipping our heads around to focus immediately on ourselves again. This technique, called spotting, is essential to all turns.

Now we're ready for the *chaînés*. We will keep our backs strong and upright and our thighs squeezed tightly together, and take little steps on our toes, turning half way round with each step, always turning the same way. Anne lines us up to cross the studio four at a time, like lap swimmers.

We're to spot on the wall directly across from us, and I'm lucky to be in a lane that can spot on the fire alarm. We first-time turners are allowed to go slowly, one step per beat of the music. When you see the Sugar Plum Fairy do these turns in *The Nutcracker*, she goes about eight times faster and stops on a dime to end with a flourishing balance.

Our foursome starts across the room. In the first turn I lose the fire alarm. Soon I lose my lane altogether, and wobble across John's lane and Nikki's lane to bump against the *barre* along the back of the studio. I shouldn't be surprised; I can't stay in my own lane lap swimming either. I hold on to the *barre* for ages before the room stops spinning in a nauseating way. As often happens in class, I feel like the love song lyric "bewitched bothered and bewildered." If Emerson was correct when he wrote "People wish to be settled: only so far as they are unsettled is there any hope for them," then ballet is working for me. Since I started this, I'm nice to bumblers and beginners everywhere, and I have an entirely new level of respect for the Sugar Plum Fairy.

Anne tells us we're building muscle memory and new neural pathways in our brains. It takes years, and most dancers begin as children. We can't expect it to happen over night. *Au contraire*, it will surely take me longer than the kids, what with my balance being rockier since menopause began. Bifocals make spotting confusing too.

But ballet class is like a 12-step meeting in that there isn't any cross talk. I can't offer menopause as an excuse because there isn't room for excuses. Ballet is a system for the perfection of the body's inborn symmetry. It is built of the careful layering of skills, taught by demonstration and explanation, in specific sequences that just keep coming. The river of class flows relentlessly on a current of music. We students take in information, try, take corrections, and try again. If you let your mind dwell on what didn't work for even a moment, you wake up to find that the class has disappeared down river and you must paddle like mad to catch up. You try your hardest or you don't, it doesn't matter, class goes on. Only you, facing yourself, know if you have given everything.

Adult beginning ballet is so popular that OBT adds a Saturday morning class, so we can study twice a week. After class, drenched with sweat and having expended every calorie of energy available to us, we plop down in OBT's carpeted foyer to stretch together. Some of us have become friends, a band of nuts who forgo sleeping in on Saturday mornings to work incredibly hard at something we have no hope of ever doing proficiently in the eyes of the world. Part of our comradery is this: It is nearly impossible to explain to someone who has never tried it why even ballet's simplest skills, like stretching the foot in *tendu* or circling the leg in *rond de jambe*, are so rewarding. Can you say to the spouse you leave alone in bed, "I'll be back in a couple of hours. I'm off to try to tap into the order of the universe?"

When we watch through the studio door for a moment, we realize that the eight- and nine-year-old kids who have class after us are doing pretty much what we were doing, only better. A year later, those kids are nine and ten and have progressed to Level II at the School of OBT. We have progressed somewhat in parallel, and OBT has had to start another class for absolute beginners.

Twenty-three people are in class today, the usual Saturday morning blend of regulars, some folks who used to dance and are excitedly returning to class, a few modern dancers adding ballet to their training, and two brave souls promoted from the absolute beginner class. Though ballet classes all follow the same format, there is room for endless complexity within the framework. Tracey Katona, our Saturday instructor, gives us more complicated exercises at the *barre* with offbeat rhythmic accents. What with holding all the basic structure we've been building—lifted muscles everywhere, abs, backs, butts and legs, turnout, strong arms— and grasping when to move what—which foot and how, the arm when and how, the tilt of the head—and striving for a graceful and musical execution which honors the pianist and the Chopin she plays, and adding the different accents, it makes for the kind of morning we love. We are so engaged just keeping track of everything that we don't notice we're exercising. And it goes well, too. I remember the combination. My feet cooperate.

At the end of class, Tracey gives a combination of *jetés, glissades,* and a *pas de chat*—the step of the cat. These are jumps from one foot to the other, and we have to launch ourselves sideways. My left knee has only become strong enough to attempt things like this in the last month, and I can't begin to follow the steps Tracey shows us. Where moments ago I was confident, suddenly I am lost. I throw myself to the right with the first *glissade*. Maybe my feet do what is required, I'm not sure, but I have no clue what to do with my arms. Tracey gives me corrections and she might as well be speaking to a brick; I can't absorb the information.

I anticipated that I wouldn't be strong enough for ballet, but I'm finding that "strong enough" is a wire always hovering just a fraction of an inch above you and you keep rising toward it. What I didn't appreciate, not even remotely, was how coordinated dancers are, though James did warn us back in our very first class that dancing was all about coordination.

Tracey directs us to repeat the set of jumps, and I flail at them again. No longer can I keep track of my body parts, let alone get them where they should be going. One of the new women from the absolute beginners class is equally confused. She wants to go to the front of the studio and watch, and I yearn to bail out with her. I'm aware that all the months my knee was weak gave me a release valve. In the very real need to protect myself from injury—an injury at 56 years old could take me out of this forever—I held back.

Tracey encourages the new students to keep trying. "I'd like to have one day where I felt like I really got it," another student says. "But that's the beauty of ballet," Tracey urges, "you always have something to work towards and something to lose yourself in."

There it is. If I want ballet inside me, I can hold back no longer. We are building good foundations, learning how the system works, layering memory into our muscles at the *barre*. Now the jumps are waiting in the air like wishes. We may bumble and fall, we may make *pas de chats* that look more like *pas d'éléphants*—but if we want to dance, the only way is by abandonment. With the most experienced of us in the front line, and the still-bewildered in the lines behind them, we fling ourselves again into *glissades* and *jetés*.

I want to celebrate today, wearing the new dance clothes I purchased this week at Goodwill—a t-shirt that isn't baggy, and size 12 (down from 16) not-quite-tights, but on this particular morning, one of us has just had news that her father is seriously ill, and another has lost a best friend to cancer. Our mood is quiet. Lavinia Magliocco is instructing. We have learned so much, the muscles of our abdomens and backs are so much stronger than they used to be, that Lavinia can give us a long, slow *dével-oppé* combination at the *barre*. It requires endless balance on the standing leg, and sustained extension of the lifted leg in front of us, to the side, to the back, and to the side. The accompanist plays *O Mio Babbino Caro* from Puccini's *Gianni Schicchi,* which perfectly suits our fragile mood, and our efforts rise to the melody. I can feel the counterbalance between grounding my standing leg and lifting my torso, and the energy, awake and trembling through my lifted leg and clear out my toes. In the studio mirror, I see that my *développé* is not thrilling, and with my limited flexibility, it never will be. But that doesn't matter. Within the structure of my body, at this stage of life, it is right. I hold the balance for a tiny extra breath, suspended in a kind of harmony, like standing inside a chambered nautilus shell or flying in the midst of a flock of geese. Outside, it has begun to snow. The swirl of soft flakes against the windows cocoons us in a subtle intimacy. We are at once elated and sad and grateful to be together, reaching for life. ◙

How Do Musicians Do
What They Do?

Tom Grant

How do musicians, especially jazz musicians, do what they do? How do they remember all those melodies and know to play those long, lush lines of newly-improvised-on-the-spot melodies? Where do their ideas come from and where are they going with them and how do the other players know when to do what and to whom?

These are the kinds of questions that I have heard over and over through the years from non-musicians—and even some (especially classical) musicians! The spell woven by an adept jazz musician can be provocative, thrilling, touching, haunting, relaxing, surprising, and infuriating. The sound from a well-made musical instrument in the hands of a master is a lovely thing. But the very beauty of that sound is as deep as the mystery associated with its making.

All music is communication, and jazz music specifies a language and a style for that communication. During my forty or so years of playing jazz music, I have thought a lot about this great mystical/musical activity. I have always (since age six) been able to play, but I think my understanding of the process has been fifty years in catching up to my abilities. The first album I recorded was in 1976 in Holland, and I gave it the title *Mystified*, probably in recognition of the fact that at that early time I didn't totally understand what I was doing! I was on the path toward mastering a language. I'm still on that path.

For years I taught an adult education class called "jazz/music appreciation." The students in the class were people with limited music experience and understanding. In this way, they were fairly typical of the general population. I was fortunate to be able to bring into the class some of the Northwest's leading musicians who would play through tunes with me and then talk with and answer questions from the class. The most commonly asked questions were 1) how do you know what notes to play, and 2) how does one know when to do things, like start or end a solo, end the song, play the main melody. These things that experienced musicians take for granted were the main source of the students' mystification. In one of these classes, the great guitarist Dan Faehnle made the point that down through the years, jazz musicians have purposely made such things seem mysterious and inaccessible to lay people so as to cultivate that special aloofness that typified the jazz subculture. Through the 1940s and 1950s, jazz musicians happily cultivated their status as outcasts and bohemians. After all, if you could "hang" with the likes of Diz and Bird, then you could stay in your cocoon of coolness and justify your poverty while at the same time blaming the "straight" world for its lack of understanding.

My how times have changed! The last few generations of jazz musicians have produced people whose openness and love of the music prompts them to teach the skills that they have learned so as to pass on the tradition to younger generations. Trumpeter/composer/teacher/historian Wynton Marsalis comes to mind as an exponent of the new openness of jazz. Here in the Northwest, another trumpeter and arranger, Thara Memory, was also a great teacher and jazz communicator. Thara was the musical director for the Mel Brown sextet, and to watch this band play can be the ultimate experience in the power of jazz to move an audience, and a great example of the interplay between musicians and the communicative skills of the director.

So maybe it's time to attempt to answer questions 1 and 2 above. First, how do we know what notes to play? The general formula is deceptively simple sounding. Musicians agree on what song to play from our mutual lists of known songs. We then play the main melody (sometimes called the "head") one time through, and then somebody steps up and solos *over the structure of the song*. Pretty straightforward. After the first soloist finishes, he or she is followed by another soloist who does the same thing until the last soloist finishes, at which time we again play the head and end the darn thing (or "take it out"). A typical jazz song or "standard" might be something like the great Cole Porter song, "What Is This Thing Called Love." It is a typical 32-bar song form. It has four sections: two A sections, followed by the B or bridge section, and back to a final A section. We refer to this form as A A B A.

> A: What is this thing called love
>   This funny thing called love
> A: Who can solve its mystery
>   Why does it make a fool of me
> B: I saw you there that wonderful day
>   You took my heart and threw it away
> A: And so I ask the lord, in heaven above
>   What is this thing called love

Now it is the soloist's job to play through the tune, making up a new melody as he goes. This is the tricky part. Because in order to make up a new melody, the soloist has to have a vocabulary. And for one to develop a vocabulary of jazzy melodic statements, a person can't avoid some serious study, which will involve lots of listening to the great established players, studying music theory, and just working it out on your own. The process can take years to a lifetime. The song above has a certain chord structure or "changes." In order to play over the changes, the soloist has to know what scales or modes fit with various chords. Most young players start by learning "licks" or "riffs," pat phrases that they might copy from records of their favorite artists. Years of study and some imitation might lead to the players gradually weaning themselves off the licks and creating their own approaches to inventing melody. This is the beginning of developing their own style.

Moreover, the soloist has decisions to make not only about where to take the solo—what notes to play and how to phrase them and at what volume—but also how long to play. The soloist can play one "chorus," which is once through the song, or several choruses depending on how verbose a particular artist is. Back when I recorded my *Mystified* album, I was on a European tour with the late tenor saxophonist Joe Henderson. Having played with masters like Art Blakey and Miles Davis, Joe had developed a tendency in his own bands to play long—I mean really long—solos, playing as many as twenty choruses, sometimes soloing for 10 or 15 minutes. He took me aside once and said, "Say, Tom, why don't you solo longer? Some day you'll be in bands where you don't get much solo space, but in this band, you can play as long as you want." But in those days, try as I might, I just couldn't solo longer than a few choruses. I just didn't have that much to "say." I would end up repeating myself and playing total nonsense in the attempt to stretch myself. I became mentally weary.

I still feel that truly gifted players can make a musical statement with an impact in two or three choruses . . . easily. Joe Henderson happened to be one of those old school geniuses who would take the audience on an incredible, albeit long, musical/emotional journey.

Attend a jam session some day and you'll witness the process and protocol of jazz musicians playing together in a casual setting. Ron Steen is one of the Northwest's best jazz drummers who for years hosted weekly jam sessions where players of all abilities come together and jam on familiar tunes. Novice players and singers are thrown together with veterans in a process that results sometimes in total magic and at other times—well, it's just short of magic. Ron does an artful job of fitting players together based on styles and abilities, balancing egos and temperaments. And he insists on players understanding the basic principles of playing together. Every player is expected to know the tune that's called, or not play ("lay out"). Everyone is expected to listen to the solos and keep their place in the song so that they know when to come in, when to "trade fours" with the drummer, when to take it out/play the head, and—one of the most elusive problems of them all—how to end a tune. Watch the eyes and body language of the players or a (self-appointed) leader who may tap his head which means play the out chorus or head. Sometimes his eyebrows are slightly raised and so this becomes more like a question: "Should we take it out now?" The piano player might point to the drummer, which would be like saying "No, not yet, let's trade fours with the drummer." In these sessions, there is an ongoing communication playing out before the audience.

And so it goes for any jazz band. For players at a high level of skill and experience, the communication becomes more subtle and cryptic. This is particularly true for bands that have been together a long time. As a piano player, I mostly give cues to my band mates by some slight head movement. (I could opt for the more theatrical one arm straight-in-the-air pointing to heaven approach, but I'll leave that to Peter Allen.) Similarly, guitarist Dan Balmer, in his band of highly seasoned veterans, often pulls his guitar slightly out in front of his body and tilts the neck up about ten degrees to signal his mates. And sometimes cues are strictly musical. A well-constructed solo will follow the short story-esque structure of development: rising action, climax, denouement, and for the next-in-line solo-ist, if he is truly listening, then there will be no doubt as to when to start his solo. Also the good listener/player can use the "vibe" or some element of the just-finished solo as a jumping-off point for his own solo.

But then sometimes the good old English language works just fine. In a slow dreamy ballad, I like to limit the whole presentation to just a few choruses, TOTAL. So I may turn to the bass player at the end of a chorus and say "go to the bridge" so as to take it out before the piece gets too long and tedious.

But there's more communication taking place on a bandstand than just that which flows between players. There is an even subtler and more mystical communing that comes from the core of the artist and goes out into the world to be picked up by the other players and the audience. It is this kind of soul-to-soul channeling of music that gives it its great power. That playing music comes from some special place deep in the conscious or unconscious being is evidenced by the sometimes odd physical mani-festations that accompany playing music. When I was young, I loved to listen to my records of the wonderful pianist Errol Garner. I noticed in these recordings that there were these strange guttural sounds that could be heard in the background while I listened. I soon learned that this was Errol himself kind of grunting and groaning along with the music. Nowa-days many musicians that I know and respect make these kinds of sounds as their "inner voice" leaks through during their playing. When I hear Dan Balmer or Ron Steen or Keith Jarrett or Elvin Jones "vocalize" along with their playing, it demonstrates that the music is not just in the head or the hands but comes from some inner place of creativity. These vocaliza-tions and sometimes-rapturous facial expressions are the byproducts of the process of creating music.

Look closer at this inner place of creative activity. It establishes in the mind and body a state that athletes refer to as "being in the zone." It's that alpha-wave-emitting, endorphin-releasing state of bliss that one feels down in the soul when engaged in whatever activity taps in to that deep well of inventiveness. It's a very spiritual place, and I'm sure that just such experiences as these were what made early mystics write poetically about the nature of God and the heavens. For musicians, when they are connect-ing on a profound level—with the other musicians and with the audience, and with their own core—there is a strong sensation of the instrument "playing itself." Most thoughts just go away and there is this feeling akin to floating dreamily through space, riding a wave, or soaring through the air. You have become a conduit for a communication whose source is almost unknowable.

Of course this magical condition is not attained every time we take the bandstand, but it is always the ideal to which we strive. We try to assemble the best players to achieve the deepest grooves to attain the highest emotional state possible. When all these elements come together, built on a broad base of knowledge and experience and crafted with empathy and sensitivity, you have the makings of a very satisfying experience. This is the magic of music. ◙

Deadheading

Lee C. Neff

Yesterday, I counted the clumps of daylilies I have accumulated: thirty-four. I finally succumbed to the tally because I was, momentarily, feeling that I just might have too many daylilies. This fleeting emotion was caused by my (perfectly normal) compulsion to deadhead every spent, bedraggled blossom. In fact, there are times when I know that I buy daylilies because I enjoy deadheading.

This perversity is not quite as peculiar as using cloth napkins because one enjoys ironing or using the silver, wedding-gift teapot because one relishes polishing, and it certainly beats letting weeds go to seed because one finds pleasure in weeding! Nevertheless, in an era of "low-maintenance" gardening, it does smack of being a make-work sort of decision. Especially when I realize that I have planted several clumps of daylilies where companionable butterfly bushes have grown so enthusiastically that my ample frame finds it difficult to reach the dangly, golden daylily tatters. Then I have to roam the neighborhood to recruit a willing child or granddaughter to wriggle through the border and carefully break off the old, damp blooms.

Nevertheless, early on a warm summer morning I revel in knowing that I will have a quiet hour to tidy this rainbow of alluring plants. Anticipation gets me through the less pleasurable ritual of watering the pots and moving the flip-flop sprinkler to its next spot. And it guarantees that I will come face-to-face with a garden full of colorful characters. Such as 'Jock

Randall', 'Yasmin', and 'Mary Todd'; 'Country Charmer', 'Dancing Shiva', and even 'Lusty Leland'. Watermelon, salmon, raspberry red, and butter yellow, daylilies come in almost every flavor from blush-pink cream to pumpkin and chocolate. And hybridizers continue to find them alluring, for elegant newcomers challenge the old-timers every year. The temptation to invite a fetching debutante to the party is almost irresistible. She won't require much to eat or drink—not nearly as much as the greedy new rose in the corner. And she will be a lot less painful to deadhead than the rose!

Still, it is a good idea to have a few remontant roses, for they will bloom again when the daylilies are done for the year. Nothing beats a rose bouquet on Thanksgiving, when every blossom in the garden is recorded and counted as a blessing. So reblooming roses must be deadheaded too, even though the gardener is unlikely to get through the task unscathed. The recollection of the battle scars earned while deadheading the Chinese rose 'Mutabilis', my favorite long-blooming rose, makes the task of deadheading the daylilies even more pleasurable.

There are all sorts of daily rituals that must be done to keep home and garden running smoothly; the trick is to find them satisfying. When I had my first child, thirty-seven years ago, disposable diapers were merely a glimmer in a marketer's eye. So I folded cloth diapers and found solace in the process. I was pleased to learn the art of folding a diaper differently for a baby boy or baby girl, for pinning it on, just so, and for doubling diapers when a child began to sleep longer at night. There was satisfaction in mastering the ordinary, in admiring the neat pile of a dozen freshly folded diapers and a sweetly fragrant baby.

But the ritual had to be repeated the next day, and the next day, and the next. Just so with daylilies; they aren't called DAYlilies for nothing. Each bloom lasts only twenty-four hours, and if the plant is to look its very best, the sad-looking detritus of the day before really must be removed. Not an onerous task, usually, for the spent blossom snaps off with ease, and even a mature clump of lilies has only half a dozen to a dozen old blooms. Mastering this ordinariness is without challenge. Enjoying it over and over again is a gift to wandering minds.

But it can be a challenge to catch up with being needed by daylilies when one makes the mistake of taking a holiday during daylily season. It is sometimes tempting to look at a plant prior to the vacation week and remove all the buds likely to bloom while one is absent, knowing that one will then cleverly arrive home with far fewer drooping shreds to attend to.

After all, when one is out of town, there's not going to be anyone home to admire the blossoms anyway.

Not that the daylily cares. Its job is the blooming, and deadheading blooms before they have had their day seems as foolish as hiding the silver teapot because it will eventually need polishing or failing to enjoy a sunny day because there will probably be another one tomorrow. One of these days we will deadhead this year's final golden daylily blossom, and an orange-red leaf or shortened evening will remind us that Thanksgiving is our next holiday and that winter is just over yonder.

In the meantime, today's quiet ritual is a gift. The familiarity of the ordinary provides the time to contemplate the possible. Deadheading yesterday is today's task. Not every shimmering bloom is seen by human hearts, but those we glimpse are a treasure. The daily-ness of deadheading reminds me to accept each day's gift. ◙

LIFE IS A MOUNTAIN

INTO THIN AIR AND BEYOND

Thomas F. Hornbein

I ONCE met a bumper sticker that read, "Life is a mountain, not a beach." For much of mine, mountains have been, among other things, my favorite metaphor. But sometimes you can get too much, even of a good metaphor.

Take, for example, the tragic events that unfolded high on the highest place on Earth in the spring of 1996. Catalyzed by a sudden, late afternoon storm, a somber drama unfolded that ended with five people dead as they were attempting to descend from the summit of Mount Everest.

A freak late afternoon storm was the last ingredient added to a brew of human factors that set the stage for disaster. Among these human factors were the limited experience and physical reserves of some clients of this guided climb, crowding resulting in backups and long waits at several bottlenecks, and the inability of guides to communicate with each other because of lack of radios, both within and between the two commercial groups heading toward the summit that day. Sometimes there is added safety in numbers, but also on Everest nowadays there are more pins standing at the end of the bowling alley when the big ball rolls.

When the game was all played out, three guides (including the leaders of both groups) and two clients were dead; two others suffered severe frostbite. Add six more deaths in other accidents, and one has the biggest loss of life yet seen during a climbing season on Mount Everest. With websites fueled by a satellite communications system that made the world aware of events almost as they occurred (including the phone-patch reassurances to his pregnant wife in New Zealand of one of the leaders, unable to descend and soon to die on the South Summit), small wonder that even those with affinity for flatter environs were transfixed by what transpired. And, as subsequent climbing seasons have confirmed, such loss of life will continue, and for much the same panoply of reasons related both to human ambitions and limitations and the inevitable vagaries of nature.

In the aftermath of such disasters, many questions abound. How do those who pursue such a seemingly useless, selfish activity justify to themselves and their loved ones the possible loss of life or limb? Do they have a death wish? What about those with more money than experience? Should they be able to buy their way into what for them is an even greater risk than for the more experienced and self-reliant mountaineer? Shouldn't we prevent such folk from putting themselves at risk, protect them from their own stupidity? Or can Everest be safely guided? What do we mean by "safely"? Many have referred to that tiny bit of the earth's surface that extends more than 8,000 meters (about 26,000 feet) above the sea as the Death Zone. Up there the barometric pressure is so low, the air so thin, that even moving slowly is close to the limit of what most can do; climbers have little left over with which to face the unexpected. When the chips are down, individual survival can be sorely tested, and even guides may be hard-pressed to get someone down who can no longer remain upright and at least wobble slowly downhill. Mount Everest is not Mount Rainier.

Even so, Everest and Rainier have much in common, including the opportunity for tragedy. An example with great personal meaning was the death of my friend, Willi Unsoeld, on Mount Rainier in 1979. In March of that year, Willi and a student from Evergreen State College were buried in an avalanche while the group Willi was leading were attempting to descend during a storm. Willi and I had shared many summits together, including Everest's. Such moments when nature is calling the shots are not limited to the Himalayan giants but are part and parcel of an uncertain destiny in many settings.

Having looked at an example of risk that some might view as verging on pathological, I have the chutzpah now to declare that, even though at times maybe we cannot live with risk, also we cannot live without it: risk is an essential dietary constituent.

So what is risk all about? The *Oxford English Dictionary* defines risk as exposure "to the chance of injury or loss." Chance means uncertainty;

it's the roll of the dice, not knowing the outcome ahead of time. Climbing mountains is a form of gambling, but metaphorically no more so than many other activities in our lives. Dick Emerson, for many years a professor of sociology at the University of Washington and a climbing partner, posited that uncertainty about outcome is what maximizes motivation; certainty either of failure or of success would diminish the intensity of commitment to an undertaking. He showed that individuals communicate in ways that maximize uncertainty, for example by countering optimistic or pessimistic information with that of the opposite kind, called negative feedback. Risk and its attendant uncertainty are essential to motivation.

I view risk like a drug, and as with any drug, dose matters. Too much or too little may not be good for one's health. Dose varies from those who are risk averse, avoiding uncertain situations as much as possible, to those experiencing symptoms of withdrawal if deprived for too long of their risk fix. Between these extremes are those of us who are risk acceptors, maybe even savoring its seasoning, yet for whom the lust for a longer, fuller life is manifest by an inclination to minimize unnecessary risks. Bertrand Russell characterized such a dose this way: "A life without adventure is likely to be unsatisfying, but a life in which adventure is allowed to take whatever form it will is likely to be short."

Although the dietary requirement may vary among us, I see risk as an essential ingredient to a variety of human endeavors that take us beyond ourselves and our present circumstances: creativity, decisive action, and the ability both to generate and to accommodate to societal change.

Creativity: Alfred North Whitehead wrote, "Periods of tranquility are seldom prolific of creative achievement. Mankind has to be stirred up." Acts of creation involve risk, whether as a climber or writer or, for example, in another realm where I was able to exploit some of my own risk affection: research. Some investigation is like mountain exploration, treading into realms unknown. Answers are sought, sometimes to questions not even posed before. The journey may be measured in months or years and the path taken, i.e., the methods, may be one not traveled before. In the end, the odyssey may result in discovery, a new "aha!" or it may lead nowhere. This kind of creativity, whether in science, the arts, business, or our relationships with each other, involves the possibility of failure as well as success.

Decisive action: As a physician, particularly one practicing a critical care specialty (anesthesiology), and also as a medical educator for nearly four decades, I have come to believe that the ability to accept uncertainty is precious to functioning in moments of crisis. As in the climbing of mountains, most of the time we are in control of what is going on. But occasionally events beyond us are calling the shots, and we must respond as best we can. Some individuals seem to be naturally endowed with the right stuff, and many of the rest exhibit an impressive capacity to learn to manage crisis. For a few, though, to stay cool under fire just isn't in the cards. Aversion to risk can paralyze action. My observation is that those who are most unsure of themselves, lacking self-esteem, commonly have great difficulty learning to function effectively in the face of uncertainty.

For some physicians, a curious opposite situation can also impair the ability to be thoughtfully decisive in managing crises. We physicians are programmed, or perhaps program ourselves, to be omniscient and omnipotent in the care we bestow. We wish to do no harm; *primum non nocere* is like an 11th commandment. Thus we allow ourselves little room for error in providing safe passage for our patients, even when the knowledge we possess leaves us far from certain. Feelings of omnipotence sit poorly with an ability to accept the possibility of failure. Willingness to allow for imperfection provides the space to learn and grow, as well as to respond with creative decisiveness when the need arises.

Coping with the unexpected can be a powerful, at times painful, learning experience whether it be in the mountains, or medicine, or other aspects of life. What one learns that may be most precious of all is about oneself, how to live with uncertainty and accompanying fear in order to be able to act. Having been there before makes a huge difference each time such vital moments are reexperienced, in no small part because one's own response is no longer unfamiliar. In both medicine and mountaineering I have seen a fair number of situations where appropriate, quick-thinking action has averted tragedy. I have also seen and known of situations where lack of such capacity has contributed to tragic outcomes.

Risk and society: Along with a higher level of affluence and comfort than we have ever before known, we Americans have come to place great value on being in a world that is safe and secure. A corollary of this urge is a diminishing willingness to accept risk, especially when imposed by acts of others. The potency of this unwillingness to allow insecurity—that is, uncertainty—into our lives has profound societal implications. In a graduation address at Princeton some years ago, its president, Harold Shapiro, said: "The willingness to risk failure is an essential component of most successful initiatives. . . . The willingness to occupy new ground always involves the risk of losing one's footing along the way. . . . " My own observation is that American society has become too risk averse for its own good. Moreover, as individuals become more risk aversive in their own lives, they become less and less tolerant of the risks taken by those in leadership positions. We are less tolerant of our leaders' mistakes. Indeed, we often speak of failure as malfeasance and sometimes accuse our leaders of lacking courage and vision. Courage, vision, and change require not only our personal willingness to shoulder the risks of failure, but also a willingness to understand that some failed projects are an inevitable part of the great successes.

As I present this pitch for a touch of risk in our daily lives, my mind keeps wandering back to the tragedy on Everest. What went wrong up there? And why? Partly I feel that at least some of those being guided up the mountain didn't belong there. They had not learned the skills and acquired the experience and judgment to take care of themselves in a crisis. But then another part of me realizes that that's what guided climbing is, whether on Mount Rainier or Mount Everest: substituting another's expertise for one's own, a way to shortcut the competence issue while lessening the risk. Guided climbing is not unlike the doctor-patient relationship, at least as I have experienced it in my own specialty. The client/patient delegates responsibility for his or her safe-keeping to another, trusting that other to possess the skills and judgment to enable safe passage, whether it be through anesthesia and surgery or to the top of a mountain and back down again. Sure, the risks are greater on Everest than in the operating room, a lot greater. But as we have seen, safe passage cannot be guaranteed in any setting, nor on any mountain. The difference in magnitude of risk between Everest and lesser summits is quantitative, not qualitative.

I ask myself, how do these clients differ from Tom Hornbein or Willi Unsoeld when they were climbing on Everest in 1963? While some had a fair bit of mountaineering mileage under their belts, others did not. But basic skills can be quickly learned, at least to some degree, and the usual route up Everest is not technically so difficult. More essential are commitment, fitness, judgment, and insight regarding one's reserves to get not only up but back down again. That, in the company of a good guide, may suffice, so long as all's well. But end-of-the-day fatigue, compounded by unanticipated bad weather, can suddenly change the whole complexion of things. When guides aren't there, one is left to make do on one's own resources of character and experience. When either is in short supply, safety margins are wafted off on the wind.

Still, I am struck by the similarities between now and then. Although by now Everest has been climbed over 3,000 times, still people are willing to risk their lives and plunk down $65,000 to try to reach the highest point on earth. Why? Exploration? Adventure? Testing personal limits? Fame? Fortune? Trophy collection? The mix of motivations seems much the same now as it did for us in 1963. Those who are bystanders have always questioned the rationality of the minority living closer to the edge, the risk acceptors. The questioning is less query than judgmental and no different now from in the past.

Risk is an ever-present part of our lives. We might wish to control the dose but, by definition, that is not completely possible. The control that we seek, then, is not of risk but of ourselves in living with and coping with risk, with uncertainty. For some of us, risk is more than essential to creative or decisive functioning. Risk helps define who we are, where we fit into the world around us, and how we relate to and influence, for better or worse, the lives of others. I think the capacity to accept risk has helped me to be a better doctor and hopefully a better teacher, father, husband, and human being. I feel blessed to have been born at a time early enough in the human relationship to Everest that the adventure could be both pioneering and lonely. Though times and the way things are done change, the needs we humans have to seek out new places in the soul to go remain the same. ▣

Surgeon's Knots

Richard Rapport

1943

Sex and love, and war and departure, and birth and memory, but not yet my memory, not what I have to tell. Those things were the preface.

1946

The house where my mother and I lived while he was gone had a closed landing at the bottom of the stairs that went to the second floor. An ordinary wooden door, like a closet door, opened into the living room, sealing off the stairs. I had to hide there, in the dark at the bottom of the landing, on the day that he returned because of the difference that he made. He came back still wearing the uniform of the Ninth Army Air Corps, before there was an Air Force. He was big, and smelled like a man who knew things, and he held my mother. All of my grandparents were there. Crying, I was coaxed out to him, and fear made the code in my memory. That was the beginning.

1948

Dewey was winning, the radio told us, as my dad made a splint for the broken leg of a neighbor who had hobbled to our house to be mended. He was still a resident then, but he had been a flight surgeon during the war and could set bones straight and prevent them from moving. He did it with a soft wrap and tape, and a couple of pieces of wood. We lived beside a lake in a house that was really a cottage. It was a country house with transoms over the bedroom doors, and the neighbor was a country boy. We sat on the long screened-in front porch, listening to the incorrectly predicted election results on a Philco radio and watching the fireflies burn around the edge of the lake while he wrapped up the leg. "Your Uncle Sam is having an election," he said. I didn't know I had an Uncle Sam, but I thought it was better than having an uncle to watch the elaborate bandaging and taping of the leg. The boy hopped away with his father for a crutch.

1950

Some Sunday mornings, he took me with him to make rounds. We stopped first at the city hospital, then the private one—always in that order. Years later he told me that all of the doctors in the city charged their private patients a few dollars more so that they could treat those at the public hospital who couldn't pay. At the first meeting of the year, the secretary of the county medical society determined how much it would cost to provide drugs, x-rays, and hospital care for the poor, and each member contributed to a fund that paid for them; there was no dissent. He never recognized this practice as re-distribution of wealth, but accepted his responsibility to care for patients who couldn't pay. Even after Medicare made him richer, he wanted that responsibility for each patient. When he made rounds, we started in the x-ray department where films were developed by hand in large vats of chemicals, and the entire department smelled like the chemicals. He showed me the shadows, and showed me what they meant. Everyone knew him there, and in the elevators and the halls and stairwells. On the wards, he left me in the nurses' station while he visited his patients. "Do you know my son?" he asked and introduced me to other doctors, nurses, and orderlies. The nurses, I thought, liked him, and some of them flirted with him.

Midsummer, and the others were somewhere else. Our flat square of a backyard required attention, and I was required to help. When we had finished, he said, "Ricky, do you want to learn how to tie a knot you make with one hand, a surgeon's knot?" He took a piece of string from his pocket and looped it around a slat of the fence and showed me, with movements as liquid as the hand movements of a Hindu dancer. His fingers twined around each other in a way that cannot be said, but can only be shown. "Daddy, how did you do that?" He showed me again and again and again. I practiced for twenty-one years, and then I could do it too.

1956

The year I could have had a Bar Mitzvah, he showed me manliness instead by taking me to watch an autopsy. I could not understand the body being examined as a thing, and the smell and the idea made me sit down. I watched two that year. In the fall, during a paper drive, I was bitten by a spider on the fourth finger of my left hand. When it swelled up and turned blue, he took me to the city hospital emergency room which smelled like alcohol, sprayed my finger with ethyl chloride, and opened it himself to drain. I still have the scar under my wedding ring.

1957

On my birthday, he took me and five of my friends to watch the Harlem Globe Trotters play a team they always beat. He took me with him to the operating room. When I began to play football in high school and college, I found similarity between the locker rooms of operating rooms and athletic teams. The undressing and dressing again in special uniforms, the secrets and smells and fellowship—the wish for success—are the same. The shoe covers, hats, and masks were all made of cloth then, not paper, and so were the drapes used to cover the patients on the operating table. I stood behind him on a squat stool that could not wobble or tip over; the scrub nurse called it a lift. I was not afraid. I watched the residents cut open the skin and accurately stop each tiny bleeding place with a hemostat and then tie them all off, dozens of them lined up together. There was no cautery. After they removed a rib and opened the chest, he took over, and he joked with them and the anesthesiologist who he told me liked to pass gas. I was surprised that people said funny things in the operating room. Now, I am surprised when they do not. He showed me the lungs and the heart on the inside of a living person and told me how they worked.

My father was a storyteller. He told things that happened and things that did not—but could have or should have happened—all in the same voice. No one knew the difference; he did not know the difference either, and it didn't matter because it was all true. He told stories in the operating room until he began to cut out the lung tumor, a "wedge resection" he called it, and then he said things I could not understand. He helped the residents close the chest with big, curved and straight needles, and they tied the sutures in the way that he had shown me in the backyard. I did not faint.

He never told me to do it, to open people, repair them, and sew them closed. He said, "Do what you love to do, and you will be happy."

1958

The summer after my first mediocre year at prep school, he taught me how to write. In a damp white shirt and loosened tie, he sat next to me at the desk in my room, a child's desk although I was fifteen, and he told me, "Tell it without saying it," as he crossed out most of my words. He could write and he could edit, but he could not imagine.

He taught me to order properly at a restaurant where children were not taken. He made sure we cleansed our palates between courses, and tipped well.

1961

I think it surprised him that I finished first at graduation.

1964

The year I was as good as I will ever be, he came to watch me play. He came to my little university for Parents' Weekend, and stood on the sidelines with the other players' fathers, the ones for whom athletics was the reason for college. He wore his hat and overcoat and the cheerleaders hung my number thirty-six around his neck. I carefully put on my uniform, smeared the black stuff under my eyes, got ready. We ran down from the locker room, through the Midwestern leaf piles and the smell of the fall, and past our fathers. He held a little transistor radio in his hand and when I ran by he shouted, "Michigan is ahead of Ohio State!" Even after I didn't answer, I don't think he could imagine his mistake. He did that sometimes, thought only about what he was thinking. It isn't easy to be the father of another man. We lost late in the game after our coach ran a play that worked and then insisted on the same play six consecutive times. A simple play: I led the left halfback off right tackle and hit their outside linebacker six straight collisions, each time for less yardage. He thought it was foolish to do that; we all thought it was foolish. Michigan lost too, but I didn't care.

1965

It surprised him again, the honors at graduation, and when I was admitted to a first-rate medical school.

1967

By the time of his first heart attack, I had already learned to call it an MI and thought I understood what that meant. I didn't understand what it meant to him, though. I drove up the snowy freeway, past the lake where we had lived in 1948, and went to see him in the hospital. He was in a bed in his own hospital, which made him a patient and he didn't like it. My mother stood beside the bed as I listened to his chest with the stethoscope I had brought with me so that I could. They both pretended nothing had happened. "You won't hear anything," he told me with a little smirk, but he was wrong. I heard the sound of his life coming and going, coming and going, lub-dub, lub-dub.

Some of the professors at my medical school knew who he was, and asked about him, especially the surgeons. The famous thoracic surgeon who had developed an operation for the repair of a fistula between the trachea and esophagus of newborns knew him, and he asked if I was Dick's son. Then he asked me if I thought I was a movie star, and if my father knew I had hair to my shoulders. Even though he had developed the operation to fix the fistula, rules prevented the professor from doing it any more because he was too old. He could be in the operating room, and instruct, and help, but he was not to be the attending surgeon. I watched one day while he showed a resident how to do his own operation. He did not cut and he did not sew, but he could not stop himself from tying the knots.

My father did not understand the Vietnam War. It was a long time before he forgave me for his failure to understand. He preferred to believe in the war he did understand, and in the myth of Communism. That war he knew because of things that had happened, or should have happened.

1969

I did not go to fight in Vietnam, whether out of fear or bravery I cannot know. Instead, I went to Chicago to be an intern and to learn surgery from a man he knew and who turned out to be like him. I learned the fundamentals of operations and of toil, sometimes working thirty-six hours straight. His friend was an old-fashioned surgeon who made demands of the house staff on his service, in his service. Morning rounds were to be done at 6:30, the skin cut by 8:00, professor's rounds at 5:00 and sometimes lasting until 7:30, then finish the work, the "scut" it was called. But the professor was there too, not in an office or a lab, certainly not at home in bed. We operated all night once to save a woman with a lacerated liver, spleen, and bowel—a girl really, who now is a woman I know well and who now lives in my new city—and when he was sure she would not die he took us all to the Loop in his own car and bought us steak and eggs. He was a man who could make a surgeon.

I went to do research, which my father thought was a waste of time. He was right, though it took me ten years to believe him.

1972

Some city people moved to the country that year, the year the war was almost over, and doctors did too. The Public Health Service sent me to Appalachia to serve the people, most of whom had been served too much and didn't want us. I learned to know which patients were sick, which ones were worried, and how to make house calls. I called on a man I knew would soon die; he knew it too, of course, though he really wasn't old enough to die. One spring day my father who was visiting called with me. The scent of hepatic failure came not so much from the patient himself, who was as yellow as paint, as from the toilet filling with brown urine that he refused to flush through several uses. The patient, like my father, had lived during the depression. The bedroom where he would die was upstairs, facing Main Street, but he kept the shades drawn all the time. He looked at a wall decorated with wallpaper that had always been there. My father knew how to talk to a man like this, and how to comfort him, because of what both of them knew.

1978

It was my fate to become a neurosurgeon, and so eventually I did. "Any operation that takes more than three hours isn't worth doing," my father said when I described craniotomies lasting half a day. I went to teach in an exotic foreign medical school on the equator. He had a coronary bypass while I was gone to Southeast Asia, but he didn't tell until I came back.

1980

"He was offered the best academic job around, but he said no and went to work at Group Health," I heard him say to another doctor at a party. That would have been his choice, too. I watched him operate one last time on that trip, although he saw patients until the day before he died. The chief resident opened the chest, but could not find the tumor. My father put his left hand into the wound, turned to the side so that he could extend his fingers a little deeper and, without looking, reached down to feel. "There it is," he said, never turning his head.

1987

He came to my hospital to drink coffee with the nurses and to watch me operate. He liked to do that, and to introduce himself to people as "the real Dr. Rapport."

1990

His town, the place he lived his life, began to die at the same time he did. Michael Moore made a movie about the economics of the place where he too had lived—Flint, Michigan—about the greed and pain when factories left the town. My father did not imagine the cause and effect, and blamed the town's failure on the movie. He never would see the film. Forty years a known surgeon, now he was old, and he ate too much because all of his other pleasures were used. He was not recognized. He was not recognizable.

1993

He sat on a stool behind me the last time I saw him, containing himself as he directed my repair of a brick walkway beside the house. I felt his eyes on the job and remembered them watching me with the same slightly uneasy concern as I washed the wheels of his car when I was five. Four and a half decades later he still wasn't sure my work was to his standard, and although he squirmed a bit, he said little. He assumed that his sitting there, in the heat and sunlight of a June afternoon with his oldest son doing the work he could no longer do, insured the repair done properly. We loved each other in that moment without saying so, and enjoyed the work together, although he wasn't enjoying his life much. "I've had seventy-five good years," he said, "and three mediocre ones."

Later that summer, he and my mother went out, and when they came home he finished a bowl of ice cream and fell off his chair in the dining room. He would have wished for that suddenness. I flew from my fashionable West Coast city where I am known, now, for a little while, to the midwestern town I no longer know. I opened his desk and, in the slot in front made for holding pens, I found his wings, the Ninth Army Air Corps wings that had meant for him so much possibility. I keep them in my desk now, and in the staircase landing of memory, closed by a door, like a closet door.

He showed me most of what I know, both how to be and how not to be. He showed me how to tie surgeon's knots. ◙

Calling the Past into the Future with Stories

Kim Stafford

Where is my neighbor, the homeless man, tonight? I mean my neighbor Phil, who called me a year ago, left a few words on my answering machine, before the tape cut him off:

Hello, this is Phil. I've just been mugged . . .

Then I heard the buzz of the dead line. I listened to that message five times in the dark of my room, reaching out with my finger to touch the play button over and over. "This is Phil . . . This is Phil . . . "

Almost a year ago now, a week after that message, Phil appeared at my door. He had a bad cut, a city wound on his forehead where someone had kicked him as he slept under the Burnside Bridge, kicked and kicked until he let go of the bag he held, and left him in a heap. After three days at my house, at breakfast—his wound healing, his humor returned—Phil was writing a letter. He turned to me.

"What is our address?" he said.

What is our address, we in the Oregon country, in the terrain of moss and sage, in the grip of fat rain and withering wind? What is our address on the map of years? Are we a young culture, pioneer babies at play in the meadows, not yet knowing the blue camas from the white, the sweet of this place from its poison? Or are we among the oldest, still living contemporary with what Lewis and Clark found, still stumbling into a world happening at salmon time, at the root feast, at the volcanic fore-edge of history?

When I am with Phil, I feel I inhabit both worlds. I drive, and he tells stories. It was like this when I went with Phil for the giveaway at Nespelem.

One day Phil told me, "My stepfather died a year ago. They will be giving his things away. But I can't get there. It's too far and too soon."

"I'll drive," I said. "I'll drive, and you tell me where to turn." So it happened we traveled some hundred miles, east up the Columbia, then north over the hills and along the Snake, into Idaho, and then he said to me, "Stop here. I want to tell you about this place." We were on the Clearwater then, a few miles upriver from Lewiston. It seemed an abandoned place. The river slid by, steady and slow. We parked where people parked to throw their litter. The grass was tall and dry. I could see in the brush of the side canyon where some trees grew. Maybe there had been a house once.

"There's where we had the garden," Phil said. "The corn grew pretty tall then. We hid there, when we got in trouble. And up there by those trees? That was my grandmother's house. Once we were leaving, and we looked back, and the house was on fire. My mother saw that over her shoulder, and we turned and went back, saved it that time."

His hand swept down toward the river. "And down there," he said, "down by that point, that is where my family fed Lewis and Clark, when they came down to the river. We fed them, and then they went on."

And then we went on, up the canyon to Juliaetta, to Kendrick, over the hills to Troy, Moscow, Pullman, and then north through the dry land.

The dry land is the landscape of stories. Stories come from far off, the bushmen say, like a wind. A story comes from far away, and you feel it. When does this begin? As an old man the poet Pablo Neruda liked to tell a story about his earliest childhood. He was in the stone-walled garden then, a young one playing alone, just learning how the world works. He was small enough then to be always close to the earth, stumbling along, getting his hands in the dirt, and there, at the foot of the wall, he found a crevice. He couldn't see through to the other side, but he knew it went through. He knew it went through to another place he had never seen.

And then he saw a little toy sheep pushed through at the crevice. Someone on the other side was pushing this precious thing through to him, without knowing him, and without a word. He took it in his hand, the warm, soft thing, and he knew what he must do. He ran to his room for his own most precious possession, a pine cone. At the wall, he pushed the pine cone through the crevice, out of sight and away. He held the sheep, and thought of the pine cone. His breath went in, and out.

That's how I remember the story, anyway. Do I have it right: the exchange of gifts is the work that knits the people and the years. Something comes out to you, and you give away, out beyond yourself. As we drove north, Phil and I, up a dry wash, where the grass was blond and stones glittered in the high sun, Phil pointed to a bank, dim and low on the far side. Wind whistled at the windows as we sailed along, and I had to strain to hear his voice.

"They were coming this way," he said, "and they were walking from Lapwai clear up toward Nespelem. The women all had their elk-teeth dresses inside out, with just the threads showing, so people would leave them alone. If they looked poor and ragged, people would leave them alone. And they came to that place, that dry bank over there. My great grandmother asked them to stop. She knew a place where her own grandmother had taught her, where she took an ax and cut into the bank, and water came out. She cut, and the water came. They rested there, washed. They drank that water. Then the old lady covered it up so the water stopped. She put dust on it, and it was dry again. Then they went on.

I am calling the past into the future with stories. I am calling to reach back through the curtain, back into the dust, reach through the crevice, and pull out a story of someone I love. We are emissaries from the future come back to make it right. I am calling the past into the future. Do you hear?

Phil is somewhere in the Oregon country tonight. Maybe he is nearby. I can't see as well as I once could. His hair is getting longer now. Someone saw him dancing at the Lapwai powwow. They didn't know who that good dancer was. Then he stopped, and they recognized him. He is making new clothes for himself, a whole new traditional outfit. I saw him last in a red shirt, red wool from the mill ends store on McLoughlin, red and trimmed with white and silver. The wound on his forehead has healed. He is older. I think he is laughing more. But his mother doesn't know where he is. His sisters can't tell me. His nephew hasn't heard. I have sent a letter to six addresses. No answer. I am trying this other way to find him: telling stories.

At Nespelem, we arrived one day too late for the giveaway. Phil was wearing black shorts and a flowered Hawaiian shirt and tennis shoes. We went to the old longhouse, the one Chief Joseph asked them to build. The roof was tattered, many shingles were gone. A man shuffled toward us, through the tall weeds, very drunk, very friendly, very sad. No one else was around. We three went inside the longhouse, from the blade of hot sun to the blue shadows of the room. Phil walked around and around the floor, counter-clockwise, the dancing way. It was a dusty place, with frayed curtains. By the window, I stood by a chair. Someone had been sitting there, looking out at the hills. The chair seat was polished. Everything was dusty but the chair.

The drunk man was saying to us over and over, "That door, that was where they took my mother the last time I saw her. They carried her through that door, the last time. No one knows the old dances any more. That door, the last time I saw her ever. They carried her out through that door."

And Phil walked around the floor and around. He stopped beside me, pointed to a corner.

"That is where I would sleep," he said quietly, "when I was a child and the dancing was late. When I was a boy that is where I slept. I remember the dancing, feeling it in the wood by my face."

"Phil," I said. "I will pay for a new roof. If the people wish it, I will buy the shingles." He listened, looked at me. We both looked up—daylight twinkled here and there.

"Some don't want that," he said. "Some want this old longhouse to fall down. Some say they will never go to the new longhouse. They are loyal to this one, even though no one comes here any more. Even though there is no dancing here. Some say the tribe will never be one, until the old long-house falls down.

"You know," he said, "how they made the new one? Everyone went to Wallowa, back to our own country, and took up earth from that place. They carried away earth in their cornhusk bags, in their pockets, in their shoes. They all brought that earth back to Nespelem, and scattered it where the new longhouse was to be. They all danced around there, beating the earth from Wallowa into the ground up here. Then they built there, so they could dance on their home ground, even this far away."

Phil walked around. I stood by the chair, where the grayed curtain swayed.

"My mother," said the man, "they carried her out there, out that door."

We sat in the shade of a cottonwood at Nespelem, waiting for the danc-ing to start.

"One time" Phil said, "I was hitching down to Lapwai. I didn't have a ride for a long time, and then I decided it was time to get a ride, and right away this car pulls over, and it was Horace Axtel. He was going to the powwow at Lapwai, too, so we got there right away. But it kept getting darker. It was getting darker all the way down the Lewiston grade, and up the river. Everything was getting darker like a storm, but strange.

"At Lapwai, I couldn't find my dance outfit. I went to my sister's house, and it wasn't there, so I went back to the school. The dancing was about to start, so I went to another house, and my outfit wasn't there. Back at the school they kept saying on the loudspeaker, 'The children don't know how to do these dances. We are waiting for someone to show them how.' Finally, I decided, even without my outfit, I should show them. So I danced. It kept getting darker, but the children danced with me. We all danced.

"Then this old, this real old woman from Warm Springs was there in a wheelchair. She started making a speech to everyone. Her daughter was translating for her. It kept getting darker, and she said. 'The world is about to turn over.' The dancing stopped, and everyone was listening to her. 'The world is about to change,' she said 'and everything will be new.' And it kept getting darker. And then the people found out it was ash, from the volcano. That was the day the mountain exploded—St. Helens—and the ash got clear over there to Lapwai. And the old woman kept saying over and over, 'The world is about to turn over.'

"And my sister said, 'Let's go to the Bear Dance the Utes are having.' So some of us got in a car and drove all the way down, all night and next day. When we got there they said, 'Who came from farthest?' And it was us. So we were honored there."

How can I honor the place I live? Sometimes I think about the old ways, how as a child I wanted to be the Indian of this place. I wanted to be Clackamas, or Kwakiutl. I whittled cedar with a flake of stone. I smoothed a stem of buckthorn with a clamshell. I made arrows and baskets. Now I make stories. I twine fragrance and friends into stories. They seem the oldest things of this place still left. And the newest. The world is about to turn over, and I am calling the past into English words. Words come out of our mouths like a chant from before: Stumptown, starlight, logger, skookum.

When the dance at Nespelem started, Phil and I sat on the dark bleachers, and watched the people go round and round to the drum, the tin bangles ringing on their dresses, beaded cuffs and bags flashing where they turned, otter fur wrappings on the women's long braids flying, their hem fringes swinging wide, the blankets over their outstretched arms like wings when they swayed and spun. Little ones danced, and old ones led them slow, in step, and fancy dancers jumped and glittered.

Then the dancing stopped, the drum and all the little bells stopped at once, and a man came into the center, carrying a bridle trimmed in silver. Everyone fell still.

"I have been with you three months," he said, "I, a visitor with you from the Cherokee." He held up the bridle. "I have been watching the passing on of traditional values from a certain grandmother to a certain granddaughter." He shook the bridle. "I would honor that with the gift of this bridle, which belonged to my grandfather. And I would honor that passing on with the gift of a saddle, which belonged to my father. And I would honor that with the gift of a mare, a young one, and fertile." He looked around the circle, then called the name of the child.

"Do you hear me?" he said. No one moved. "Do you hear me?"

Phil had left the bleachers quietly, and was circling around back toward the announcer's booth. The dancer called a second time the name of the child. No one moved. I saw Phil talking in the shadows with the announcer. The dancer called a third time, a fourth, a fifth, and then a little girl in beaded doeskin dress came shyly forward, and let the dancer lay the bridle about her shoulders.

Then the drumming started, and everyone was dancing again.

"What's happening?" I whispered to Phil, as he climbed to his seat again.

"When this man started giving," he said, "I looked to see who among us would think of a gift for him. No one moved, and so I saw it was me. I gave the announcer some money for him. And I gave some for the announcer, too."

The drumming was steady, thick in the air. Everyone in traditional dress came into the circle moving in the dust. I saw the dancer who had given. I saw the girl dancing with the bridle. I saw the grandmother dancing slow. And no one looked at her, or at the child, or at the Cherokee dancer, but everyone was dancing where they turned and turned.

When I turned twenty-eight, I was living alone in Port Townsend, Washington. I spent my birthday alone, looking out at the water. I watched a loon dive, and come up. I watched it go down into the green world of the water, and then come back to the light. As I watched, something came clear to me. My parents had given me this life, and I was grateful. But I could not give back to them. I could only give away. The bargain of the generations is not a trade, but a giveaway, a passing on.

Phil, I am calling you with stories. My brother has gone away. I need you to hear me now. I am calling you with these few stories. Will you go driving with my people now? When the moon is full, at Wallowa, we can turn the headlights off again on the valley run. We can turn four ways and swim at the lake before dawn. You can show how to burn old pine to make a place pure. At noon you can tell again about the hawk's shadow crossing the hood of the car, how that brings balance—the right things and the wrong things we have done coming to a new balance when the shadow crosses over.

I have a beading needle for you. I have bought thirteens, hanks of blue and red beads, cut beads that glisten. Tell me about your grandmother, beading with her one good hand. Remind me about the good days when you stitched in a hi-hi bead, a white one for joy. Teach me to turn without stumbling at Young Joseph's grave. Tell me about the people camping a last free time at that lake near Grangeville, before giving up their rights.

If you wish, tell me what they remembered the day they named you. Tell about the whipman. Tell those stories about the ordinary places as we pass them, how someone's life made that place worth looking at always. Tell about Vietnam, and coming back, and not having a car, and racing bareback to the river, how they stole your shirt in Seattle, after you won at the dancing, the shirt with ermine tails. Tell me again about the buffalo, the little buffalo come dancing two by two from the high lake, singing. Sit on my daughter's bed again, and tell more of the story that put her to sleep with seven brothers and their sister, Morning Star, traveling and horse-trading, in love and in disguise. Tell her, and let me listen, how a man cries, and a woman cries, but they have different ways.

I am calling you now. Tell me, in the hills and canyons of this place, in the years of this life, on the homeless vagabond road that takes you everywhere, at home no one place but everywhere, tell me, what is our address? In this country, what is our way of belonging, what is our flag, and our blessing?

You called me on the phone machine. I call you with stories. I want you in the future, for the future will starve without your stories. The future is a twig that doesn't yet know where to cut the dust with its root for water. The right story knows where. I call you with stories.

Hear me. ◙

III

WHAT DO WE KNOW
ABOUT THE ISSUES
WE FACE?

If Thoreau had merely left us an account of a man's life in the woods or if
he had simply retreated to the woods and there recorded his complaints
about society, or even if he had contrived to include both records in one
essay, *Walden* would probably not have lived a hundred years. As things
turned out, Thoreau, very likely without knowing quite what he was up
to, took man's relation to Nature and man's dilemma in society and man's
capacity for elevating his spirit and he beat all these matters together, in a
wild free interval of self-justification and delight, and produced an original omelette from which people can draw nourishment in a hungry day.
—E.B. White, *A Slight Sound at Evening*, 1954

An Impromptu
on Owning Land

Jarold Ramsey

I own some land, in the western foothills of the Ochoco Mountains in central Oregon. Somewhere or other I have a packet of papers indicating that I have title to it. I pay yearly county taxes on this property; if I stop paying them, the county will claim the property, and eventually auction it off "for back taxes," which is exactly how my parents bought our home-place at the end of the Depression. So we pay taxes, on what we own.

Actually, I hold joint title to this foothill property with my brother and our wives. It's understood in this arrangement that we share it equally, undividedly, right down to the smallest indivisible unit, an acre, a square foot, a grain of sand. What's ours is theirs, and vice versa. No problem there, because we're close; but most of the time, when I think about the place, or walk around it, it's as if I'm the owner, and I imagine my brother thinks of it in the same way. When the place makes us a little money, on timber or pasture rental, we share equally, and likewise the expenses of keeping it up.

This easy arrangement is going to become more complicated, I think, when the place passes on to my brother's three children and their spouses, and my three children and theirs. Can ten or twelve owners carry on as easily as four, pay the taxes, keep the fences and the old farmhouse in repair, resist the temptation to "develop" and make deals? I worry that possession of the place will not mean to all of them what it means to this generation. And in the next generation, after them . . . ? Maybe we should form a "family corporation" now, so that conflicts-to-come can be settled, even by buy-outs if need be. But that seems awfully dramatic, even dynastic, for an old worn-out sheep ranch that up to now has been maintained by a kind of neglectfully possessive love.

When my father bought the place over sixty years ago, from the original homesteader, the latter (who had mined for gold in the Yukon) insisted on retaining the mineral rights. A strange feature of law is that mineral rights can be perpetually separated from real property rights—so now, after all these years, I'm not really sure who holds the former. It may be a dentist in San Diego, who probably doesn't know what he owns up here. It's a serious vexation: if my life depended on it I couldn't show you where our real property rights end and his mineral rights begin, but if he suddenly found the deed to our place and decided to prospect on it for oil and natural gas, he could come through our gates willy-nilly and set up drilling rigs wherever he pleased on an acre of ground for each well, and drill as deep as he wanted, using our water as necessary! Who would ever think of dividing land up that way? My dad must have wanted the place very badly, to have accepted such a deal. I hope it doesn't turn around and bite us one of these days.

Thinking about those buried, alienated minerals, I brood sometimes about the air over my property. Do I own it; how much? Probably about as high as I can reach up and fan with my hat, no more. Maybe I should test this assumption by erecting a 300-foot flagpole and flying a proprietary flag on it. But for all intents and purposes I've conceded that what I own, really, is the gritty mineral skin of the land, which I share with the ants and lizards, sagebrush and trees, and enough air and sunshine for all of us to live. When it rains, I get to keep what soaks in. Fair enough.

Long before it was homesteaded the place was visited by Paiute and probably Chinookan Indians on hunting and root-gathering expeditions. I doubt that they settled in for long, up here, although we still find their arrowheads and hide-scrapers, especially on sandy south-facing hillsides, where they could make sun-warmed camps. Once I found the bottom of a very old bottle: the glass, sun-blued and full of bubbles, had been expertly chipped to make a sharp scraping edge! That would date it around 1860, at the latest. Did the Indians who came up here then or before think this stretch of country "belonged" to them? No more than they would have claimed any other parcel they regularly traveled through. More likely, so far as they reflected on it at all, they held that the land owned them, as a mother owns her children, and so they possessed the freedom and the duties of being owned: that would have been the basis of their allegiance.

As late as the 1920s, Indians from the Warm Springs Reservation used to ride up here in the fall, with their kids, pack horses, and dogs, and camp in the willows along one of our creeks. Probably they were on their way to hunt deer and elk in the Ochoco Mountains farther east and south, but they would stay long enough here to build and use sweat lodges in the willows. A very old lady who grew up on this part of our place told me this years ago, just before she died. She remembered that her father always welcomed them onto his land, and usually traded whatever he had to offer for buckskin gloves and moccasins. She also remembered that her family's neighbor over the hill, who ended up owning both properties before we bought all of it, had some trouble with the Indians early on and told them never to come onto his place, and they didn't.

This meant, I guess, that they stayed outside the fences he'd put up to keep his sheep in, and Indians out. Judging from the evidence he left us, he wasn't a very exacting fence-builder. Most of the thirteen miles of four- or five-wire barbed fences around and across our land are still, despite our improvements, no better than they have to be, the rusty wires and the old juniper and cedar posts holding each other up mutually. And on some sectors, we've discovered, the fence lines do not correspond to anything in the county courthouse records. For years, according to the legal description of our place, we didn't really own our front gate, or the summit of the hill above the house; a neighboring rancher farmed some of our land on the wrong side of the fences between us, and we grazed some of his on our side! Recently, through a series of land trades, we've "rectified our frontiers," and that's a comfort.

Our fence line must seem even more arbitrary to the deer and elk, whose immemorial trails often cross the fences at right angles, as if challenging them. As a consequence, each spring we go around with rolls of barbed wire and staples and fencing tools, and repair the considerable damage done by these wild herds jumping over or crashing through the lines. Once I found the carcass of a young buck, its limbs, head, and horns woven into the wires in a horrible knot. But usually the deer vault right over, without doing more damage than breaking or loosening a top wire or two, and so we keep on cutting and splicing our fences, and when I'm done with the job each year, I feel good about it, as if an unequal truce between the two-legs and the four-legs has been renegotiated for another year.

During the early fall hunting season, when there are still cattle on the place, we're pestered by deer hunters straying across our boundaries and sometimes cutting our fences. So like all ranchers hereabouts, we've put up signs saying POSITIVELY NO HUNTING OR TRESPASSING on prominent fence posts facing out, for would-be trespassers and poachers to see. It's hard to say whether this "posting" of the property does much good, and I confess I'm not fond of putting up such blunt challenges to any and all visitors. They must seem like insults to innocent, gun-less hikers. On the other hand, most of our signs around the place are shot to pieces every few years and have to be replaced, indicating I guess that their message is reaching the right people, whether it stops them from trespassing or not. Only a few times have I ever confronted a total stranger on our lands, but others in the family have had some ugly encounters with poachers, and after one of these, my father actually got himself deputized by the county sheriff, and carried a worn silver deputy's badge in his shirt pocket during hunting season, in case he had to invoke the law.

Beyond our northeastern fence line lies another man's property, which I covet. My father could have bought this place from the son-in-law of the original homesteader, but declined, reasoning that we had enough land up here already. He was right, but coveting land is not rational, and I do covet this other place. It's much smaller than ours, only about 800 acres, but being mostly above our highest land, it's densely timbered with ponderosa pine and Douglas fir, and embellished with springs and creeks and meadows. It's not been logged in recent years, and walking through it (trespassing!) is like walking through a forest park. The blue lily-blossoms of camas appear along the creeks in June, and even in the heat of August you can always walk in the shade, and come upon little meadows full of scarlet gilia in bloom.

Once for the better part of an hour, at the edge of a meadow back in the pines, I watched a young coyote playing with a pine cone as if it were a mouse, flinging it high into the air, retrieving it with great galumphing leaps, pointedly ignoring it, and then pouncing on it again. When finally, having promises to keep, I walked into the meadow and broke the spell, the coyote ran off—but when I looked over my shoulder a few minutes later, here he came behind me, discreetly keeping his distance, fellow traveler through the woods, probably expecting me to flush out a chipmunk.

Back there at the edge of the meadow, watching the coyote at play, I had coveted nothing—what more was there to want? But later, of course, far away, I resumed my brooding over that land, and everything on it, under it, and over it, wishing that I owned it and had the undivided title to it in my safety deposit box, and could pass it on to our children, along with our place just over the hill. For shame: thou shalt not covet thy neighbor's property, let alone his wife, and if the sin applies to land as well as to human flesh, I am guilty as sin. What if I could turn my ownership-complex inside out, and really accept the proposition that the land owns me, gives me my life, requires my devoted service? The habits of thinking otherwise run very deep, but I remind myself that when Thoreau felt that universal urge to build and live in his own house, he built his Walden cabin on land he neither owned nor rented. I wouldn't want to try that now, on the shores of Walden Pond, but like everything else in Thoreau's story, it shows what you can try to do without.

Meanwhile, I keep looking for images of being in place, in the right place, without ownership. Two years ago, before he died, an oldtimer here made a final request to a neighboring rancher, one of his best friends. The friend owns and flies an antique biplane, and the oldtimer's wish was for his friend to take his ashes up in the old plane and scatter them over a rocky pinnacle known to locals as "the Dry Island." So late in spring, as the sidehills above the creek were greening, the oldtimer's extensive family assembled close by, and the pilot took off with his cargo and flew over the Island. In the calm morning air, the oldtimer's ashes came straight down in a faint ribbon of white, and vanished, reclaimed, in the bitterbrush. ▣

Oregon Land Use Planning

THE FAIRNESS CHRONICLES

Richard P. Benner

Two travelers, worn out by the heat of the summer's sun, laid themselves down at noon under the widespreading branches of a Plane-Tree.
As they rested under its shade, one of the Travelers said to the other,
"What a singularly useless tree is the Plane! It bears no fruit, and is not
of the least service to man." The Plane Tree, interrupting him, said, "You
ungrateful fellows! Do you, while receiving benefits from me and resting
under my shade, dare to describe me as useless, and unprofitable?'
    Moral: Some men underrate their best blessings."
                                    —"The Travelers and the Plane Tree," Aesop

O UR use of land says a lot about who we are. More than arguments
pounded home in courtrooms and stakes driven into the ground, land
use is the place where histories, interests, and visions of the future intersect,
too often with disheartening results. From the Middle East to the American
West, we are still fighting over land. Not surprisingly, our various views of
the land arise from conflicting narratives, reflected in the language we use:
homestead/investment, park/development, wilderness/property. The same
dichotomy is revealed in the way we see its use: private rights/public trust.
The past few years have seen a Supreme Court decision and a number of ballot measures trying to resolve the issues raised in this continuing conflict.

Much of this history reflects at least two narratives creating two very different kinds of heroes. The first we call the "rugged individualist," tamer of the wilderness and morphed in more urban settings into the self-made man. From James Fenimore Cooper' s Natty Bumppo to Ayn Rand's Howard Roark, he makes his own success from brains or brawn, courage, hardship, and ingenuity, and he takes pride in having done it all with no help from anyone else. His strength carved out the homesteads of the West and his self-interest worked with market forces to develop our economic structure. In the world of land use, he stands with private rights.

The second narrative we call the "social contract." From Teddy Roosevelt to Tom McCall, real characters whose mythic words and deeds inspired some and irritated others, this hero reminds us of our duty to each other and to future generations, and that "with benefits come responsibilities." But as with so many lofty ideas, "the devil is in the details," or perhaps more accurately in the implementation. In the world of land use, he stands with the public trust.

Though some have pledged their allegiance fully to one or the other of these narratives, most of us have a bit of both in us and perhaps it is at this juncture that solutions lie.

This brings us to yet a third narrative. America is the land of the fair. From playground on up, the plaintive "That's not fair!" can be heard almost any time a limitation is put on personal freedom, and it is a complaint which engenders a lot of sympathy—especially when it strikes home. The value of the sacrifice of the individual to the greater good is often not appreciated by the individual involved. To be perceived as fair, the sacrifice has to be shared and to be perceived as shared fairly.

The current web of property laws, environmental laws, and land use regulations reflects our efforts, over the course of many years, to blend these narratives into one story. As recent developments at the federal and state level illustrate, we are still looking for a happy ending.

A LITTLE WORLD HISTORY

Our early ancestors simply wandered where terrain and temperature allowed, taking what was needed and available—fish, game, plants. Increases in population led to expansion of hunter-gatherer territories aided by a growing ability of people to make clothing and shelter and thereby endure more variation in climate, and to make the tools and weapons necessary to feed and defend themselves.

The wandering continued as extended families formed into tribes, expanding languages and social organizations, forming societies, and developing art and culture. Group by group they learned to cultivate the land. In so doing, they discovered they could support growing populations with agriculture, as revealed, for example, in the remains of one of the first farming villages discovered near a spring-fed oasis at Jericho in the Jordan Valley. Believed to be 10,000 years old, the village covered an area of almost 6 acres and supported a population of at least 300 with crops of barley. More villages grew in the Jordan Valley near what we call Damascus and along the Euphrates River in present-day Iraq. People were able to settle permanently and in higher densities. Other tribes threatened, and the settlers began to protect themselves and their work. Thus wandering tribes grew into villages, cities, and states with boundaries and borders fencing themselves in and others out. In nearly all these societies, land was recognized as sustenance, and people took care of their resources, often giving thanks through festivals of harvest to gods and goddesses of forests and fields. In societies where it existed at all, the concept of ownership was often as tenuous as the lives and power of those who claimed it.

A LITTLE U.S. HISTORY

As Europeans immigrated to North America, they adopted English common law (except for Louisiana, which is still bound by law derived from the Napoleonic Code), under which land they owned, their "property," meant a place in which they held a bundle of rights:

1) to control and use the property,
2) to benefits from the property,
3) to transfer or sell the property, and
4) to exclude others from the property.

These rights were not absolute; they were, and still are, subject to the rights of society, often codified in law. In the early history of the United States, society placed few limitations on the use of land as it seemed an endless resource, especially with a limited population base. From Thomas Jefferson's Corps of Discovery to the Homestead Act to massive federal subsidies for irrigation, railroad, highway, and energy projects, the challenge was not limiting use of land but rather getting it settled, cultivated, and developed. However, as the population increased and people began to congregate in cities, the need arose for local governmental control to put some limits on the movement of industry and commerce into residential areas and to keep residents from becoming nuisances to each other. These limitations generally took the form of zoning to regulate incompatible uses, building heights, setbacks, and densities. As population grew and spread, some began to recognize a need for planning. Noting the changing times, Theodore Roosevelt told his audiences in the summer of 1910: "Every man holds his property subject to the general right of the community to regulate its use to whatever degree the public welfare may require it."

This concern reached a peak in the 1960s and 1970s as members of Congress observed that the balance between economic growth and development on the one hand and protection of natural resources on the other had tipped too far in the direction of the former. As a result, Congress enacted federal laws to stem the loss of natural resources and environmental degradation: the National Environmental Policy Act, the Wilderness Act, the National Forest Management Act, the Endangered Species Act, the Clean Water Act, and the Clean Air Act. Many states passed their own versions of these laws.

Intentionally or otherwise, the new laws affected the balance between the public interest in environmental conservation and private interests in economic development of property. This is particularly true in the area of land use, when state regulations on behalf of the general welfare without paying property owners for lost rights butt heads with constitutional requirements that property owners be "justly compensated" when their property is "taken."

OREGON STRIKES A BALANCE

At the same time Congress was enacting these new laws, Oregon was also addressing the balance between public and private interests in land. Governor Tom McCall was spearheading an effort to establish a land use planning system that would serve as a model for the country.

Nowhere has land use been more of an issue than in Oregon. From the passage by the Oregon legislature of the first Oregon statewide land use planning laws in 1969, when inquiries came in from across the country to use the legislation as a template for planned and limited growth, to its threatened demise through Measure 37, enacted by voters in 2004, when inquiries came in from across the country on how to avoid it, Oregon has been at the center of the action.

And no one is more associated with Oregon's land use laws than Governor McCall. It was during his tenure in office (1967–1975) that Oregon gained its reputation as a national leader in innovative land use policy.

The McCall era saw Oregon protect public access to virtually all of its beaches; adopt the nation's first bottle bill; clean up the Willamette River; and enact the country's first statewide land-use planning system. Not all these concepts originated with McCall. But he was the catalyst and provided the leadership to make them a reality.

Born in Massachusetts, where his grandfather had been governor, McCall divided his time between his family's Massachusetts estate and his father's ranch in Prineville, Oregon. When he was nine, he settled permanently at the ranch in the midst of a family that read the classics and played music together, and for whom lively political discussion was a regular part of life.

Gregarious and dynamic through his college years, McCall was conscious of being solidly part of the establishment. But he admired and befriended those on campus who challenged the establishment, particularly those involved in campus journalism, his chosen field. He said, as he grew older and saw more of life, he became more sympathetic to their point of view. It was as a young journalist in Moscow, Idaho, that he first became actively involved in environmental issues. His years on the ranch had given him a respect for the land and an appreciation of its spiritual as well as practical value. It was in Idaho that he became publicity chairman of the Latah County Wildlife Federation, which advocated for the outdoor life including hunting, fishing, and conservation. It was also there, in the middle of the FDR administration, that he started a Young Republican club.

Many of these early experiences coalesced when, after a stint as a Navy war correspondent in the South Pacific, he got a job in Portland as a talk show host on KEX radio. Over the next twenty years, McCall built a statewide reputation as a journalist. In 1962 he produced the award-winning documentary *Pollution in Paradise*, which called for measures to clean up the Willamette River. In 1967 he began his first term as governor and tackled many of the issues he had raised as a journalist. But it was in a 1971 speech to the Jaycees that he uttered his famous line: "We want you to visit our State of Excitement often. Come again and again. But, for heaven's sake, don't move here to live." A bit later adding the slightly mitigating, "Or if you do have to move in to live, don't tell any of your neighbors where you are going."

Bolstered by tongue-in-cheek warnings to tourists—"Last year in Oregon 677 people fell off their bikes, and drowned"—these sentiments reached the national press, which dutifully spread them. The governor's office began receiving inquiries asking whether special permits were required for out-of-staters to visit Oregon.

But McCall was seriously and deeply concerned about growth. He worried Oregon would become the center of a megalopolis ranging from Seattle to San Francisco, "committing some of the richest farmland in America to supermarkets and suburbs." With the rising tide of environmental consciousness, he thought the timing might be right for a major effort to preserve the awe-inspiring natural beauty of the Oregon landscape.

McCall was convinced that "unlimited, unregulated growth leads inexorably to a lowered quality of life." In 1969 the Oregon legislature passed Senate Bill 10, which required every city and county in the state to have a comprehensive land use plan that met state objectives prescribed in the bill. In 1973 State Senator Ted Hallock, chair of the Senate Environmental and Land Use Committee, and State Senator and farmer Hector Macpherson sponsored Senate Bill 100, which created the Land Conservation and Development Commission (LCDC) to oversee and implement Oregon's land use laws by approving or rejecting city and county land use plans. Opponents argued that the bill would interfere with and confiscate private property. One group referred to the bill as "the biggest land grab since our great-grandparents took this land away from the Indians." On May 29, 1973, McCall signed the bill into law.

Far from being a draconian instrument, the legislation was designed to provide flexibility. General statewide goals were established by LCDC. Then it was up to cities and counties to designate the land within their boundaries for uses that they, knowing the area, thought were most appropriate (zoning the best farmland for farm use, for example). Urban growth boundaries were established around every city, with provision for expanding them if the need arose. There was recognition that the future would bring change, and city and county plans were to accommodate those changes. Whether that accommodation was fair was to be a matter of implementation.

In 1976, 1978, and 1982, McCall actively opposed initiatives to repeal SB100. All three initiatives were defeated, the first two by large margins. The vote was close in 1982. Opponents of the land use program blamed it for the prolonged recession of the early 1980s. In the 1982 campaign, as he was dying of cancer, McCall said: "If the legacy we helped give Oregon and which made it twinkle from afar—if it goes, then I guess I wouldn't want to live in Oregon anyhow." Many credited McCall with saving the program.

The votes on these initiatives did not settle the debates between the property rights and social contract forces. Nearly three decades later, Oregon's many new residents have never heard of Tom McCall and do not understand the debt owed to the land use laws resulting from his and others' efforts for the farms and forests and open spaces they enjoy, or how easily that legacy can be lost. Despite continuous adjustments to the land use program by the Oregon legislature and LCDC through its rulemaking authority, the friction between the two tectonic plates—property rights and the social contract—has not abated. As the plates grind against each other, they create new edges that re-define fairness.

OREGON RE-BALANCES

The push for changes to the land use planning program has come from various directions. To be sure, some are speculators, who look forward to taking advantage of land whose development value has been greatly increased through the years by the very land use laws they seek to circumvent. But it has been individual landowners who have drawn most of the attention to unfairness they perceive in the program. Many landowners believe they have borne a disproportionate share of the burdens of those laws and want the burdens to be more widely shared by others.

The tension between these forces produced an earthquake in 2000, when Oregon voters passed Measure 7, a citizens' initiative that restricted the power of state and local governments to limit development. The Oregon Supreme Court struck the measure down on a constitutional technicality, but aftershocks followed. Riding a wave of anger over the court ruling, program opponents rewrote Measure 7 to avoid constitutional problems and persuaded voters to enact Measure 37 in 2004. Measure 37 required state and local governments to pay landowners for any reduction in property value resulting from land use regulations, or to drop the restrictions.

Litigation to overturn the measure failed. State and local governments began implementation in 2005.

Meanwhile, property rights advocates across the nation saw passage of Measure 37—in the bastion of statewide land use planning—as an opening for efforts in their own states. They were further energized by the overwhelmingly negative reaction to the 2005 U.S. Supreme Court ruling in *Kelo v. City of New London*. The Supreme Court supported the city's use of eminent domain in an urban renewal scheme that had resulted in condemnation of several homes whose owners had refused to sell to the government, even though the condemned properties were to be transferred to a global pharmaceutical company's 100-acre manufacturing complex.

A multi-state campaign to place initiatives on the November 2006 ballot in six western states—Arizona, Washington, Montana, Idaho, Nevada, and California—quickly got underway. *High Country News* reported that the Los Angeles-based Reason Foundation had set forth a 64-page strategy entitled "Statewide Regulatory Takings Reform: Exporting Measure 37 to Other States." The basic strategy was to ride the *Kelo* wave but expand the narrow eminent domain issue to land use regulations as a whole. The Natty Bumppo/Howard Roark rugged individualist narrative was on a roll. Or so it seemed.

Then the Measure 37 story began to unfold. The media carried a steady stream of stories about claims involving big developments in surprising places. Multiple claims were filed by out-of-state timber company Plum Creek to subdivide 32,000 acres in Lincoln and Coos Counties on the Oregon coast. *The Oregonian* told of a claim for a 640-acre subdivision—or $6.4 million in compensation—near Fish Lake on the slopes of Steens Mountain in southeast Oregon, a treasured landscape and part of a protection area established by Congress in 2000.

Property owners filed 7,500 claims by the deadline in the measure. Portland State University estimated it would cost state and local governments $15 billion to pay off the claims. A stark reality emerged: because the measure provided no funds to pay the claims, state and local governments had only one option: give up the regulations. It began to dawn on neighbors of claimants that, in the absence of money to pay claims, they were going to have new "neighbors." Instead of the children of the grandmother of the Yes on Measure 37 Campaign ads who was denied the right to build houses for the kids on her property, the new "neighbors" might be aggregate mining operations, big subdivisions, shopping centers, apartments, and billboards.

Besides focusing on surprising beneficiaries of Measure 37, newspapers across the state also drew attention to studies that cast new light on the fairness of compensation for landowners. The Portland-based American Land Institute released a study that showed reductions in property taxes on farmland, intended by the legislature to compensate owners for new regulations, saved farmland owners $3.9 billion between 1974 and 2005. These taxes had been shifted to urban taxpayers, often seen by rural landowners as the chief beneficiaries of regulation of rural lands. Another study found that the values of agricultural land in much of the state increased from 1975—when the state farmland protection program took effect—faster than investments in the stock market, despite the regulations.

The national media also took note of the unfolding story. The *New York Times* reported a $203 million claim associated with a pumice mine on private property surrounded by the National Volcanic Monument at Newberry Crater in central Oregon. The *New Yorker* published a review of Jared Diamond's book *Collapse,* which searched for explanations for societal decisions over the ages that proved to be suicidal. Written by *Tipping Point* author Malcolm Gladwell, the review drew a parallel between Diamond's stories and Oregon voters' approval of Measure 37. Polling in Oregon indicated a shift of sympathy against Measure 37. The drumbeat of stories was taking a toll.

It occurred to many people that Measure 37's new tilt on the property rights–social contract balance was not fair. Not only had many claimants been compensated for the loss of development opportunities by dramatic property tax reductions over many years, but also the big new developments, now allowed because the regulations that limited them would have to be abandoned, would impose harms upon the public and reduce the values of neighboring properties. And what about the fact that some of the property value claimants said they had lost to regulations came not from their hard work, but from investments in roads and other public works?

Support for ballot measures similar to Measure 37 in western states also began to wane. But there was more going on than lightbulbs about the real beneficiaries of the measures. The strategy to "piggyback" an attack on land use regulations on the anger generated by the Supreme Court's *Kelo* decision on eminent domain failed as opposition campaigns pointed to overreaching. All the measures across the nation aimed solely at the *Kelo* decision passed. Of the six measures in the West aimed at eminent domain and land use regulations, only the Arizona measure passed.

The tension at the colliding edge of the social-contract and property-rights tectonic plates yielded more than aftershocks in 2006. It brought advocates of the two positions back to the table at the 2007 Oregon legislature. Statewide polling heading into the session showed disenchantment with Measure 37. But the polling also revealed continuing concern with the effects of land use regulations on individual property owners. Rather than seek outright repeal of Measure 37, supporters of the land use planning program asked for referral to the November 2007 ballot of a measure that revised Measure 37 to allow a limited number of new dwellings on agricultural and forest lands and other regulated lands. After intense debate over the number of dwellings to allow, the legislature sent newly minted Measure 49 to the ballot.

Voters passed Measure 49 by a 62–38 percent margin, a larger margin than passed either Measure 7 or 37. A collective sigh of relief whispered across the state. The *Oregonian* said it was "wonderful to be back . . . to a long-lost place, a kind of Brigadoon where the state's environmental achievements still shimmer." Property rights advocates sensed they had achieved their principal objective and announced they would work to ensure Measure 49 delivered on its promise to individual property owners.

And so concluded a seven-year run of earthquake and aftershocks at the edge of the colliding tectonic plates. Before passage of Measure 7 in 2000, the "fairness edge" was found at the Fifth Amendment to the U.S. Constitution and Article I, section 18, of the Oregon constitution. With passage of Measure 49 in 2007, the property-rights plate had ground into the social-contract plate, yielding a new reconciliation between the two narratives. Voters seemed to say: "We need Aesop's Plane-Tree to limit the sometimes rapacious behaviors of large development interests. But we also need to prune the Plane-Tree to allow some sunshine on property owners who use their land for homes for their families." ▧

From "River Soldiers"

David James Duncan

I WAS born in a hospital located, of all places, on a volcanic cone. . . . My birth cone's slopes are drained by tiny seasonal streams which, like most of the creeks in that industrialized quadrant of Portland, were buried in underground pipes long before I came on the scene. . . . I was born, then, without a watershed. . . .

I didn't rebel against my situation. Little kids don't rebel. Rebellion comes later, along with the hormones. What I *did* do, from as far back as I can remember, was start handbuilding my own rivers—and in the process broke all neighborhood records for amount of time spent running a garden hose. . . .

I built minuscule hazelnut rafts and elderberry canoes, launched them on my river, let them ride down to the growing driveway puddle that served as my Pacific. I stole a three-inch blue plastic cavalry soldier from my brother's Fort Apache set, cut the stock off his upraised rifle so that only the long, flexible barrel remained, tied a little thread to the end of the barrel to serve as fly-line, and sent the soldier fishing.

I don't know how it happened . . . , but that little guy has become me. I'm trapped in him, now. I have become a River Soldier.

It's a strange profession to try to describe at cocktail parties:

"Hi. Glad to meet you. What do I do for a living? Well, I'm a River Soldier."

"Hmmm," some say. "Is that more of a Republican thing, or a Democrat thing?"

"Different spectrum," I answer. "Democrats and Republicans exist on a left to right, liberal to conservative spectrum. River Soldiers exist on a high to low elevation, mountain to ocean spectrum. Humans are seventy-eight percent water. So. Being true to this seventy-eight percent of everyone, regardless of anyone's left to right spectrum—that's the job of the River Soldier."

How does that work out in day-to-day life? Here's one small example:

My dentist in Montana loves rivers. My dentist also proudly calls himself "as right wing as you can get." This is not a good description of how I happen to think of myself. But it's my dentist's gentle hands, not his right wing, that so painlessly and skillfully fix my teeth. A River Soldier, in such a dentist's chair, endeavors to be like a river. You oxbow and meander away from the hot buttons, find the shared passions, home in on the water molecules, the trout the dentist caught, the otter you saw last week, and you talk about that. Why judge, why argue, why alienate the best dentist you ever had because of an alleged right wing you can't even see?

Another example of day-to-day River Soldiering:

Back at that same cocktail party, somebody says: "I *love* Rush Limbaugh."

Somebody else turns crimson and says: "Well *I* love Dave Foreman."

Or probably they both already *were* crimson, if they love Rush Limbaugh and Dave Foreman. My response to both: "Well, Rush and Dave, like you and me, are seventy-eight percent clear clean water and a hundred percent dead without that water. So let's focus on the inarguable. Dave and Rush, like it or not, are seventy-eight percent molecularly identical."

What can anyone say in objection? The worst case scenario is: "Seventy-eight percent, eh? Well, I twenty-two percent disagree with everything you're saying!"

I can seventy-eight percent live with that.

Life is short. There are people and animals and songbirds, there are crayfish and herons and caddis fly larva and swimming and splashing and accidentally-gulping-the-creek children, there are sentient beings on watersheds everywhere worth knowing and serving by watching over their lifegiving waters. The River Soldier's allegiance is not to political parties: it's to the unjudgeable seventy-eight percent of every human and the entire planet: the seventy-eight percent that no creature from the least to the greatest can live without.

Norman Maclean's father was one of us. Reverend Maclean loved to carry a Greek New Testament in his wicker creel when he flyfished the Blackfoot near my home in Montana, because his River Soldiering habit was to catch a few trout, clean them, then sit down under a pine by the river, pull the Greek Gospels from his creel, put the trout in the creel where the gospels had been, then read Blackfoot and good book at once, enabling himself to turn from sunlit riffles to hovers of insects to water running over stones to the primordial Word, *logos*, and know that he was reading a single beautiful text.

Norman Maclean was one of us. Of the same Blackfoot, in *A River Runs Through It*, Norman writes: "Heat mirages danced with each other, and then they danced through each other, till eventually the watcher joined the river and there was only one of us. I believe it was the river."

James Dickey, sober, was one of us. He called his favorite river "a holy hallway." Tom McGuane is one of us: he calls "every refractive glide of water a glimpse of eternity." Izaak Walton was one of us: he wrote that while fishing he was sometimes "lifted above earth, and posses'd [of] joys not promised in my birth." Lorian Hemingway is one of us. Returning in her forties to the rank home creek of her Mississippi childhood, she wrote, "I looked down the clogged channel—at the sedge broom, wild holly, sawgrass, brambles knotted up like barbwire, and watched the clean red feather of a cardinal drift from the open limbs of a sweet gum tree, spin like a maple seed caught on a draft of wind, and land on water just short of my outstretched palm, an invitation home."

Jim Harrison is one of us. In "Cabin Poem" he writes:

I've decided to make up my mind
about nothing, to assume the water mask,
to finish my life disguised as a creek,
an eddy, joining at night the full
sweet flow, to absorb the sky,
to swallow the heat and cold, the moon
and the stars, to swallow myself
in ceaseless flow.

River Soldiers. All dangerous people in their way, I suppose, mucking peacefully around in the rivers and creeks out there. . . . Caretaking the waters shared by liberals, conservatives, ouzels, mink, trout, and bottomfish alike. Creekophiles. Stone skippers. Aquatic insect watchers . . .

We're not anti-progress, anti-profit, anti-politics. We're not anti any-thing except lifeless, deadly, child-betraying, wildlife-exterminating water. We just happen to have discovered that once you start spending time in holy hallways, glimpsing eternity in glides of water, seeing invitations in cardinal feathers, and being lifted above earth by unpromised joys, all thanks to nothing but clean, clear H2O, you tend to stop obsessing over the Gross National Product. Less gross but equally national products such as baby fish, mayfly swarms, and kingfishers start to tilt your needle instead. You turn off CNN and turn to side channels, holding pools, frog ponds, spring creeks. You grow happily haunted by the sound of the English words *riffle, rise, rain*, the Indian words *Clackamas, Chewana, Celilo, Wallawalla*, the primordial Greek word *logos* coupled with the sound of primordial water purling over equally primordial stone.

We're not in the phone book, but you can find us on most any creek and river. Don't call us. Let the creek or river call you. The life and health of the waters flowing into our lives; the life and health of the waters flowing out of our lives; the clear, lovable seventy-eight percent of all our neighbors: this is the news that absorbs us. Our absorption doesn't make many news headlines, but there's a newsworthy reason for this: eventually there may be only one of us. Norman believes it's the river.

We call ourselves the River Soldiers. ▣

WATER IN THE WEST

Charles Wilkinson

W E all have our mentors, people who give us their wisdom and comfort and teach us about our worlds and ourselves. I've had two principal mentors and, although both are gone now, they have remained with me.

The first was Paul Roca, a great lawyer in Phoenix, a lawyer who charged the highest fees between Houston and Los Angeles and who claimed that he had to keep it that way because his clients wanted proof that they had retained the best.

That was 1965, when I had just joined Lewis & Roca, where Paul was a senior partner. I was new to the region—I'd never been out west before going to law school at Stanford—and it was Paul who was the matchmaker in my love affair with the American West. He told me that in order to be a great lawyer in Arizona you had to know Arizona as well as you knew the law. He taught me more than I could ever say, sending me clippings, recommending books, drawing maps of river systems in the desert sand with a stick during early morning hunts for doves, and telling me late-night stories over *toros bravos* (one part kahlua, three parts tequila), stories of labor strikes in the Arizona copper mines, and of bold TR himself coming out in 1911 to christen Roosevelt Dam, its rock carved by Italian stone masons and its water bringing green fields and statehood, stories of the Mogollon Rim, Fray Marcos de Niza, the Mormon settlement of the Arizona strip, ironwood, and crooked land deals. I left Phoenix eventually, but Paul stayed with me.

In 1977 I first read Wallace Stegner, our greatest western writer, who in time would become my second mentor. *Angle of Repose* was the book. I was entranced by the way he captured the West with his plain words and by the scope and depth of what he knew. I bought an armload of Stegner books and dove in.

I was teaching at the University of Oregon at the time. Water law, public land law, and Indian law—western courses, all—were my subjects. Yet Wally's writing was telling me more about the law than the court decisions and the statutes. He wrote about the western mind and experience, and about the land and rivers and aridity, and I began to see how those things shaped the laws of the American West.

A few years later I wrote Wally a letter asking him if we could get together. I had inadvertently stumbled onto one of the West's best secrets, which is that Stegner was such a gentleman that he'd answer anybody's letter, usually by return mail and always with a generous spirit. In time, Wally and I became good friends, and it was one of the greatest blessings of my life.

Together, Paul and Wally showed me that law is organic, that it grows out of a society. To learn about law, learn about the society and its distinctive qualities, its history, peoples, lands, and waters, its possibilities and limitations.

Law, in other words, has a habitat. And, in time, as society—law's habitat—changes, so does the law, responding to evolving priorities, new stress points, and higher dreams.

THE TRADITIONAL WATER SYSTEM

The notion that law grows out of a society is writ especially vividly in the American West, where we have created so many distinctive western legal institutions. Most of these deal with our relationship to the waters and land that are so essential to defining society here. So we have distinctive laws for public land mining, grazing, and logging; for Indian tribes; and, perhaps most notably, for water.

The prior appropriation doctrine, the core of western water law, was created to meet the felt needs of the mining camps during the California gold rush. Under this doctrine, the person first in time to divert water from a stream for a beneficial use is the person with a right "senior" to, or having priority over, all subsequent water users on that particular stream.

The gold rush was an extraordinary time. Americans virtually invented a new society. When James Marshall made his historic find in January 1848, there were about 15,000 non-Indians in California. Just four years later, the figure was 250,000. One historian of the gold rush titled his book *And the World Rushed In*, and he had it right. It was one of the largest migrations in human history.

Water law in the eastern United States and in England employed the riparian doctrine. Riparian law viewed the watershed as an integral natural unit. Export out of the watershed was prohibited or disfavored. Keeping water in the streams was valued as an amenity that enhanced the worth and beauty of all parcels of land along the watercourse.

This was nonsense to the utilitarian miners who flooded to the gold- and silver-bearing deposits of the West in the middle of the nineteenth century. They were there on business, not in pursuit of amenities. Water was the linchpin of the miners' operations, whether they were washing river gravel away from the gold dust and nuggets with pans, sluices, or long toms: blasting away at hillsides with high-power hydraulic hoses; or transporting water twenty miles or more to remote mining towns such as Mokelumne Hill or Columbia by means of the serpentine canals that still wind across the California gold country.

Thus western mining was water intensive from the beginning. In addition, water was scarce in those hot, dry foothills. The mining camps had no use for a riparian law, developed thousands of miles away in country where water was plentiful, that called for most water to be left as is. Water was not an amenity in gold rush times; it was an engine. Mining—that is, society—could not proceed unless water could be assured in sufficient and certain quantities. Riparian law made little sense in the western habitat.

The miners developed their own customs. Just as the first miner to stake a claim was accorded the right to work the area, so too was the first user of water considered to have an absolute right of priority. In 1855, the Supreme Court of California promptly approved the miners' rules in *Irwin v. Phillips* and made "first in time, first in right" the law of California. In this justly famous opinion, the judges stated that "courts are bound to take notice of the political and social condition of the country which they judicially rule."

The prior appropriation doctrine quickly became the deeply ingrained water law of every western state, although Washington and California retain remnants of the riparian scheme. Prior appropriation rejects the riparian doctrine wholesale. The first user gets a guaranteed supply of water. In times of shortage, junior users are cut off according to their order of priority. There is no sharing of water. There is no need to preserve water in a watercourse. A stream or lake can be drained low or dried up entirely as has occurred with hundreds of western rivers and streams.

These rules reflected the deeply held belief that the wisest state policy is a passive one: decisions on water use were best made by individual private water users. The first users could decide the future for the stream, for its associated wildlife and wetlands, and for present and future landowners in the watershed.

Farmers, and later ranchers, made up the next waves of settlers in the westward expansion. They, too, needed water as the essential resource in their operations. In most of the arid region west of the 100th meridian, annual precipitation averages fewer than twenty inches, the amount of water needed to farm without irrigation. Almost everywhere in the West, water must be taken out of watercourses and applied artificially to the fields by irrigation. Prior appropriation law guaranteed early appropriators of legal rights to a sure supply of water to put on their fields. Irrigation quickly became the dominant water use in the West. Even today, eighty percent or more of all water in the western states is used for irrigation, with twenty percent going to municipal and industrial uses.

But many western farmers required more than a legal doctrine to get water to their fields. Crops needed water in the late summer and early fall, long after snowmelt from the mountains had flowed past. Potentially fertile farming areas often were located far from the rivers or on benchlands high above steep canyon walls. Private enterprise in the form of farming and ranching cooperative associations was inadequate to raise the capital needed to build large storage reservoirs or to construct canals and laterals for transporting the water. Wallace Stegner's novel *Angle of Repose* told the heartbreaking story of a family's fruitless attempts to make a go of farming in the arid Boise Valley in the late nineteenth century.

The federal government, keen to complete the settlement of the West, stepped in. The Reclamation Act of 1902 authorized funding for most of the big irrigation projects that now dot the region. Homestead entries boomed as new waves of settlers moved west to capitalize on the offer of nearly free farmland and water. Reclamation was heavily subsidized from the beginning—billions of federal dollars have been expended to provide cheap western water.

Traditional western water law, then, has been dominated by the themes of extreme deference to individual decisions to the exclusion of larger societal concerns: stable priority for historic uses; preferences for consumptive, usually commercial, uses; a lack of protection for instream flows; and the provision of subsidized water for irrigators. Furthermore, the state laws made no place for Indian rights.

It goes without saying that this range of nineteenth- and early twentieth-century priorities is not as broad as the spectrum of considerations that must be accommodated in current water policy. In many respects, this system is radical today. Yet it made sense to those people, in those times, in those places, and my guess is that modern westerners, myself included, would have made the same decisions if we had been alive then.

There is no doubt that traditional western water development, including reclamation, accomplished many worthy things. Although homesteading is commonly associated with the nineteenth century, in fact the greatest flood of homestead patents, driven by the Reclamation Act, occurred between about 1900 and 1920. Reclamation directly irrigated 9.2 million acres of arid land, nearly one-third of all irrigated terrain in the West, and thus effectively opened them for settlement.

The impact of this irrigated land went far beyond the actual acres watered. Farms create jobs in farm employment and in the equipment businesses that supply farms. Whole communities then grow up around the agricultural base. The good that came out of reclamation is evident in the many solid farming and ranching communities across the West, whether on the Snake River Plain, in the lower Yellowstone River valley, in the Gunnison River valley, or in southern Washington.

THE POST–WORLD WAR II ERA

We often think of the nineteenth century—triggered as it was by the colorful and explosive California gold rush—as being the decisive period in the history of the West. Now we can see, however, that the profound demographic changes wrought during the period since World War II—the period we are still in—have transcended even the dramatic events of the nineteenth century.

For a century and a half, the American West has hitched its destiny to rapid population growth. And most people would agree that wide-open boosterism had its place and time. The West, after all, was the nation's last place to be settled, and civic infrastructures—whole economies, really—had to be built out of rock, sand, and stingy rivers.

But now, for the first time in history, westerners are directly questioning growth—its high price tag and the way it is remaking communities and the land itself. We hear these concerns all across the region, from Denver to Reno and from Phoenix to Seattle. We hear them, too, in the farm, cattle, and tourist towns.

It is no wonder. In just two generations, since World War II, the West has industrialized and urbanized in a way perhaps unparalleled in world history.

It has come on so fast. Civic leaders had always wanted much, much more population and wealth, and beginning in 1945 they got it. The Cold War was a bonanza for the West, which had the open land required for military installations and defense industries. The soil, when irrigated, could grow any crop from alfalfa to hops to apples to pears to cherries. The land was magnificent, perfect for locating subdivisions and companies.

Perfect also were the postwar politics. Washington, D.C., picked up the bill, building the military installations, subsidizing water projects, and underwriting the interstate highways. Federal largesse carried few strings: there was minimal oversight of health, environmental, or budgetary matters.

In 1945 the West's population stood at 17 million. Today it is over 60 million. Nearly all of the growth has come in the cities. The state of Washington has boomed from 2 million at the end of the War to 5.5 million today, with most of the 3 ½ million increase coming in the Puget Sound area. The Denver area has boomed from 475,000 to 2.5 million. Phoenix, a dirt-road settlement of 5,500 people in 1900, grew to a metropolitan area of 250,000 by 1945. Today the Valley of the Sun is pushing 3.5 million. Las Vegas could not even qualify as a city for the census, which required a minimum of 2,500 people, until 1920. At the end of the War, Las Vegas had about 20,000 people. In 1995 it reached 1 million. And Los Angeles. . . .

Though the population is urban, the postwar boom has taken a heavy toll on the rural West. The resources couldn't come from the cities themselves. They had already exhausted their own water supplies. Coal-fired power plants near the cities would make the smog—a word invented in postwar Los Angeles—even worse.

So the cities reached into the interior West. For the southwestern urban areas, the main target was the Colorado Plateau, the Four Corners Area,

the spectacular redrock canyon country, home to the nation's most traditional Indian people. The plateau's deep canyons would make superb reservoirs. The ages had laid down some of the best coal, oil, gas, and uranium
deposits on earth.

Almost before anyone knew it, the Colorado Plateau was laced with
dams and reservoirs up to two hundred miles long, power plants with
stacks seventy stories tall, 500- and 345-KV powerlines spanning hundreds of miles, and uranium operations that required mining, milling,
and, almost as an afterthought, waste disposal.

In all, this big build-up of the Colorado Plateau—its heyday ran from
1955 through 1975—was one of the most prodigious exercises of industrial
might in human history.

Among the few competitors was the furious post–World War II build-
up of hydroelectric and nuclear energy in the Columbia River Basin, where
inland dams and power plants were built to supply energy to the cities. We
all know the stresses in the Northwest. We are fast losing open space in
general, and forest and farm land in particular. We are losing our rivers,
too. Above Bonneville Dam near Portland the term "Columbia River" is a
euphemism. All the way to Canada, nearly six hundred river miles, there
is virtually no river; instead, a succession of reservoirs backed up nearly
flush against one another, leaving only fifty miles of open water in a few
chopped-up segments. We did that to the River of the West in a strobe-light
blink of time, just twenty-five years. And we know the effect on the quick,
strong, silvery Pacific salmon, the Northwest's essential animal, the runs
now at just five to ten percent of historic levels. Of course, events of that
magnitude will change not just the natural habitat but also the views and
determination of the people. The habitat of the law in the Pacific Northwest has been fundamentally altered by the state of the salmon.

We also face an intangible cost: we are losing the West, both the slow-
moving, uncluttered way of life and the spirituality that lies thick and
sweet over every river, every high divide, every green orchard and farm,
every big expanse of open sagebrush range.

We have not yet lost the West. But a question now looms over the land:
Suppose we do for the next fifty years, or even the next twenty-five, what
we have done since World War II; if we do that, will we still have the West?
These questions hang in the air over us now, over the discussions we have
and decisions we make for our rivers and lands.

WESTERN WATER LAW AND POLICY IN TRANSITION

At the end of World War II, the traditional system of water law remained essentially intact across the West. But as the habitat—the societal habitat as well as the natural habitat—began to change, so did the law. Some of the main forces that have driven this change are:

1. The public's determination to become involved in water decisions—a shift away from the right of an individual water user to make unilateral decisions toward a full recognition of public interest.
2. Objections, in an era of tight government budgets, to the cost of water projects, especially when subsidized.
3. A deep-running concern over the many environmental consequences, including the waning salmon runs, that have resulted from water development.
4. An understanding that the natural beauty of the West has many economic benefits, including its value as a magnet to tourists and to light, clean, community-oriented business.
5. Sympathy over the loss of farmland and farm communities that can result from water transfers to urban use.
6. The felt need to fulfill Indian tribal *Winters* doctrine water rights, which are usually senior, because they arose when the federal government reserved the land.

There are more abstract, and deeply emotional, concerns that plainly influence policy, including the ideas that a river is a place of beauty and mystery, that a western canyon can have a mystical quality, and that rivers and canyons are rare and sacred. These are important ideas and have been explored in an upswelling of good writing, as good as any in the world.

We can see a new perception of land and water, too, in the mind of William O. Douglas, former Supreme Court justice, who grew up in, and loved, the Yakima Valley in Washington. When he was just six, Douglas lost his father, whom he idolized. At the funeral in Yakima, the young boy fell into melancholy and terror during the indoor services at the church. Once the small congregation moved outside to the cemetery, however, the Cascades—as this landscape does—brought him some healing:

Then I happened to see Mount Adams towering over us to the west. It
was dark purple and white in the August day and its shoulders of basalt
were heavy with glacial snow. . . . As I looked, I stopped sobbing. My eyes
dried. Adams stood cool and calm, unperturbed by the events that stirred
us so deeply. Suddenly the mountain seemed to be a friend, a force for me
to tie to, a symbol of stability and sovereignty.

When Douglas finally left the court, old and infirm, having served
longer than nearly any other justice, he wrote his farewell to his fellow
justices by treating their explorations of the nation's constitution and laws
as a metaphorical river journey:

I am reminded of many canoe trips I have taken in my lifetime. . . . There
were always a pleasant camp in a stand of white bark birch and water
concerts held at night to the music of the loons; and inevitably there came
the last camp fire, the last breakfast cooked over last night's fire, and the
parting was always sad. . . .

The greatest such journey I've made has been with you, my Brethren,
who were strangers at the start but warm and fast friends at the end.
The value of our achievements will be for others to appraise. Other like
journeys will be made by those who follow us, and we trust that they will
leave these wilderness water courses as pure and unpolluted as we left
those which we traversed.

What William O. Douglas knew, and what each of us knows, is that the
land, rivers, and canyons are the soul of the West.

The last of the realizations about water and the natural world that has
been imprinted on us since World War II is something I'd like to separate
from environmental consequences generally, though it is fundamentally
related to the loss of habitat, both land and water. That is the matter of species loss. This is a complicated matter, but I'd like to allude to some basic
facts.

Edward O. Wilson, a biologist from Harvard, is the world's leading
authority on biodiversity—species diversity. Wilson, who emphasizes
that his figures are conservative, squarely addresses the loosely discussed
idea that over the course of geologic time we have always had species loss
and that our problems today are nothing new. In fact, the scale of extinctions is far beyond anything that has gone before. Wilson estimates that

ten percent of all species have gone extinct since human beings have populated Earth. The rate of extinction has increased, especially since the Industrial Age, and especially since World War II. At current trends, another twenty percent of all species will be lost by 2025. This would amount to extinction of thirty percent of all species during the tenure of humans. The current rate of extinction is between 1,000 and 10,000 times the rate of extinction before humans. Worldwide, we are losing a species every 15 minutes.

So there is a host of economic, environmental, and social concerns that has changed the way water policy law proceeds. The past decade or so has been a dynamic time of change, with westerners reacting to new circumstances in fundamentally the same way that they did in 1902 with the Reclamation Act and in the mid-nineteenth century when prior appropriation was created.

Most basically, it has become a difficult matter to get a water project funded and built, especially when subsidies are involved. And senior water rights are not as secure as they once were. The law now recognizes substantial limits on water rights, including the states' established right to regulate for efficiency; the increasing use of various water pollution laws to alter existing uses; the public trust doctrine; various instream flow laws; the seniority of Indian tribal rights, when established; and the Endangered Species Act.

These changes have come because of the enormous stress on western waters. Our rivers simply cannot give us all the things we want from them. Farmers too often feel like targets because the largest block of water has been dedicated to irrigation and because long-established patterns of water use are now called into question. Yet other westerners feel every bit as much put upon. Indian tribes rightly believe that treaty promises, upheld by the Supreme Court in the 1908 *Winters* decision, have never been honored. Conservation and sportsmen's groups think we have made a grievous mistake by developing the rivers too hard and too fast. The tragedy is that we seem inevitably to be in for a long period of stress that will not finally abate until the West's out-of-control population growth levels off.

But we have begun to develop strategies to deal with the excesses of the post–World War II era, and I'd like to turn to a hopeful set of developments.

INNOVATIONS ON WESTERN RIVERS

Westerners have invented new, flexible approaches to deal with water as one organic part of natural resources policy. Increasingly, now that water policy has become so intensely public and raises so many different kinds of issues and concerns, we have begun to proceed in a new way that is fundamentally different from the traditional system in which water users made separate decisions on their own.

The traditional structure for western watersheds has had two main layers: general federal laws—the Federal Power Act, the reclamation acts, and modern federal statutes such as the National Environmental Policy Act, the Clean Water Act, and the Endangered Species Act—and state laws, such as water laws and state forest practices acts, which typically were much looser. In many cases, however, we have broken the traditional mold and moved into much more flexible, creative, and individualized approaches focusing on specific natural systems. The federal government is less dominant, sometimes serving mainly as a convenor. The state water agencies are involved, and the third group of sovereigns, the tribes, have become extremely active, both in advocacy and in scientific research and management. For the first time, the conservation community has established state offices, several under the aegis of Trout Unlimited, that approach scientific policy and legal water issues on a state-specific basis. There are now water trusts, nonprofit organizations similar to land trusts, that purchase senior water rights and retire them so that the water can remain in the stream. The new approach is collaborative, with all affected governments, interest groups, and disciplines at the table. These groups are commonly called watershed councils.

The objective is sustainability of some natural system. The traditional multiple use–sustained yield management regime measured outputs, such as acre-feet, kilowatts, board-feet, and animal unit months. Sustainability today is broadly writ, encompassing a much broader range of things to be sustained, including salmon, eagles, wolves, humbler animals such as voles and chubs, archaeological sites, good rafting water, long vistas, wetlands, open space, solitude, beauty, and the cultures of traditional societies, whether they be Indian tribes, Hispanic towns, or ranch and farm communities. We have rightly begun to adopt an ambitious definition of sustainability.

We've made impressive progress in this kind of decision making, which is local not national, particular not general, open not closed, creative not cookie-cuttered, messy not neat. In this setting, dealing with a specific place, usually a watershed, the affected parties can negotiate issues such as environmental protection, recreation needs, the timing of irrigation withdrawals, instream flows, conservation measures, groundwater storage, water transfers, and the need for new construction.

We see this approach, always with refinements because these are bottom-up agreements, at Lake Tahoe, on the Truckee River, in the Sacramento Bay delta, at Mono Lake, in the Grand Canyon, on the Clark Fork in Montana, along the Columbia River Gorge, on Oregon's Umatilla River, in the Nisqually River watershed in Washington, and at numerous other places around the West. We have responded to changing times and have opened up the process to try to achieve sustainability. It is an accomplishment we ought to take pride in.

WATER FOR THE FUTURE

Yet we have an uneasiness in our hearts and minds and viscera about whether making collaborative decisions based on natural systems—valuable though the approach may be—can be enough in the long term. Take the groundwater situation in metropolitan Phoenix. Arizona has taken strong, progressive action—the Groundwater Management Act in 1980, the limits on water farming in 1991, the 1995 rules on "assured water supplies." The current groundwater overdraft is said to be about 350,000 acre-feet, down from about 1.3 million acre-feet in 1980. Yet that figure is misleading because a depressed agricultural economy has reduced the demand for water, and Phoenix has had some recent wet years. The true reduction of the overdraft is considerably less.

So Phoenix remains far from safe yield, even though it is now receiving Colorado River water. It is uncertain how much future water Phoenix can acquire from farmers and tribes. Meanwhile, the people continue to pour in. Arizona is one of the nation's fastest-growing states.

Water transfers, one of today's purported panaceas, can have steep costs—some of the same costs as old-style projects, others that we have not learned how to address in a serious way. Water policy is social, as well as natural resource policy. It always has been. Transfers can take irrigated land out of business and debilitate farm and ranch communities. We have seen that at Owens, along the Arkansas River in Colorado, and in some Arizona rural areas before the water farming debacle was largely arrested in the early 1990s. Today farms up and down the Colorado Front Range operate as tenants, waiting for Colorado Springs, Thornton, and other cities to call in their leased rights when new subdivisions want the water.

Water marketing can also debilitate traditional communities. In northern New Mexico, acequia associations—the Hispanic water distribution collectives—already feel the pressure from Albuquerque, which is growing apace with no significant water conservation program. As a *mayordomo* from an acequia in the Chama Valley told me, "Since a ditch system must be maintained by the collective labor of its users, each time a parcel loses its water rights, a proportionate amount of labor and ditch fees is also lost to the system as a whole. . . . Each member is a link in the chain of community water use and control, and each time a member and his quota of water and labor are lost, the overall chain is weakened." The integrity of our legal system could not hold when it came to recognizing Hispanic ownership of their land grants, supposedly guaranteed by the Treaty of Guadalupe Hidalgo, but the Hispanic communities have by and large held on to their water. Can our system of water laws have the integrity to assure a fair treatment of the acequias when the cities and their developers come calling?

The uneasiness about Phoenix groundwater is replicated for aquifers and river systems across the West. The apprehension about transfers in Hispanic communities is found on many reservations. Perhaps worse, the process for Indian water settlements is in shambles, leaving those tribes without quantified rights wondering if they will ever see their long-promised *Winters* water. The pressure to supply water for urban growth continues to build. Six other western states join Arizona among the ten fastest-growing states.

We know we can produce enough molecules of water for population growth in virtually any magnitude imaginable. But we also know that we can never escape the glare of geologist John Wesley Powell's stern visage, put forth in his landmark work, *Report on the Lands of the Arid Region of the United States* (1878). Thirteen percent of the West is desert and most of the rest of it is arid. Water is scarce, distinctive, valuable. Yes, we can bring enough water to the cities for the new subdivisions, but is this the wisest use and are we willing to bear the costs? The next century will bring different specifics from this one, but if we have learned any lesson, it is that from now on we must ask the question we never bothered to ask in water policy during the Big Build-up: we can do it, but is it worth it?

The most dramatic signs that we are stepping back for a moment and considering such questions come from the Pacific Northwest, where a dam removal movement is well underway. Coalitions of tribes, conservationists, and people who just plain love free-flowing rivers have generated broad public support to assure that Pacific salmon will once again surge into the prime habitats in the upper reaches of watersheds. Several small dams have already come out. Work is ready to begin on large structures on the Elwha River, flowing from Olympic National Park into the Strait of Juan de Fuca, and the White Salmon River, running south into the Columbia. Savage Rapids Dam, on the Rogue River in Oregon, has been decommissioned. The most ambitious restoration effort of all is on the Klamath River of Oregon and California, where magnificent historic salmon runs have been pushed to the brink. All parties have now agreed to take out four hydroelectric dams by 2020. This restoration effort on the Klamath will be the largest dam removal project ever undertaken in any country.

In the modern West, then, rivers have many uses, but fundamentally westerners want them to be rivers, not engines. We are even questioning Glen Canyon Dam, the behemoth that drowned 180 miles of red rock canyons and energized and symbolized the Big Build-Up of the Southwest. Wallace Stegner has written of this, urging us to finally move beyond the impacts and psychology of old-style western water projects:

> Behind the pragmatic, manifest-destinarian purpose of pushing western settlement through federal water management was another motive: the hard determination to dominate nature. . . . God and Manifest Destiny spoke with one voice urging us to "conquer" or "win" the West; and there was no voice of comparable authority to remind us of [the] . . . quiet but profound truth, [stated first by Mary Austin writing of the Owens Valley in *The Land of Little Rain*] that the manner of the country makes the usage of life there, and that the land will not be lived except in its own fashion. ◙

A River Runs against It

america's evolving view of dams[*]

Bruce Babbitt

During the New Deal, President Franklin Roosevelt and his interior secretary, Harold Ickes, toured the West, dedicating dams before large, enthusiastic crowds. Now, I am out touring the country with a different message: it is time to un-dedicate some of those dams by removing them and letting the rivers run free. For we now have too many of these dams, some 75,000, the equivalent of one every day since Thomas Jefferson wrote the Declaration of Independence. Along the way I am asking questions: Is this dam still serving its purpose? Do the benefits justify the destruction of fish runs and drying up of rivers? Can't we find a better balance between our needs and the needs of the river?

In some places the case for removing a dam is so easy to make that one wonders why it took so long. In December 1997 I took a sledgehammer to the Quaker Neck Dam on the Neuse River in North Carolina. As dams go, Quaker Neck isn't much; it's only six feet high and it doesn't generate power. But to the American shad trying to spawn upstream, that six feet might as well be six hundred, blocking off 900 miles of upstream spawning waters. Now biologists and engineers have figured out an alternative water diversion method and the dam has come down. And, just a year

[*] This article was originally published in 1998, while the author was Secretary of the U.S. Department of the Interior.

later, the shad are spawning seventy miles upstream all the way to the city of Raleigh.

Onward to the Kennebec River in Maine. In June 1998 I joined Governor Angus King and local officials in Augusta to announce an agreement for the removal of Edwards Dam. Standing on the riverbank we could see the dam up to our left, a stone and timber crib structure built clear back in 1837 at the start of the Industrial Revolution. On the bank above the dam, we could see the brick skeleton of the long-abandoned textile mill. In the river below the striped bass were swimming haplessly in circles searching for a way through the dam. An osprey circled overhead, then plunged into the waters to scoop up a stranded fish.

The textile mills were eventually abandoned, but the Edwards Dam refused to die. It was converted to produce the electricity that powered the first electric lights in Augusta. But by 1997 the dam was producing less than one half of one percent of the power used in the city. Residents began asking the inevitable question: Is that trickle of electric power worth destruction of the legendary runs of Atlantic salmon, stripers, and six other species of migratory fish? And now, after 157 years, Edwards Dam is coming down.

Each stop on these dam-busting tours stirs enormous local, regional, and national attention. And I always wonder, what is it about the sound of a sledgehammer on concrete that evokes such a reaction? We routinely demolish buildings that have served their purpose or when there is a better use for the land. Why not dams? For whatever reason, we view dams as akin to the pyramids of Egypt—a permanent part of the landscape, timeless monuments to our civilization and technology.

Those 75,000 dams are the cumulative result of two centuries of innovation and progress, accompanied by indifference to the natural world of river ecology. What started out as reasonable and desirable went on and on beyond all logic, overstating benefits, ignoring the damage to fisheries and river systems, and understating the financial costs. At the extreme, dams were built with government subsidies simply to add glamour to real estate developments. It even happened in Yosemite where park officials added a dam at Mirror Lake to raise the water level, thereby "enhancing" the reflection of Half Dome for visitors.

In the twentieth century, dam building was transformed from local project into national enterprise. Edison and Steinmetz started it with electric lights and long-distance transmission. Water power transformed into electricity could be sent instantaneously to every community in the country. Hydro dams became cash registers overflowing with money to finance ever larger projects. It remained only for Franklin D. Roosevelt and the Works Progress Administration (WPA) to build dams on the scale of the pharaohs—first came Bonneville Dam and Grand Coulee Dam on the Columbia, then the Tennessee Valley Authority, then Shasta Dam on the Sacramento. Dam building became an unstoppable, runaway political juggernaut of spending, job creation, and local pride.

As the juggernaut rolled on, we paid a steadily accumulating price for these projects in the form of fish runs destroyed, downstream rivers altered by changes in temperature, wedges of sediment piling up behind structures, downstream erosion, and delta wetlands degraded by lack of freshwater and saltwater intrusion. The great salmon runs of the Columbia River and the Snake drifted toward extinction. The Colorado River ran dry, its great delta, celebrated in the writings of Aldo Leopold, reduced to barren salt flats. The Platte River, once "a mile wide and an inch deep," shriveled, threatening the existence of the vast migratory flocks of sandhill cranes.

For decades dam building remained unstoppable. Even John Muir at the height of his powers was unable to stop the City of San Francisco from invading Yosemite National Park to construct the Hetch Hetchy Dam. Then in 1956 the dam builders selected a site within the National Park System, Dinosaur National Monument on the Colorado River. This time the opponents mounted a national campaign and won. But their victory came at a heavy price—as a tradeoff the dam was relocated outside the park, on a little known stretch of the Colorado River called Glen Canyon.

In 1963, as the dam gates closed and the river backed up and inundated hundreds of miles of river and canyon, we came to understand that the issue involved more than just keeping dams out of national parks and lamenting the loss of nice scenery. At stake was the integrity and life of the river system itself.

I began to reflect on these issues over the course of many days and nights spent in the Grand Canyon over the last half century. I hiked and boated and camped beside the Colorado River before Glen Canyon was built in the 1960s. In those years the Colorado River was a wild, unpredictable, red-brown, sediment-laden torrent, "too thick to drink, too thin to plow," flooding in the spring, languishing in the summer, always reflecting the seasonal weather across its vast Rocky Mountain watershed.

When the gates of Glen Canyon Dam, a few miles upstream from Grand Canyon, closed in 1963, we started to notice the downstream changes. The warm silt-laden waters turned jello green and cold. In the depths of the Grand Canyon the waters rose and fell on a daily cycle, in response to the heating and air-conditioning demands in Phoenix and Los Angeles.

Over time, as I floated down the river, I saw trees high on the talus slope wither and die for lack of water from seasonal flooding. I saw sandbars, once covered with arrowweed, willow, and cottonwood, disappear as the silt-free waters scoured the banks down to granite boulders. I saw the once plentiful native fish—unlike those anywhere else on earth—driven back into a few isolated tributaries, threatened with extinction.

Remorseful river runners and canyon lovers, inspired by the writing of Edward Abbey, began to talk of a campaign to remove the dam and empty Lake Powell. Barry Goldwater ruefully acknowledged that his support for the dam was the one vote of his career that he most regretted. The elegiac photographs of Eliot Porter in *The Place No One Knew* inspired people in different parts of the country to look at their own rivers with new vision. Gradually the tide of national opinion turned and projects began to come under question. The two dams proposed in Grand Canyon were killed by the Congress. In California, Governor Reagan halted a project on the Eel River, and the legislature followed with protections for the remaining wild rivers in northern California.

Thus it was that the Glen Canyon experience awakened long-dormant dreams of river restoration and dam removal. In 1992 Congress took a tentative step in the direction of dam removal by authorizing the National Park Service to examine the feasibility of removing two dams on the Elwha River on the border of Olympic National Park in Washington. The two dams, Elwha and Glines Canyon, present a textbook case for dam removal. The Elwha River rises in the snowfields of the Olympic Mountains, thunders down a narrow canyon toward the Pacific, and then slows to a dead halt against the concrete barrier of Glines Canyon Dam. A few miles below Glines Canyon, the river gathers force once again, only to come against the second barrier, Elwha Dam.

The structures at Elwha and Glines Canyon were erected early in the twentieth century to provide power for a then-isolated community on the Olympic Peninsula. Today, however, that community, Port Angeles, has access to the regional power grid in a region where there is a huge surplus of power hanging over the market. Meanwhile the two dams have elimi-

nated one of the great chinook salmon runs of the Northwest. A few of
this salmon stock linger on in hatcheries, awaiting either restoration or
probable extinction. Also awaiting dam removal are over seventy miles
of streams radiating downward from the heart of Olympic National Park.

In 1996 the Park Service completed an environmental impact study
demonstrating the feasibility of taking the dams down. In 1997 I signed
a formal decision recommending removal. Having requested us to study
and make a recommendation, the Congress is now equivocating, refusing
to appropriate the full sum necessary to carry out dam removal. But with
strong support from Washington residents and Governor Gary Locke, and
partial funding extracted from Congress under threat of presidential veto,
it now seems only a matter of time until the dams come down and the
salmon once again make their way upstream into the living heart of Olympic National Park.

The next big test for river restoration is approaching on the lower Snake
River and its four salmon-killing dams. And it will be an epic debate, rival-
ing the great controversies of past years over Hetch Hetchy and Dinosaur
National Monument. This time it will not be about protecting scenery
within a national park. It will be about restoring a river ecosystem and its
salmon runs. That fact alone demonstrates how we as a nation have come
to comprehend that our stewardship obligation extends beyond park borders to encompass entire watersheds and landscapes.

The Columbia-Snake is one of the most industrialized river systems
in America. The largest of its dams, Grand Coulee, cuts off more than a
thousand miles of salmon streams in Washington and British Columbia.
Bonneville Dam, dedicated by President Roosevelt in 1937, initiated the
damming of the lower river. After that the dams marched relentlessly up
river—the Dalles, John Day, McNary, Priest Rapids.

Through all this dam building the salmon managed to hang on, continuing their annual migration rites up the Columbia, then into the Snake
and on into the Salmon River system of Idaho. Fish ladders helped some.
Hatcheries were built by the dozen to boost production of declining stocks
and offset fish ground up in turbines and eaten by predators in the long
stretches of slack water.

Then the scales tipped toward extinction in the 1960s with congressional authorization to build four more dams—Ice Harbor, Lower Monument, Little Goose, and Lower Granite—on the Snake River upstream
from its confluence with the Columbia. The four dams together were pro-

jected to add only a small increment of additional power to the Northwest grid, and by then the rationale for adding still more power was wearing thin. Enter a bold new justification—an inland seaport for Idaho.

Idaho would have a seaport from which to barge Montana wheat down to the Pacific. Never mind that the Burlington Northern and Union Pacific were already shipping grain by rail on tracks that parallel the river. By 1975 the four Snake River dams were complete, and barges were on the river from Lewiston, Idaho, to the Pacific.

The salmon runs plummeted. In 1988 just one sockeye salmon managed to find its way back to Redfish Lake in the Sawtooth Mountains of Idaho. The following year it was six. Almost none have been seen since. The over-the-edge effect of these four dams can also be seen in eastern Oregon where the John Day River, a tributary of the Columbia, still has viable salmon runs, while to the east the Grand Ronde, a tributary of the Snake, is virtually devoid of fish. A key difference is that the Grand Ronde enters the Snake above the four dams.

One approach to the collapse of salmon runs is to manipulate natural systems even more intensively. Take the fish out of the river and put them in trucks—even as we take the grain out of trucks and put it in the river. Shoot the sea lions that congregate at Ballard Locks in Seattle to feed on salmon and steelhead. Get rid of the flocks of birds on Rice Island on the lower Columbia that prey on salmon smolts. Offer bounties for fishermen to catch more of the squawfish that prey on smolts in the lakes behind the dams. More hatcheries.

This tinkering in the name of "mitigation" has now gone on for over two decades with little sign of success. It may not be possible to have all the dams and viable salmon runs in the upstream river stretches. There are economic considerations on both sides. Barge transportation does provide a marginal saving over rail transportation. Even small amounts of hydropower have value, as do the disappearing salmon fisheries.

But there are also values beyond calculations with pencil and green eyeshade. In 1856, Isaac Stevens, the governor of Washington Territory, set out to make treaties with Northwest Indian tribes. The Columbia River tribes ceded land and agreed to reservation boundaries on one condition—that they would be entitled for all time to use customary fishing sites and to share equally in the salmon harvest. Yet without fish there can be no harvest, and the tribes are demanding that the United States, in exercise of its trust responsibilities, take steps to protect and restore the salmon runs.

The salmon runs of the Northwest, for both Indians and non-Indians, are an emblem of hope, an object of reverence. Like the sound of migrating geese in autumn or the scent of a campfire, wild, native salmon are a part of us, a link to an older, mysterious world. They are swimming, spawning, biological coordinates that give us a sense of where and who we are. Lose that and you lose something basic, something that all the museums and mitigation projects in the world can never repair.

The national debate over the Snake River dams is underway. All parties, including the states and the Indian tribes, are turning to the scientists for an objective look at the alternatives. And the fisheries biologists are moving toward a consensus assessment: marginal mitigation projects are not enough. We probably cannot have salmon runs up into the Rocky Mountains and maintain four dams on the lower Snake River. We have reached the point where the arteries are so clogged that surgery to reduce the blockage may be the only hope, and it will finally be up to the people of the Northwest, their governors and other elected representatives to decide.

In July 1998, I participated in a dam-busting event in California, the removal of McPherrin Dam on Butte Creek, a tributary of the Sacramento River. A farmer who had helped construct the dam in the 1950s told me he was sorry to see the dam go, but that the new substitute water delivery system would probably work, although he wasn't entirely convinced. And then he got to the point. "Are you going to try to take down all the dams?" I told him not to worry, that we had so far taken down only about a dozen structures, all with community support, and that, by my reckoning, meant that we had 74,988 more to go. Those dams are still blocking 600,000 miles of what were once free-flowing rivers. That's about seventeen percent of all river mileage in the nation.

No, we're not taking aim at all dams. But we should strike a balance between the needs of the river and the demands of river users. Where the balance should be is something I can't predict. We have no comprehensive inventory of the dams in this country, much less knowledge of the benefits and environmental costs associated with each. In all probability the process will continue on a dam-by-dam basis, with states and community stakeholders making most decisions. But there can be no doubt that we have a long way to go toward a better balance. ◙

POEM

Ann Ware

The Thunder has been talking softly
From mountain to mountain
All evening
Like grownups in the next room
Finishing dinner at the big table
And telling family jokes.

ONE'S VIEW OF MOUNT RAINIER

Eric Redman

WHEN I was growing up in Seattle, my father, who'd come from Maine, one day asked whether I expected to live in Seattle as an adult.

"Of course!" I replied, surprised he'd ask.

"Then you should consider going east for school," Dad said. "Easterners have a lot of influence in society. They make the rules. They run the country. You should get to know some."

To reinforce this, Dad gave me a copy of *Taras Bulba*, Nikolai Gogol's tale of a Cossack chief (Yul Brynner in the 1963 movie version) who sends his son (Tony Curtis) to be educated by the Poles, then great European powers, in order to add depth to the Cossack chief that the son, in turn, will one day become. I recall the movie better than the book, particularly the scene in which an outraged Polish father, whose men have seized Tony Curtis, slowly draws his sword and menacingly declares, "I won't kill you, Cossack, but I will make sure you never dishonor another Polish woman as long as you live."

Nonetheless, I took the risk, and eventually, for thirteen years, while at school or working in Washington, D.C., I lived in the East. Still, it never occurred to me not to return to Seattle. I must have transmitted strong signals on this point. Decades later, a woman in D.C., whom in 1970 I'd tried hard to convince to marry me, finally explained why she'd refused: "I knew you would drag me out to Seattle and a life in the rain."

This recalled another movie scene: Liza Minelli explaining to Michael

York in *Cabaret* why she'd refused him and chosen to remain in Berlin—he would have dragged her off to Cambridge, and life in a flat as a mother and the wife of a don. For both of us—Michael York and me—a woman we'd loved providing this too-late explanation of why we'd lost her stung bitterly, and prompted two inconsistent thoughts: I would not have dragged you there. And besides, you would have liked it.

The first time I met a Seattle native who felt differently from me, rain had nothing to do with it. James Quitslund, a Rhodes Scholar who'd grown up on Bainbridge Island, a short ferry ride across Puget Sound from Seattle, became a teacher at Andover in 1965, during my senior year. I was very young, far from home, and felt a bond; I even knew some colorful folks who lived near Jim's. But he rebuffed my attempt to found a friendship on an insider's appreciation of the Queen City (as it was then known, before civic boosters, uneasy about gays, re-nicknamed it the Emerald City).

"In Seattle," Jim said, "no one cares about anything except whether his view of Mount Rainier is blocked."

That extraordinary and succinct observation has haunted me for years. In it, Seattle parochialism is neatly captured and forever exposed, like a butterfly on a pin. My father and Taras Bulba thought: spend time with the Others, and improve the qualities of mind you bring home. Instead of the Greeks' slogan over the academy door, "Here we develop the mind without loss of manliness," they hoped for something slightly different: "Here we develop the mind without loss of rootedness." Jim Quitslund's observation conveyed the opposite objective: spend time with the Others, improve your qualities of mind, and that way you can escape into their midst.

Of course, there's something incomplete about Jim's observation—and Jim himself, after many years, eventually came home. But what he said remains troubling and difficult to dismiss, unlike the dated words of the famous conductor Sir Thomas Beecham, who, when he headed the Seattle Symphony, exhorted the city's leading arts patrons in 1941 to redouble their efforts, lest Seattle be known as "an aesthetic dustbin." That snobbish remark (usually characterized, wildly out of context, as an intentional insult) now seems merely quaint. Jim Quitslund's pronouncement, although snobbish, too, can't easily be brushed aside. It carries a whiff of Eternal Truth.

In my unfinished novel, set in Seattle, the Quitslund-troubled characters spend a good deal of time musing about the view of Mount Rainier, and whether concern (or regard) for it somehow symbolizes the small-mindedness of the city. One character considers the view the reason for living here; another, the reward. A third considers it a form of compensation, and meager. The protagonist considers it emblematic. Like Turgenev, he's chained to the earth, and his view of the mountain, on clear days, reminds him of the links. (This summary suggests good reasons why the novel remains unfinished.)

In real life, Jim's observation naturally troubles me most when, as now, I am in fact actually worried about someone blocking my view of Mount Rainier. I've become the person Jim despised. It's not the only thing I care about, I hasten to emphasize. But I do care about it. Even at the Quitslund risk of my immortal soul.

I believe—and this is my Provocative Thesis—that nowadays people in Seattle take far less care than formerly to avoid blocking someone else's view of Mount Rainier, and that this decline in neighborly consideration and sensitivity, while reflecting national trends, can be traced more or less directly to the impact on Seattle, in recent years, of sudden new wealth. This thesis is so difficult to prove that it may be wrong. But when, as today, our views of Mount Rainier are threatened by happy new homeowners with too much money and too little judgment (or, as realtors say, "MMNT—much money, no taste"), I can perhaps be forgiven for framing it. And the recent shrinkage of sudden new wealth, driven by the stock market, may even provide evidence to test it.

The Provocative Thesis, asserting that today's Seattle residents act differently from their predecessors, and offering a causal explanation, depends on what a sociologist might call "time series" data. Mine are in anecdotal form. But before trotting them out, it's worth noting a curious bit of "cross-sectional" data, an unchanging frame from the ever changing movie: except when it comes to someone else blocking their view of it, Seattleites are remarkably blasé about Mount Rainier. Am I the only person here who wonders, on a clear day, how any work gets done, how traffic even moves?

Physically and visually, Mount Rainier dominates Seattle as no other mountain quite dominates any other city. (I'm ignoring Tacoma, of course, as Seattleites generally do; "Tacoma" actually means "Mount Rainier" in local Native American dialect.) For one thing, almost no other mountain has Mount Rainier 's sheer mass. It rises as a huge mound, its profile from Seattle a perfect bell curve, an astonishing 14,410 feet tall. (A whimsically precise figure; the mountain's snow-capped, after all.) Rainier is so high and so white that, from Seattle, it appears to float in the sky, its forested lower slopes atmospherically painted out in the sky's own blue.

The Colorado Rockies, visible from Denver, include individual peaks taller than Mount Rainier, but they rise from a mile-high plateau and stand in serried ranks, unlike Mount Rainier, which rises in solitary splendor from sea level near the Cascade Mountains but not quite in them. Mount Whitney in California is taller, but what city's skyline does it dominate? Mount Hood, the most prominent volcano in Portland's view, resembles a sharp fang. Mount Rainier's a graceful cone, and much larger, twenty miles in diameter, symmetrical as a Sumo version of Mount Fuji bulked up on Kobe beef and steroids. Mount McKinley, also called Denali (a Native word I suspect means "big two-named mountain"), is taller and visible from Anchorage, but achingly distant. Mount Rainier sometimes looks as if it could fall on Seattle—as bits of it have, in the past (and may again, volcanologists warn).

One might expect such a brooding omnipresence in the sky, particularly one capable of killing us, to inspire homage—if not, indeed, idolatry. That's the curiosity. Except in the residential real estate market, Mount Rainier remains largely unsung, more or less taken for granted.

The name *Rainier* appears relatively rarely. You'd expect a Rainier Bank, but it was swallowed years ago. The Rainier Brewery, just south of downtown, has morphed into the roasting plant of Tully's Coffee. This particular transformation, with yuppy symbols displacing those of the working class, seems to typify Seattle these days, and reinforces my Provocative Thesis. (Another example: Amazon taking over the former U.S. Public Health Service Hospital, which served merchant seamen, and later the poor.) In my youth, when first-generation Scandinavian immigrants were still profuse here, comedians made a staple of Ole and Arne jokes, in one of which Ole calls Aunt Lena from the Rainier Brewery with the sad news that Arne's drowned in the main vat. "Did he suffer much?" Aunt Lena asks. "Yach, I'm afraid so," Ole replies. "We had to drag him out five times."

Where the Rainier name persists, it does not necessarily refer to the mountain, at least directly. At the Rainier Club in downtown Seattle, the featured portrait is not of the mountain but of Lord Peter Rainier, Admiral of the Blue, for whom Captain George Vancouver named it. The Rainier Valley is a Seattle locale celebrating concave topology, not convex, and most uses of *Rainier* refer to it. Rainier Beach, an adjacent neighborhood, celebrates a lakeshore, another antithesis of a peak. Mount Rainier Drive is a Seattle street, but only a short one, and in a neighborhood named Mount Baker, nestled in among Cascadia Avenue, Mount Adams Way, and Mount St. Helens Place.

But where it really matters—Seattle's residential real estate market—Mount Rainier need not speak its name. A fancy advertisement might mention "stunning views of the Cascades" or "stunning views of the Olympics." But if it says "stunning Mountain views," it means only one thing: you have an opportunity to purchase, now for a fabulous sum, your very own piece of the particular anxiety Jim Quitslund identified long ago. Buy it today, and someone else will try to block it.

In theory, and to some extent in practice, a high percentage of Seattle-ites can see Mount Rainier from their homes. The mountain is some fifty miles southeast of Seattle. Like Rome (we were taught in school), Seattle is built on seven hills. From south- or east-facing slopes, or any level spot, Mount Rainier is readily visible. (North-facing slopes afford views of Mount Baker, a white volcano on the Canadian border, and western slopes face the Olympics.) Moreover, the hill count is arbitrary and understated: had Rome been built on twenty hills, we'd say Seattle is, too. There are many places from which to see the mountain.

Blocking someone else's view of Mount Rainier takes two forms, only one of them new. Blocking the view with new construction, clearing a lot, and then building the first house on it is as old as Seattle itself. As a child, I lived on Bella Vista Avenue. The street name, a bit odd for Seattle, reflected that Bella Vista runs along a ridge-top that could afford sweep-ing views of Mount Rainier and the entire Cascade range to the east. All houses with Bella Vista addresses were on the west side of the street, however. Their only views were of houses on the east side of the street, with Cascadia Avenue addresses. From a bedroom in our attic, through a decorative quarter-moon window between chimney and sloping roof, our family could spy Mount Rainier floating in stately grandeur above the Cascadia Avenue rooftops. Completed in 1916, our house had enjoyed a better view for only a decade, until new houses were built across the street.

Fair enough, this view-blocking new residential construction. For the most part, and as a practical matter, the adverse impacts were inevitable. It would not have been reasonable to leave one side of every street unbuilt. Given our Northwest trees, plenty of views would still have been obscured. Besides, it's ancient history: today, Seattle has few vacant lots.

In retrospect, what might have been done differently, and better, would have been to require larger lot sizes, allow each house less lot coverage, and demand bigger setbacks—things that occurred to the city only late in life. With such limits on scale and bulk, light and views can peek through what's otherwise a wall across the street. Seattle is a city of single-family dwellings, in which apartments and condominiums are comparatively recent arrivals (and regulated to protect views). But traditional Seattle homes stand on small lots, and cover them quite completely. The old houses are tightly packed—but not tall.

The dread form of view-blocking in Seattle is not construction on vacant lots, but rather the "tear-down": the razing of existing houses by new owners and their replacement with inappropriately tall, big, blocky new ones. (In Denver, I'm told, a "tear-down" is known as a "scrape-off.") Two variants are possible. In the straightforward approach, the owner admits the new house represents "new construction" for purposes of the building code. Even so, the owner can build a house that stuns the neighbors. Like many cities nationwide, Seattle simply hasn't caught up with people's willingness to deface a neighborhood by designing a house to cover every permissible square inch of a lot and extend that coverage upward to the last inch of the code's height limit. Today's lot sizes, height limits, lot coverage limits, and setback requirements were devised with an entirely different style of house in mind.

Worse is view-blocking through the pretense of "remodeling" an existing house. Forgoing the code's technical terms, realtors and architects tell prospective buyers how to create "pop-up" houses or "telescope" homes. The scam—and that's what it is—begins with buying an older, one- or two-story house, with which Seattle abounds (remember, this is a city with working-class roots). Unfashionable now, such houses are comparatively inexpensive. But these older houses have more lot coverage, and smaller setbacks from lot lines, than the code allows for new construction. Naturally, these pre-existing "nonconformities" of older houses are grandfathered into the code, and lawful to maintain. Naturally, too, it's also lawful to remodel a nonconforming house.

Here's the form a typical "remodel" takes: with no warning to the neighbors (an important tactic of the buyer), a bulldozer arrives and, in an hour, completely demolishes the old house. Part of a wall, or perhaps the chimney, is left standing—this fig leaf signals "remodel" and not "new construction." A new house is then built on the footprint of the old, which covers too much of the lot and has setbacks too small for new construction. Most important, the too-wide new house also "pops up" or "telescopes" and extends the pre-existing nonconformity vertically: one or more new stories are added, up to the city's height limit of thirty-five feet for pitched roofs. The new house is to the old as Mount Rainier is to a hill. (A final insult: the tidbit of wall or chimney initially left standing is often "remodeled" away some months later. Perhaps embarrassed by such silliness, the city changed the building code to allow "remodels" of wholly demolished houses.)

Of this particular view-blocking abuse, many things can be said, but I will limit myself to a choice few. First, the city could stop the practice cold, simply by rejecting the emperor's-new-clothes notion that brand new houses are somehow remodels of the houses torn down. "We had to destroy the village in order to save it." What self-justification from our era, not related to sex, better symbolizes indefensible absurdity? It should be easy to recognize, and flatly state, that one does not demolish a house in order to remodel it. This is new construction, pure and simple, and nothing in existing law prevents the city from simply saying so. The city doesn't because . . . well, that's a different story, and partly a mystery.

Second, this is all about money, and primarily new money. Okay, it's partly about traffic—in car-clogged Seattle, people value in-city neighborhoods more than suburbs—and partly about the shortage, in our city, of the really big houses that really big money has nowadays made possible, hence fashionable, coast-to-coast. But buying a house, tearing it down, and building a new one—whether "new construction" or a "remodel"—wouldn't generally make sense, except for people with money to burn.

Let's say the old house costs $450,000 (many cost much more). Leaving aside demolition expenses, new residential construction in Seattle these days runs about $200-$300 per square foot for well-to-do owners. The new house, built on the ghost of the old, is generally huge—4,000, 5,000, or even 6,000 square feet—although it shelters no larger a family than the old. In the end, something between $1,000,000 and $2,000,000 is spent for a big bulky box with its own great view. This is done by people who want to live in the house, not by speculators. As an investment, it's not entirely rational; the new house generally can't be sold for what it cost. It is, in fact, a self-indulgent form of consumption. The only people who spend money this way are people with too much money to spend. In Seattle, that didn't used to be a problem. A few years ago, it became one.

Third, this is an ugly thing to do to your neighbors. Substantively, it strips views, light, and property value (often hundreds of thousands of dollars per neighbor) from nearby homes. Procedurally, it depends on stealth, a lack of notice, the *fait accompli* of the old home demolished before anyone can protest, check the building plans, challenge the permits. (When demolition takes place before permits are granted, the city may shrug: "The owner will just claim the structure was unsafe," one official said.) Precisely because this is done by people who want to live in the new house, the insensitivity involved, and the lack of neighborly solicitude, are all the more stunning—and un-Seattlelike.

For the past few years, chunky new construction and the demolition/ remodel scam have played out weekly in every Seattle neighborhood with good views. Perhaps the economic slowdown, the plummeting of NASDAQ, will prove to have come just in time. Still, it's sad to rely on a recession to slow what the city could halt at once, had it the will. It's even sadder to depend on recessions or officials—or the courts, presumably the next and last resort—to restrain conduct that used to be restrained by manners alone.

Face it: we became a gold rush town, with gold rush sensibilities.

Two East Coast friends of mine worked in Washington State for Eugene McCarthy in 1968. One said, "Seattle is a city where everyone waits for the light to change before crossing the street." The other said, "Seattle is a city where strangers converse in elevators." I would have said, then and especially later, "Seattle is a city in which wealth is neither despised nor celebrated, a place where money simply doesn't occupy much psychological space."

I knew, at the time, that Seattle could absorb newcomers only so rapidly—that too-fast growth led to rude driving, for example. But "newcomer," then, was a geographic concept—easterners, New Yorkers, Californians—not an economic one. I would not have said that Seattle was a city in which no one would deliberately block another's view of Mount Rainier. Much less could I have blamed any change on sudden wealth, too much wealth, too much wealth in the hands of the still too young, for none of that existed then. In the old days, to say, "Seattle is a place where no one would deliberately block another's view of Mount Rainier" would have been like saying, "It rains here," or "Boeing's here." It would have illuminated nothing about Seattle that people did not already know or expect.

Enough ringing assertion, I can hear my history teacher bellow; time for credible demonstration. I offer the following tales.

In 1976, as baby lawyers, my then-wife and I bought our first house, a modest (1,900 square feet) brick home on Queen Anne Hill. The view of Mount Rainier, the harbor, the city lights—all of it was simply incredible. Bad weather in Seattle comes from the southwest, up the long reach of Puget Sound; we could see it approach, before it battered us like a giant fist. On crystal clear days we could spot, far south of Mount Rainier, a tiny white pinnacle. My father disputed that this was Mount St. Helens until, one day in 1980, it went up in smoke.

Unfortunately, in those days I wasn't perfect, tending somewhat toward anxiety, and in buying that house, I had spent (a) a lot of money to own a view of Mount Rainier, and (b) a lot of time mulling over Jim Quitslund's words. Our beloved house stood perched on a south-facing slope. It had a house below it. That other house had only two stories, and an unattractive, flat, pea-graveled roof. In my fears, I saw those two stories and raised them one. Legally, the owner of the house was entitled to do it. She could have blocked our view.

We consulted an architect friend, Doug Zuberbuhler. He spent a long time looking down at that flat-roofed house from ours, and a long time on the street below it, looking up. "Structurally, I think she can do it," Doug said. "She wouldn't have to tear it down to add another story." At the time, when people had less money and spent it sensibly, not having to tear down the existing house in order to add another story signified that adding that story would be economically feasible—and, in fact, a sensible investment.

So we began courting that neighbor, Mrs. Hyslop. We wanted to buy her air space, her upward development rights, pay her not to raise her house and block our view. We decided to ask her outright, offer her a deal. I shudder now to think of it.

Mrs. Hyslop could not have been more friendly, or colorful. A tall, aged widow, in some pain from wasting illness, she wore a terrible wig and poured a stiff Jack Daniels for herself and every visitor. Using an aluminum walker, she'd inch her way forward from kitchen to living room with the drinks, lifting each glass and carrying it forward, then setting it down on a counter another foot ahead of her before taking her next step. She told dirty jokes, and laughed loudly. But she was not about to sell us any of her rights.

"Your house was already there when my husband and I built this house!" she insisted. "We designed it not to block the view! We didn't add a third story not to block your view! We built it with a flat roof not to block your view—and when that darn roof leaks, I remember that! So don't worry, you don't have to pay me anything! I'm not going to block your view!"

We did not find this reassuring. We just didn't get it, my wife and I. She was from the East, I'd been away those thirteen years; we weren't socialized yet as Seattleites. We thought, "Great, but she's really old, and she's sick. One day she'll die—then what?"

Mrs. Hyslop answered the unspoken question for us. "I'm leaving this house to my niece," she promised. "She's going to live here. I've told her about not adding another story, or raising the roof. She understands completely. You don't have to worry, I tell you. No one is going to block your view."

"Great again," we thought. "Just great. How will we ever hold the niece to that?"

The unwelcome day arrived too soon. At the hospital, Mrs. Hyslop and Death circled one another quietly. "Can you hear me, Mrs. Hyslop?" the doctor said, leaning closer, thinking her gone. "Can you HEAR ME?" he said more loudly, leaning closer still. He put his ear down to her face, listening for her breath. "Come any closer, doctor," Mrs. Hyslop whispered, "and I'll kiss you." This was a woman with a lot of character.

Her character may have had a genetic component. The niece, Margaret Dees, promptly moved to Seattle from Illinois. "Uh-oh," we thought. "This is an outlander." We decided to approach her at once.

Like many midwesterners, Margaret seemed quiet, cautious; she was also in mourning. Like her aunt, she could not even begin to understand our concern, or why we'd raised it.

"Why should you pay me to forgo a right I'll never exercise?" she asked, a bit bewildered. "My aunt would never have raised this house. She told me never to raise it. It would not occur to me to raise it."

"Besides," she added, "I'd rather have you as friends."

That is the fundamental choice. Nowadays, of course, it's resolved differently. But back then, anticipating a selfishness Seattle hadn't yet seen, we managed to insult two very fine women and neighbors, one right after the other. That's why the story makes me shudder: I'd taken Jim Quitslund's words to heart, but a heart that still had much to learn.

However extraordinary the decisions of Mrs. Hyslop and her niece by today's Seattle standards, they were common then: our friends told similar tales. And at least some members of earlier generations went even further.

We knew this, because the record was right there, in the history and title report of our own house.

Our house had been built in 1906 as a wood-frame structure with clapboard siding. At the time, it was three stories tall, and perched on a natural hillock, as old photos showed. Although near the summit of Queen Anne Hill, it was not at the summit, and there was room for another house above it. By 1911, someone had decided to build that house.

The record shows that the owners of the new house paid the owners of our house $200 to do three things: remove our house from its lot, grade the lot to reduce its elevation ten feet, and remove the third story from our house before returning it to the lot. All this was done not to protect the view from the new house, but to create it. That neighborly transaction—inconceivable today—explained why the house we bought in 1976 had two stories instead of three, and why the staircase to the attic seemed so incongruously grand.

The folks who made that 1911 deal had lawyers. The lawyers intended to create a height restriction on our house that would "run with the land" and bind all later owners. That's why the information showed up in our title report nearly seven decades later. But creating covenants that run with the land can be tricky. As lawyers ourselves, we weren't sure the earlier lawyers had succeeded. When our first child arrived, in 1982, we felt we needed more space, and took a hard look at creating it by "restoring" the original third floor. (I shudder again: we toyed with justifying this as "historic preservation.")

We thought, legally, we could pull it off. The old agreement seemed unlikely to bind us, and our house wasn't nearly as tall as the code allowed. We knew the structure could support a third story—it had already done so. And the economics looked very, very favorable.

But we'd finally learned our lesson, if only barely, from the examples of Mrs. Hyslop and Margaret Dees. We had, as D.H. Lawrence put it in his poem The Snake, something to repent ourselves of: a pettiness. It was time for us to grow. We sold the house and moved to another, larger one, with a lovely view that just happened not to include Mount Rainier.

Not surprisingly, this story lacks a happy ending. I drove past our old Queen Anne house not long ago, and guess what? It's been "remodeled." Now it has a third story once again. The vertical addition happens to be amazingly ugly: historically, it's inauthentic, and architecturally, it ruins the house. But that's not the point. A long thread has been snipped: ninety years of solicitude for the neighbors has finally come to an end.

There's little more to say. Once Western civilization starts to decline, there seems to be no stopping it. But there's time for one last tale.

Twenty years after buying my first house with my first wife, I bought my first with my second. Heather called me when she toured it. "It's lovely," she said. "It's got an incredible view of Mount Rainier. The only thing is, it looks down on a lot of rooftops."

The rooftops were those of one-story houses, about ten of them. Could they be raised, we wondered? Our realtor thought not, as a practical matter. The houses were small but nice; it would be too expensive to buy them and tear down. And unlike Mrs. Hyslop's house, their structures wouldn't support additional stories.

We consulted Doug Zuberbuhler, our architect friend. We consulted the contractor who'd built, in 1991, the house we were considering. Both came over and took a look. "Naw," the contractor said, "it wouldn't make economic sense to buy those houses, tear them down, and build new ones. That's what someone would have to do in order to raise them."

We bought the house in August 1996 and were married there on November 2. During our one-week honeymoon, someone demolished a house in front of us, about ten feet to the left of our view of Mount Rainier. I walked over to meet the new owner on the site. The remarkable thing is this: I wasn't anxious, both because I was newly married and happy with the world, and because I had not even begun to imagine what the owner might have in mind. I expected another tasteful, relatively small house on the relatively small site, something probably two stories tall but certainly no view-blocker.

"Building a new house, eh?" I asked in a friendly manner, signaling my willingness to share the enthusiasm of a neighbor I expected might become a friend. It was just a conversation starter. It was also an obvious comment: although the basement walls remained, above ground level not one bit of the old house still stood. This was a vacant lot with a deep, wide hole in it.

"No!" the owner, a total stranger, quickly snapped. "It's not a new house! It's a remodel!"

That first occasion on which we spoke promptly became the last.

Admittedly, once that owner decided to build an inappropriate new house, he could have demolished the old one and undertaken "new construction." Seattle's building code, as noted, hasn't caught up with the bulky visions of today's homebuilders. But by calling it a "remodel," he signaled his intent to make it even bigger and chunkier and more view-blocking than the code would otherwise allow. In other words, he wanted to harm his neighbors even more.

When that house "telescoped" in front of us—it became, literally, a giant cube—people were puzzled, and considered it a tasteless fluke.

"It still doesn't make sense economically," our contractor friend told us. "The only way this could happen was that someone with a lot of money and no taste wanted to build his dream house, and didn't care about the economics—or the neighbors."

That, it turns out, could be the epitaph for our once-distinctive city. Now other houses in our neighborhood have begun popping up, as if from a toaster. Typical is a planned "remodel" with a 33-foot pitched roof—although the house will have only two stories, each with 9-foot ceilings. We can still see Mount Rainier, but perhaps in the future we might see it only from our upper floor, over rooftops that are higher—many, like this one, gratuitously so. Some of our neighbors are already losing their views entirely.

Of course, the new owners of these houses are walking into a beehive of hostility, if not lawsuits. We've tried to warn them. "Don't worry about the neighbors," a realtor countered, trying to reassure one couple with "pop-up" drawings in their hands and stars in their eyes. "The neighbors will get over it." Wrong: the neighbors have never gotten over the giant cube house. But also upsetting: how can any Seattleite offer such advice to other Seattleites?

We recounted all this to our peripatetic friend Deb Fallows, who recently spent eighteen months enjoying a view of Mount Rainier her-self. "Can't you talk to them?" she asked, referring to the newest owners of a nearby tear-down. "Can't they see they are making a mistake?" Yes, I replied, we can talk to them, but no, they can't see they are making a mis-take. They are too young, and they have the money to do what they want; the combination seems to make people oblivious.

I remembered, of course, my youthful errors with Mrs. Hyslop, with Margaret Dees. In fifteen years, I predicted to Deb, the new owners will regret what they've done, but not now. It takes time to become wise enough to avoid such mistakes. In the old days, however, it also took time to earn enough money to make them. When today's young millionaires mature, many may look back and say "Ooops." That—or the stock market making them feel poor again—seems the most we can hope for.

And so, things have changed a lot since Jim Quitslund declared, thirty-six years ago, that in Seattle no one cares about anything except whether his view of Mount Rainier is blocked. Nowadays, it seems, in Seattle no one cares a thing about blocking someone else's view of Mount Rainier. Jim would have liked to see Seattle transformed. But not this way. ◙

Volcanoes and Superquakes

LIVING WITH GEOLOGIC HAZARDS
IN THE PACIFIC NORTHWEST

Stephen L. Harris

For most residents of the Pacific Northwest, the region's spectacular landscape—from rugged coastlines to towering, glacier-clad peaks—seems permanent and unchanging. For the Native Americans who inhabited the area for millennia before Anglo Americans settled it, however, the land's apparent stability and tranquility were recognized as a dangerous illusion.

As their oral traditions testify, many Native tribes knew what contemporary scientists have only recently discovered: the Pacific Northwest owes much of its scenic beauty to almost unimaginable geologic violence, catastrophic earthquakes, and devastating volcanic eruptions. Geologists studying deposits left by prehistoric earthquakes and tsunamis—giant sea waves tens of feet high—have learned that the coasts of Washington, Oregon, and northern California are vulnerable to the same kind of quake-generated tsunami disaster that killed about 200,000 people around the Indian Ocean in December 2004. During the last several thousand years, giant temblors have repeatedly convulsed the Pacific Coast from near Eureka, California, to Vancouver Island, British Columbia, most recently in January 1700.

The 1700 event—dated by a combination of radiocarbon techniques, the counting of annual tree rings, and written records of a tsunami that struck Japan in late January that year—registered a magnitude of 9.0, at least 30 times more powerful than the quake that shattered San Francisco in 1906. Tribal memories of that cataclysm include a northern California tale in which intense shaking was accompanied by floodwaters that swept away an entire village, sparing only those who had fled to high ground before the tsunami rolled ashore. On the Olympic Peninsula of northwest Washington, the Hoh and Quileute tribes interpreted the upheaval as a fierce battle between two supernatural forces, Thunderbird and Whale.

In creating tales about the geologic events and processes that shaped their physical environment, Native storytellers typically presented a united worldview that encompassed both material and spiritual components. In the Bridge of the Gods legend, which celebrates a love triangle involving three volcanic peaks bordering the Columbia River—Hood, Adams, and St. Helens—the snow-capped mountains were not merely inert piles of rock; they were living presences with distinctive personalities.

Although it is now difficult to disentangle later Caucasian embellishments from the original tradition, a Klickitat version of the story preserves the important elements. According to Klickitat lore, long before white explorers arrived on the scene, Native tribes were able to cross the Columbia River, near the present site of Cascade Locks, via a land "bridge" that was *tomanowos*, a creation sacred to the gods. But when the tribes became noisy and quarrelsome, Tyee Sahale (commonly interpreted as the "Great Spirit") took steps that eventually led to the bridge's demolition. First, he caused all the fires in their lodges to go out. Only the fire kept by Loowit, an old woman who avoided the violence that divided her people, remained burning, so all her neighbors had to come to her to rekindle their campfires. When Tyee Sahale asked Loowit to claim a reward for her generosity, she did not hesitate to name her choice: youth and beauty. Transformed into a lovely young maiden, Loowit inadvertently reignited the fires of war by attracting two aggressive suitors, both sons of the Great Spirit.

The first son, Pahto, ruled over territory north of the Columbia, while the second, Wy'east, led the Willamette people south of the river. When Pahto and Wy'east contended furiously for Loowit's favor, hurling red-hot boulders at each other, Tyee Sahale separated them by overthrowing the bridge linking their two realms, its fragments creating the cataracts for which the adjacent Cascade Range was later named. The Great Spirit also changed the three lovers into volcanic mountains: Pahto became the broad-shouldered giant that white settlers called Mount Adams; Wy'east became Mount Hood; and Loowit, the beautifully symmetrical Mount St. Helens. It was said that Loowit (whom some tribes named Tahonelatclah or Louwala-Clough, "fire-mountain") secretly favored the more graceful Wy'east, who burned with passion longer than Pahto, who soon fell asleep under his ermine blanket.

Besides explaining the volcanic nature of the three Guardians of the Columbia, the Bridge of the Gods tradition also evokes tribal memories of an enormous avalanche, the Bonneville landslide, that completely dammed the Columbia River only about three centuries ago, forming a rocky causeway that allowed travelers to cross the river dryshod. (Because the local tribes had no word for "bridge," the notion that this formation was a soaring stone arch is a Caucasian invention.) It is possible that some of the large basaltic blocks forming the dam remained in place considerably after the river cut a new channel through its southern toe, about a mile south of its pre-slide course. If so, the famed Bridge of the Gods was in fact a jumbled pile of lava slabs, much as a Native informant described it to a French missionary—"a long range of towering and projecting rocks"— before it collapsed, possibly in the earthquake of 1700.

By far the most frequently—and violently—active of the volcanic trio overlooking the Columbia River, Mount St. Helens opened a new chapter in her legendary career in March 1980, when she began a series of minor eruptions that culminated in a cataclysmic outburst. Shaken by a magnitude 5.0 quake at 8:32 a.m., May 18, 1980, the entire north side of the volcano suddenly collapsed, triggering the largest debris avalanche in recorded history and unleashing a ground-hugging lateral blast that devastated 230 square miles of pristine timberland. In minutes, St. Helens' classically perfect cone was transformed into a horseshoe-shaped wreck that faced northward toward a moonscape of gray desolation. During the initial phase of the day-long eruption, ash clouds soared almost 100,000 feet into the stratosphere, where winds carried the ash plume eastward, turning day into night across eastern Washington, northern Idaho, and western Montana. Deadly lahars, volcanic mudflows that resemble churning waves of liquid concrete, streamed down valleys heading on the mountain, destroying bridges, logging camps, and more than 200 houses and other structures before emptying into the Columbia River, temporarily closing it to shipping.

Although St. Helens' 1980 outburst killed fifty-seven people and thousands of animals, including about 7,000 deer and elk, and caused approximately $1 billion in property losses, the eruption was relatively small compared to others in its recent geologic past. In 1479 (according to tree-ring dating), the volcano produced an explosive paroxysm six times larger than that of 1980, beginning an eruptive cycle that continued intermittently for at least 250 years. About 3,300 years ago, St. Helens disgorged so much pumice—creating a yellowish ash layer known as Yn that lies a foot thick at Mount Rainier National Park, 50 miles to the north, and extends as far northeast as Banff, Alberta—that many Native Americans had to abandon their former settlements and migrate to sites farther from the volcano's lethal reach.

Even St. Helens' tempestuous behavior, however, is dwarfed by the explosive violence of Mount Mazama, a volcano in southern Oregon that virtually destroyed itself.

About 7,700 years ago, Mazama, which then towered more than 12,000 feet above sea level, erupted so large a volume of material—perhaps forty cubic miles of frothy volcanic glass called pumice—that its former summit collapsed, forming the basin, five by six miles in diameter, that now holds the azure waters of Crater Lake. In the first phase of its suicidal paroxysm, Mazama ejected a column of ash that rose 30 miles into the air, showering orange-colored pumice over 500,000 square miles in eight western states and southern Canada. As new vents encircling the entire cone opened during the eruption's second stage, roiling avalanches of incandescent pumice swept down all sides of the mountain, some traveling as far as 35 miles from the volcano. With its internal storehouse of molten rock rapidly emptied, the volcano's upper cone subsided to fill the void, transforming a towering peak into a vast hole in the ground. As geologists observe, a comparable eruption today would create a regional disaster.

Like those of the Columbia region's volcanic sentinels, Mazama's tremendous outburst inspired a Native tradition involving mountain deities. In 1865, Lalek, an aged Klamath chief, confided his people's tradition to William M. Colvig, a young soldier then stationed at Fort Klamath, Oregon. According to Lalek's story, in ancient times Llao, an underworld god who lived beneath Mount Mazama, fought against Skell, a sky god who inhabited Mount Shasta, 125 miles to the south. In their titanic conflict, all the spirits of earth and sky waged war, searing the land with sheets of flame that intermittently lit up the ash-shrouded darkness. When Skell at last prevailed, he beheaded Llao's mountain, confining his opponent to a subterranean prison. (Although some anthropologists believe that this story of Mazama's collapse and the origin of Crater Lake was transmitted orally from generation to generation for the last 7,000 years, others suggest that it was invented to explain the strange presence of a huge basin in a range of high peaks.)

Mazama and St. Helens are but two in a chain of geologically youthful volcanoes in the Cascade Range, which extends for 700 miles from Lassen Peak in northern California through Oregon and Washington to Mounts Garibaldi and Meager in British Columbia. During the last 350 years, at least eight have erupted: Baker, Glacier Peak, Rainier, and St. Helens in Washington; Mount Hood in Oregon; and Mount Shasta, Lassen Peak, and Cinder Cone in California. Geologists are particularly worried about future eruptions at Mount Rainer (14,411 feet), which supports a cubic mile of glacial ice, the nation's largest single-peak glacier system south of Alaska. Hot rock ejected onto the volcano's icefields causes rapid melting, producing enormous lahars that rush at speeds of twenty-five to forty miles an hour downvalley before spreading out into the eastern Puget Sound lowland. About 150,000 people now live atop Rainier's recent lahar deposits—directly in the path of future mudflows—but many more of the area's 2.5 million inhabitants are likely to be affected when the volcano next erupts. Extensive deforestation of the Puget Sound lowlands has removed barriers that previously restricted a mudflow's lateral extent, ensuring that future lahars will travel faster and farther than ever before. Even in locations untouched by lahars, the loss of crucial highways, bridges, businesses, residential developments, and shopping centers will disrupt innumerable lives.

Because its future activity will impact a densely populated region, including the Seattle-Tacoma area, Mount Rainier has been officially designated the most dangerous volcano in America.

Why does the Pacific Northwest's scenic splendor involve so much geologic violence? The region's propensity for both giant earthquakes and volcanic eruptions results from its geologic setting, a vulnerable position where two huge slabs of the earth's crust collide about 30 to 90 miles off the Pacific Coast. Washington and Oregon form a link in the notorious Ring of Fire, a belt of intense seismic and volcanic activity encircling the Pacific Ocean. The circum-Pacific Ring of Fire, in turn, results from a worldwide geologic process known as plate tectonics. Pulsating like a living organism, the earth's crust is fragmented into about sixteen major and several minor tectonic plates, rocky barges that carry continents or ocean basins on their backs. Heat circulating through the earth's interior keeps the plates in constant motion, pulling apart, rubbing against each other, or colliding together as they slide over an underlying zone of hot plastic material, the mantle. Deep beneath the earth's surface, the highest concentrations of internal heat form convection cells, similar to those in a pot of boiling water. This cycle of currents in the mantle, the 1,800-mile-thick region between the earth's metallic core and its brittle outer shell, keeps the plates moving, buoying the crust in one place and tugging it down in others.

Linear rift zones at which plates separate are called divergent boundaries, or spreading centers, where magma (molten rock underground) oozes up through long fissures in the crust, creating submarine mountain ranges such as the Mid-Atlantic Ridge and the East Pacific Rise. As the magma rises along linear spreading centers in ocean basins, such as the Juan de Fuca Ridge off the Pacific Northwest coast, it shoulders the surrounding rock aside, pushing opposite sides of the ocean floor away from each other and toward the neighboring continents. When the dense, relatively thin seafloor, composed of basaltic lava, collides with the much thicker and lighter granitic rock composing the continents, the heavier, denser ocean floor is forced downward, gradually sinking into the mantle beneath the continental margins. Where ocean and continental plates converge, a subduction zone typically forms. As the water-saturated oceanic plate plunges deeper into the mantle, the descending slab encounters increasingly high temperatures. The addition of water to subterranean hot rocks lowers their melting point and generates new magma. Hotter and lighter than the surrounding rock, the magma rises into the continental crust, typically forming underground reservoirs called magma chambers. When the chemically evolving magma becomes more buoyant than the surrounding rock and migrates to the earth's surface, a new volcano is born or an old one revives.

Plate convergence forms subduction zones around most of the Pacific basin, triggering some of the world's greatest earthquakes and volcanic eruptions, including those in Alaska, Japan, Indonesia, Central America, South America, and the Pacific Northwest. The two most powerful earthquakes ever recorded—a magnitude 9.5 event in Chile in 1960 and a 9.2 quake in Prince William Sound, Alaska, in 1964—both centered at subduction zones and both generated deadly tsunamis that swept thousands of miles from their source.

At the Cascadia subduction zone—which extends about 700 miles from northern California to British Columbia—two relatively small fragments of the Pacific plate, the Juan de Fuca plate and the even smaller Gorda plate to the south, are sinking beneath the northwest margin of North America, moving eastward at a rate of one or two inches a year. Partial melting of these descending slabs generates the magma that fuels the Cascade volcanoes from Lassen to St. Helens to Canada's Garibaldi.

Subduction of the Juan de Fuca plate also produces the colossal earthquakes that have catastrophically jolted the Pacific Northwest at least a dozen times in the last 7,700 years, most recently in 1700. Geologists believe that the Cascadia subduction zone generates particularly high magnitude earthquakes because the Juan de Fuca slab does not descend smoothly or continuously beneath the continent's edge. Instead, the two plates become locked together, causing stress to build until the descending plate breaks free and plunges suddenly many tens of feet downward, commonly pulling sections of the coastline down five or six feet with it. In the 1700 earthquake, which ruptured the fault for most of its length, subsidence was greatest along the northern Oregon and southern Washington coast, where large tsunamis also swept far inland, inundating townsites from Grays Harbor to Coos Bay. During quiet interludes between major quakes, the coastline rebounds gradually, rising about 1.5 inches per year—until the next great convulsion yanks it down again.

Although the interval between Cascadia superquakes averages about 550 years, they do not occur regularly; interludes between them vary from 200 to 1,000 years, making prediction of the next magnitude 9.0 temblor impossible.

As if a vulnerability to gigantic subduction temblors were not enough, the Pacific Northwest also has two other major sources of seismic threat: ruptures within sections of the already subducted Juan de Fuca slab and fault movement in the brittle continental crust. Perhaps because of a bend in the subducted slab beneath the area, intraplate earthquakes tend to center in the Puget Sound region. Washington's three most damaging quakes in historic time—those of 1949, 1965, and 2001—originated when parts of the already subducted slab fractured far below the surface. Because their foci were so deep, about 30 to 35 miles underground, seismic waves had lost much of their energy by the time they reached the surface, muting their destructiveness. Even so, the magnitude 7.1 temblor of 1949 killed eight people and caused $25 million in damage, a financial toll that would be much larger if the quake were repeated today. Another seven people died in the 1965 event, which was centered between Seattle and Tacoma. The Nisqually quake of February 28, 2001, originated at almost the same underground location as that of 1949, but had a magnitude of only 6.8. State officials tabulated its cost at between $2 and $4 billion.

The third category of Pacific Northwest earthquakes originates on faults in the North American plate. Historically, the strongest earthquake from this source (estimated magnitude of 6.8) occurred in 1872. Centered near the town of Entiat, Washington, about 17 miles north of Wenatchee, it was felt on both sides of the Cascade Range, from Walla Walla in eastern Washington to Port Townsend, Tacoma, and Olympia in the western part of the state. Because quakes originating in the continental crust typically occur at much shallower depths than those in subducted slabs, they cause much more intense shaking at the ground surface and are more damaging to human-made structures.

When previously unknown active faults in the continental plate were discovered crossing the Puget Sound area a couple of decades ago, geologists realized that the region's largest cities run a high risk of seismic disaster. The Seattle Fault, which slices at least 40 miles through the crust from an area east of Lake Washington across downtown Seattle to Bainbridge Island, produced a topography-changing jolt about A.D. 900. Some locations were suddenly raised as much as 20 feet above their previous levels, while others dropped an equal distance. Like water sloshing in a bathtub, tsunamis swept inland over the shores of Puget Sound, including what is now the Seattle waterfront.

A recent study envisioning damage from a magnitude 6.7 event on the Seattle Fault estimates a loss of $33 billion and fatalities and injuries totaling almost 8,000. Renewed activity at some of the Cascade volcanoes, particularly those near large population centers, could exact an even larger toll. If Mount Rainier were to stage a major eruption—or even a small eruption that generated a large mudflow—the economic and human losses would be staggering. Although not as volatile as Mount St. Helens, Rainier threatens more densely populated areas on valley floors many tens of miles from the volcano. About 5,600 years ago a relatively minor explosive event caused Rainier's former summit to collapse, triggering the Osceola Mudflow—a cubic mile in volume—that streamed 65 miles from its source and buried 210 square miles, including the sites of Buckley, Enumclaw, Auburn, Sumner, Puyallup, and Tacoma, under thick muck. In a matter of hours, rocks that had once stood more than 15,000 feet above sea level were submerged beneath the waters of Puget Sound.

Although the largest known, the Osceola is only one of approximately 60 similar lahars that Rainier has produced during the last several millennia. About 600 B.C., part of Rainier's west face collapsed, opening a wide scarp known as the Sunset Amphitheater and generating the Round Pass lahar, a wave of rock and mud initially 1,000 feet high, that poured many miles down the Puyallup River Valley. Only 500 years ago, avalanching rock from the same area high on Rainier's west side produced the Electron Mudflow, which entombed a forest at the site of Orting before streaming down the Puyallup Valley at least as far as Sumner. Although Orting has installed a warning system to alert residents that a lahar is on its way, people would have little more than 45 minutes in which to evacuate to high ground.

Rainier's eruptive activity commonly produces destructive mudflows on several sides of the mountain at once. Between about A.D. 900 and 1000, eruptions produced a series of voluminous lahars that swamped both forks of the White River on Rainier's east side, as well as the Nisqually River Valley on the south flank, depositing a thick fill that raised canyon floors 60 to 90 feet above their present levels. During this extended eruptive episode, some mudflows traveled 65 miles into the Puget Sound basin, covering the lower Duwamish, White, and Puyallup valleys in rocky sludge up to 30 feet deep and inundating the sites of Auburn and Kent. Water draining from the lahar deposits, which contained numerous pumice fragments, transported large quantities of sand to bury tidal flats in what are now Seattle suburbs near the Boeing aircraft company. These reworked sands extend as far north as the Port of Seattle Terminal 107, about two miles from Elliott Bay, the inlet along which downtown Seattle is built.

Mount Rainier's latest minor activity, which scattered pumice over the east flank between about 1820 and 1854, apparently triggered no significant mudflows. Continuing heat and steam emission in the two overlapping summit craters, however, remind us that Rainier is only napping between eruptions. It has produced more than 20 outbursts during Holocene time, the last 10,000 to 12,000 years since the end of the last Ice Age, and geologists fully expect the volcano to revive, perhaps with catastrophic consequences to people living in its shadow.

Although the range north of Mount Rainier is essentially nonvolcanic, the two highest peaks in Washington's heavily glaciated North Cascades— Mount Baker (10,781 feet) and Glacier Peak (10,541 feet)—are volcanoes that pose serious threats to towns and cities located far from their ice-shrouded summits. In March 1975, exactly five years before St. Helens began the series of steam explosions that culminated in the cataclysm of May 18, 1980, Baker abruptly intensified its heat and steam emission, ejecting minor quantities of ash that thinly veneered the Boulder Glacier on its east flank and increasing its release of hydrogen sulfide gas. As ice melted to form an acidic lake in Sherman Crater, a bowl-shaped vent located a half mile south of the main summit, the U.S. Geological Survey (USGS) closely monitored the volcano, eventually closing the Baker Lake recreational area, at Baker's eastern foot, to public access. Steam and sulfur production declined after 1976, and resorts and campgrounds were reopened, but the discharge of steam and heat remains significantly above pre-1975 levels.

Baker's largest historic eruption occurred in 1843, when steam explosions blew fragments of old rock from Sherman Crater and deposited layers of ash for four miles northeast of the volcano. The historic episode, which lasted intermittently until about 1880, emitted no fresh magma, but partial collapse of the east rim of Sherman Crater directed avalanches and lahars down the eastern slopes toward Baker Lake.

As at Mount Rainier, Baker's chief hazard—that most likely to affect populated areas many miles downvalley from the volcano—consists of debris avalanches and lahars. According to a 1995 USGS hazards evaluation, partial collapse of the upper cone 6,500 years ago caused a lahar that traveled down the Nooksack River into Bellingham Bay, burying the sites of several small towns, including Deming, Everson, and Lynden. If the west wall of Sherman Crater were to fail, the resulting mudflows could pour into Lake Shannon, perhaps causing dam failure and floods that would sweep down the channel of the Skagit River, inundating larger settlements on its flood plain, including Sedro Woolley and Mount Vernon.

Because of its location deep within the rugged North Cascades 70 miles northeast of Seattle, Glacier Peak, invisible to travelers on busy Interstate 5, is perhaps the least known volcano in the range. It is also one of the most potentially dangerous. Like Mount St. Helens, Glacier Peak is highly explosive, erupting two of the largest and most widely distributed pumice layers of any Cascade volcano since the most recent Ice Age glaciers began to retreat. Besides blanketing vast areas of the Pacific Northwest and southern Canada in thick ashfalls about 13,000 years ago, the volcano has repeatedly produced large-volume avalanches of hot pumice and extensive mudflows.

Glacier Peak has been sporadically active during Holocene time, erupting thick viscous lava that piles up to form lava domes similar to that now growing in St. Helens' crater. When steep domes high on the cone collapse or are disrupted by steam explosions, they form avalanches of hot gas and incandescent rock fragments—pyroclastic flows—that rapidly melt glacial ice, generating the floods and mudflows that have characterized the volcano's behavior during the last few thousand years. Last active during the eighteenth century, when it ejected ash that now covers nearby ridgetops, Glacier Peak is not expected to erupt in the immediate future.

A more likely candidate for renewed activity during our lifetimes is Mount Hood, at 11,239 feet Oregon's highest peak and most recently active volcano. Although Hood had enjoyed a long sleep of almost 12,000 years before it reawakened about 1,500 years ago, it has been one of the more vigorously active Cascade volcanoes since then, a fact abundantly documented in Native American legends. About A.D. 500, magma rising into Hood's erosion-scarred cone caused the volcano's south flank to collapse, initiating avalanches and mudflows that traveled down the Sandy River all the way to the Columbia. Like Glacier Peak, Hood produces a viscous magma called dacite, which, flow-resistant, typically piles up to form bulbous lava domes that shatter and collapse, generating pyroclastic flows and lahars. During this extended eruptive cycle, known as the Timberline episode, rising and collapsing domes at a vent south of Hood's summit gradually created a broad debris fan that now mantles the volcano's southern flank. Built in 1937 near the debris fan's eastern margin, elegantly rustic Timberline Lodge now draws tens of thousands of skiers, snowboarders, and other winter sport enthusiasts every year to the unusually smooth expanse of the volcano's south slope. Located at an elevation of 6,000 feet, the Timberline resort provides the nation's only developed ski center open throughout the year, a distinction partly owed to the nature of Hood's late Holocene activity.

Hood's most recent eruptive period—the Old Maid episode—began during the winter of 1781–1782, only a decade before Robert Broughton, first lieutenant of George Vancouver's 1792 exploratory voyage down the Pacific Northwest coast, named the peak for Lord Samuel Hood, admiral of the British navy. Arriving too late to witness the eruption, Broughton nonetheless observed some of its effects, which included a long submerged sandbar extending from the mouth of the Sandy River across the Columbia and logs that were stranded up to twelve feet above the river's surface. When Lewis and Clark arrived at the Sandy River thirteen years later, Clark described the Sandy as so full of sediment that it ran only about four inches deep. Attempting to wade across, he was astonished to find "the bottom a quick Sand [sic] and impassible." The Sandy River, which presently runs through a deep, narrow gorge to the Columbia, was then choked with debris from a large mudflow originating high on Mount Hood.

The Old Maid period, named for typical mudflow deposits it created at Old Maid Flat on Hood's west flank, apparently began with explosive eruptions that blasted away the dome formed during the Timberline episode. When fresh magma rose into the vent, located about 1,000 feet below and south of the summit, it erected a new dome, Crater Rock, the prominent lava knob now seen at the apex of the south-side debris fan. Hot rock avalanching from the growth of Crater Rock initiated pyroclastic flows that traveled down the White River on Hood's southeast flank, as well as onto the Sandy Glacier on the volcano's west side, causing the massive lahars that filled the Sandy River gorge. Searing clouds of ash-permeated gas— pyroclastic surges—sweeping downslope from Crater Rock killed stands of trees near timberline, creating the silvery Ghost Forest now visible on a ridgetop east of Timberline Lodge.

Although both Vancouver's crew and the Lewis and Clark expedition of 1805–1806 missed seeing Hood in action, later settlers recorded minor explosive events during the mid-nineteenth century. Writing in the *Everett Record* (1902), W. F. Courtney offered an account of activity in September 1859:

> We were camped on Tie [Tygh] Ridge about thirty-five miles from Mt. Hood. . . . It was about 1:30 o'clock in the morning when suddenly the heavens lit up and from the dark there shot up a column of fire. With a flash that illuminated the whole countryside with a pinkish glare, the flames danced from the crater. For two hours we watched, the mountain continued to blaze at irregular intervals, and when morning came Mt. Hood presented a peculiar sight. His sides, where the day before there was snow, were blackened as if cinders and ashes had been thrown out.

Six years later, John Dever, a soldier stationed at Vancouver, witnessed an early morning eruption, which he described in a letter to the Portland *Oregonian* (September 1865):

> Between the hours of 5 and 7 o'clock, and as the morning was particularly bright for this season of the year, my attention was naturally drawn

toward the east. Judge, then, of my surprise to see the top of Mount Hood enveloped in smoke and flame. Yes, sir, real jets of flame shot upwards seemingly a distance of fifteen or twenty feet above the mountain's height, accompanied by discharge of what appeared to be fragments of rock, cast up a considerable distance, which I could perceive fall immediately after with a rumbling noise not unlike distant thunder.

Although the deposits have not been positively correlated with observed historic events, Hood's upper cone is littered with fragments of lava and pumice stones, some of which may have been erupted in 1859 or 1865.

In an unpublished letter of January 28, 1866, Portland resident Franklin A. Hinds noted that Mount Hood had been "smoking" for the previous three months and was then still active. Laconically, Hinds also noted that Oregonians were not overly impressed by an active volcano located 50 miles distant, remarking that Hood's occasional flare-ups did not "create so much excitement here as you would naturally suppose, the morning paper speaks of it as an item of news and it is soon again forgotten in the hum of business." Hinds's observation about the public's attitude—determinedly ignoring a potential volcanic threat while pursuing business as usual—is still valid and identifies a major social impediment in preparing Pacific Northwest residents for the disastrous effects of a more powerful outburst in the future.

Although they do not yet have the techniques to predict the timing of future great earthquakes or volcanic eruptions, geologists agree that they are inevitable. Superquakes in the Cascadia subduction zone occur irregularly, but the certainty of their suddenly rearranging the coastal landscape, triggering tsunamis that will drown bays, harbors, and estuaries from Humboldt County, California, to Vancouver Island, make long-term planning for their recurrence a necessity. The Cascade volcanoes typically produce two or more significant eruptions per century—at least four erupted between about 1800 and 1860—making it likely that young adults in the Pacific Northwest will experience a volcanic crisis at some point in their lifetimes.

Among their many gifts to Anglo American settlers, the region's Native inhabitants transmitted their memories of convulsive temblors, huge sea waves, and mountains that thundered and blazed, manifestations of the irresistible forces that rule nature and impose limits on human striving.

As Native traditions about the Bridge of the Gods and the battles between Llao and Skell made clear, the now deceptively quiet gods of earth, sea, and mountain could reassert their destructive power at any time. ◙

No Longer a Hunter

John Struloeff

High on the mountainside
I peered through binoculars
across the hazy valley
into the spiked timber.
See it? My brother whispered.
He was as still as a deer beside me.
As if looking through a glass ball
at my own hand, I saw blurred color,
but nothing else. *Right there.*
I shook my head, straining.
The view wobbled and reeled.
Boy, look at that, my father whispered
as if seeing the Holy Spirit.
I saw flashes of pale, upturned leaves,
drooping branches, black tree trunks.
I can't see it, I said. They both moved.
Oh. There it goes, my father said, louder.
Yep, my brother said. *You scared it.*
I scared what? I asked, lowering the binoculars.

Salmon and the Northwest

Roy Hemmingway

THERE is not much of it left. Of untouched salmon habitat there is almost none. Although salmon once occupied almost every ocean-seeking stream in the Pacific Northwest, the map where salmon go has been shrinking for over a hundred years, sometimes gradually as human forces slowly worsened the habitat, sometimes suddenly when millions of acres of habitat were blocked by dams.

Now to see the headwater-to-the-sea habitat where the salmon thrive in abundance, one must go to Alaska. Here in the Lower Forty-eight, and in much of western Canada, it has almost vanished. A century and a half of logging, farming, ranching, mining, damming, road building, and urbanizing activity has taken its toll. Much that civilization demands for its sustenance has had a consequence in the fate of the salmon.

THE ABORIGINAL HABITAT

Only in a handful of small pockets, miniature and isolated ecosystems, can there still be found habitat as it once was. On the Oregon coast, just south of the town of Yachats, is a little untouched watershed, barely eight miles from the headwaters to the ocean. Cummins Creek winds through a narrow, steep-sided valley. There, protected under the Wilderness Act, trees many feet thick rise to the sky, almost blocking out the sun. Over years, as trees have died, some have fallen into the creek. Although the creek is small and shallow in many places, even in the low water of summer it is a struggle to walk the streambed. Tree trunks are everywhere in the creek, creating dams over which the water must plunge, digging out pools that could soak a person up to the neck. Gravel bars have built up where the creek slows. The fallen trees push the creek from bank to bank, undercutting, and causing more trees, rootwads and all, to end up in the creekbed. All this adds up to stream "complexity," a diverse set of stream conditions that create the conditions needed for healthy salmon.

In other streams, where the trees have not been allowed to mature and die and end up in the creek, what we see is a far more simplified stream. What most of us now think of as a pristine natural stream, bubbling along unimpeded to the sea, is not what the pioneers saw in many of the Northwest watersheds. Instead, west of the Cascades, they found creeks so choked with trees that in places they could not reach the water. On the larger rivers, log jams were common barriers to navigation, which had to be blown up or painstakingly picked apart by men who risked their lives not knowing when the jam would give way. Whether for aesthetics or practicalities, man in the American West has systematically rid both large and small streams of the logs, boulders, and other "debris" that shape the stream and give life to salmon.

Abundant beaver in aboriginal times built dams on the smaller streams. The ponds behind the dams gave refuge to juvenile salmon from the high currents of winter floods and the warm waters of summer droughts. Beaver, now trapped and driven from much of their previous range, once were as ubiquitous in the Northwest as salmon. The simplified stream channels which have such dire consequences for salmon are in no small part due to the absence of beaver.

Before the effects of man, creeks and streams and rivers moved across their floodplains, changing course as high water cut new channels and dammed up old ones. Floods spread out into multiple channels, where the over-wintering juvenile salmon could find refuge from the fast water. In summer, these streams, slowed and directed by logs and boulders near the banks, dug deep channels, where the water stayed cool throughout the hot days.

It was into these conditions that the salmon evolved. Although they were home throughout the Columbia River and Pacific Coast states, from the coastal rain forests to the high deserts, the streams in which they began and ended their lives all shared these attributes. Vegetation along stream-banks provided shade and engineered the variety that salmon need during the freshwater phases of their life cycle. The rivers "interacted" with their flood plains by changing channels as flows increased and decreased. Small spawning streams were narrow, deep, and cool, with riffles, pools, and gravel bars. In the arid areas east of the Cascades, where fewer firs and pines grow, willows, aspens, locusts, and cottonwoods along the banks provided the stream complexity.

The few places where untouched salmon habitat can be found today are small. In our imagination we expand these places to an entire aboriginal landscape as a conceptual salmon Eden. Anecdotal pioneer stories of salmon, body-to-body across an entire stream channel, are universalized to every Pacific Northwest stream. We imagine the landscape before European contact as uniformly pure, unsullied, and unchanging through time. Even without humankind's intrusion in the salmon's life zone, however, change is the one constant. In fact, salmon cannot live without change. Floods wash spawning gravels out of the stream. These can only be replenished by new landslides, which occur most frequently when slopes are bare after fires like those that once swept through the fir forests west of the Cascades every few centuries. After fires, salmon suffer initially as the sediment fills the interstices in the gravels, suffocating the eggs. Silt and mud fill the deep holes in the streambeds where cooler summer waters are present. With time, the winter rains push these fine sediments down the river to ocean, leaving the gravels and digging again the deep holes behind a rock or a tree trunk brought down by the slide. The watershed heals itself, slowly renewing the tree cover, slowing the progress of sediment into the stream. As the smaller sediments wash away, the gravels first become home to the species, such as coho, able to make use of a stream without strong riffles and deep pools. Over time, as the stream becomes more complex, other salmon species like steelhead come in to use more of this diverse habitat.

Even without man, natural change was so constant that no more than a third of the zone west of the Coast Range, for example, was likely to have been "prime" salmon habitat at any one time. The rest of the landscape was still either recovering from a major disturbance or in need of disturbance in order to begin anew the conditions right for salmon. Not every stream teemed with fish, only those that were at the right stage between major devastating events. A third or more of all streams may have had no salmon at all. But there were enough streams with abundant runs of salmon to give early European immigrants the impression that the fish resource was unending.

MIGRATION

Different species and runs of salmon take advantage of the different conditions presented by the Northwest's rivers and streams. Almost all salmon spawn in fall to early winter and hatch out in winter or spring. Some salmon species, such as chum and pinks, spawn in the estuary and the low reaches of creeks close to saltwater and rear there for a short time as juveniles before going to sea. Most other salmon make a long upstream journey to reach spawning gravel, timing their run to when there will likely be water in the stream where they will lay and fertilize their eggs. Salmon moving upstream to spawn cannot move into a creek that has low flows or high temperatures during the summer and early fall. Other streams, like the Willamette River at Oregon City, have cascades or waterfalls that only during the spring have flow enough for salmon to pass. Others lack enough cool summer pools to hold spring-migrating fish until fall spawning and are populated only with fall and winter run fish.

The spring chinook move into the rivers during the high spring and early summer flows. Not spawning until fall, and often ascending into high reaches of the watershed, it has high fat reserves to give it stamina. Having swum through thousands of miles of ocean and struggled upstream in freshwater for sometimes hundreds of miles, this most driven of animals reaches the river of its birth. Then it stops, and waits. It finds a deep hole or a spring-fed pool in the stream where cool water remains throughout the heat of summer. Against the slight current in these holes, the salmon swims slowly in place. For months at a time, the fish is still, rarely moving more than a few feet from this chosen place, conserving energy. One can see them crowded together in these holes, their dark gray backs parallel to the current, like a flight of zeppelins, until a disturbance, a shadow, spooks them into dispersal, only to return within minutes one-by-one to their vigil.

During this time, their bodies are changing, from trophy athletes to reproductive engines. They shun even the slim sustenance these small creeks afford fish this large. Their flesh decays, their energy slowly consumed to produce eggs in females and fighting equipment in males for the mating competition to come. An adult female salmon may have over 20 percent of her body mass taken up by eggs by the time she spawns.

ANADROMY

Anadromy, ascending rivers from the sea for breeding, is salmon's great adaptive tool. It is achieved through very complex physiological changes to keep internal electrolytic balance as the fish moves from freshwater with a salt content less than its own tissues to the ocean with a salt content that is greater, and then back again. By laying eggs in freshwater and maturing at sea, salmon take advantage of the best that both habitats offer. The secure gravels of freshwater allow salmon to reproduce with fewer, but larger, eggs that are more likely to survive.

Some salmon species may spend more than a year maturing in freshwater before venturing to the ocean. In saltwater, the salmon's diet radically changes from the small insects and other invertebrates of the river to a predator's diet of smaller fish. This access to an abundant food supply at a time when salmon are mature enough to handle larger prey has a profound effect. A salmon which in freshwater may have taken a year to grow to six inches in length and barely over an ounce in weight will grow rapidly once it reaches the ocean in the spring. After the first summer, it will likely be a fifteen-inch fish.

Salmon species take advantage of the wide range of ocean habitats, just as the different varieties of salmon take advantage of almost all the riverine habitat at one time or another. Some salmon roam over thousands of miles of ocean, leaving the Columbia River and ranging to the Gulf of Alaska and out to the fringe of the Aleutians before beginning the journey back to the streams of their birth.

A creature that swims a thousand miles upstream to reproduce and then die says much about the drive to survive and create progeny. To people it seems like a waste for an animal to struggle so much to reproduce, only to meet death soon afterward. Why would nature not have given this animal just a little more muscle mass, or a little more stamina, so that it could survive spawning and follow the downstream current back to the ocean?

However, dying after spawning allows salmonids to take advantage of all their body mass to get to the spawning grounds and leave large numbers of healthy fertilized eggs and, consequently, produce greater numbers of juveniles and eventually adults. They need not hold anything in reserve for a return trip to saltwater. Dying after spawning also allows the spawned-out salmon to play a critical role in the ecosystem. The small creeks and streams where the salmon spawn are often devoid of nutrients. In a dramatic example of the circle of life, young salmon feed directly on the carcasses as well as on the other organisms that find food in the dead adults. Vegetation along salmon streams also depends on dead salmon for vital nutrients. This role of spawned-out salmon is now believed to be so important, in fact, that carcasses from salmon that have been spawned in the hatchery are placed in some streams where lack of nutrients inhibits the growth of the emerging wild salmon fry.

HABITAT DEGRADATION

Most of the habitat available in the Pacific Northwest and not closed off by dams has been degraded in slow increments. A valley farmer cannot efficiently use his bottomland because of the stream meandering through it. He fills in the curves and pushes the channel against one hillside, thereby speeding the current and eliminating the alcoves young salmon and steelhead need to survive winter streamflows. A culvert on a logging road plugs up with debris in a heavy rain, sending a flood of water over the road, starting a slope failure and a debris avalanche that fills the river with silt. A homeowner, realizing a dream of living next to a river, cuts the brush and trees obscuring his view and plants a lawn down to the water's edge, thereby allowing summer sun to heat the stream. A potato farmer, wanting to take advantage of the sandy soils and intense sun of the Snake River plain, withdraws the equivalent of six feet of rain from the river to put on his acreage each summer.

Each new habitat alteration seemed small at the time compared to the abundant numbers of fish. However, incremental damage has been a calamity for salmon habitat. These disturbances, collectively on a much wider scale than provided by nature, have left little habitat that is ideal for salmon. It is tempting to cast blame, as many do, on corporate greed and a purposeful lack of concern for the environment. But most of the damage was not done willfully. Even the Columbia River dams, each one dooming more salmon than any other cause, were built with the idea that all the losses could be replenished in hatcheries.

THE SPIRIT OF THE SALMON

When our distant ancestors stopped investing objects and animals with spiritual value, they began to see themselves as detached from nature. No longer bound up in a web of spiritual relationships with the natural world, they were then free to see in terms of cause and effect, to view the world "objectively." They began to think of the natural world as there to serve humankind's ends rather than humans serving the numinous purposes of the natural world. They believed that the quality of human life could be influenced by human action and was not solely at the caprice of the gods.

This detachment from nature is so intricately interwoven with our culture that it is difficult to find terms to describe natural phenomena that do not encompass our objectification of the natural world. The study of nature, which for many people originates in a sense of the contribution that nature makes to a person's sense of place in the world, marches quickly away from these personal values as soon as one delves very deeply into the disciplines. Latin taxonomy and interrelationships according to objective laws leave no room for notions of how nature affects our subjective experience.

Yet despite this rational creation of an objective world, we have still not lost our attachment to the earth. Our lives reflect the tension—often starkly felt—between our modern rationality and our primitive relationship with the natural world. We go out into nature to seek spiritual renewal. Although man is one of the most gregarious of animals, we harbor a belief that cities are unnatural and unhealthy. We surround ourselves with plants and flowers, both indoors and out, as much as we do with human art. We send our children to summer camp, in the belief that encountering nature will prepare them better for the rigors of adulthood. We bring animals into the household, even though many of them—fish, birds, hamsters, snakes—interact very little with their human keepers. In the dark of winter, we cut down a tree and bring it inside the house and decorate it with lights.

We are, after all, animals ourselves. We too experience the rhythms of life, and we sense when we have gotten out of balance with our natural selves. We feel we are more whole when we can retreat to the quiet of nature as well as exercise our physical selves. It is not possible to describe rationally the attachment to the earth that we feel, but in many people's lives the experience of nature is as important, if not more so, as the pleasures of civilization.

For people in the Pacific Northwest, this connection with nature seems particularly important. While every region and every state has its scenic beauties, people of the Pacific Northwest take environmental quality more seriously than people almost anywhere else in the country. Although most of the people of the region live in cities, the opportunity for recreation outside the cities is highly valued. If there is any litmus test for most Northwest politicians, it is being in favor of environmental quality.

The Pacific Northwest does not provide the greatest of scenic spectaculars. The coast is beautiful, but not as stunning as Big Sur or Point Reyes in California. The mountains are high, but only Mount Rainier rivals the Alaskan high peaks or the Sierra Nevada in grandeur. Mount Hood is the highest point in Oregon and complements the Portland skyline, but every other western state has a taller peak. The region's deserts are small and not very dramatic. What may be attractive here is the balance that can be experienced: among mountains, deserts, seashores, and green agricultural valleys. Balance between work and recreation. Balance among the seasons. Balance between the civilization of Portland and Seattle and the nature that abounds outside the urban areas.

The salmon are emblematic of the role of natural forces in the lives of Pacific Northwesterners. To have this spectacular wild creature in our midst allows us to maintain the connection to the wild that is within us. Take salmon away, and Pacific Northwesterners lose claim to being able to live within a natural environment. To lose the salmon is to confess that civilization is all-encompassing, that the only nature that can survive is that which is complementary to man's economic impulses, that humankind's connection to the earth must necessarily be sacrificed to the rationality of making maximum use of society's tangible assets, including those provided by nature.

It is the sense people have of the spirit of the salmon that has given them importance today well beyond their commercial and culinary attributes. Here is an animal which can only be regarded as beautiful in human terms. It has the sleek clean lines of a modern sculpture and is the color of polished silver. Its endurance is legendary. It roams the far oceans. It will swim upstream sometimes for over a thousand miles, leaping cascades and waterfalls, to reach the place where it was born. It will fight for a mate and engage in a ritualistic courtship. To reproduce, it will brutalize its physical self and then make the ultimate sacrifice, its flesh providing nourishment for the continuation of the circle of life. Courage, steadfastness, beauty, strength, sacrifice—these are all human ideals. It is no accident that we exalt a creature with these qualities.

CO-EXISTENCE

Is it folly to expect that the wild salmon, any more than the grizzly bear and the cougar, can co-exist with an expanding urban populace? It has been said that there are more deer in America than when the Pilgrims landed, because rural homesteads and large-lot suburbs create good habitat and provide freedom from predators. But are the salmon compatible with human development?

The evidence is conflicting. Salmon are one of the most resilient and adaptable of creatures. Despite their instinct to return to their natal stream to spawn, they have enough inclination to stray that they manage to repopulate areas after natural (and even human-induced) disasters have wiped out all habitat for a period of time. After the forty or so Missoula floods of the Pleistocene, which periodically sent walls of water up to a thousand feet high down the Columbia River Gorge, the salmon somehow recolonized the entire reformed Columbia River basin in 10,000 years, an evolutionary blink of an eye. After Mount St. Helens sent a torrent of hot mud down the Toutle River and into the Cowlitz in 1980, salmon and steelhead quickly came back to spawn. The Pacific Northwest is the most geologically active region in the contiguous United States. The surface of the land is some of the newest on earth, yet the salmon have been able to adapt and survive and occupy almost all the available habitat.

What we do not know is twofold: how much habitat degradation salmon can take and still survive through generations, and what it takes to restore the habitat that has been damaged (beyond removing all works of man and not returning for a century or two). We have never been successful in restoring self-sustaining runs of salmon to a watershed from which they were extirpated. It is not known how much of this difficulty is due to our never having restored a damaged watershed sufficiently to allow salmon to return, as against the unique genetic characteristics of the stocks of salmon in each watershed that cannot be replaced.

Where dams blocked access to spawning habitat, it was originally thought that fish ladders for adults migrating upstream would be enough to ensure that salmon could get to the habitat that was left. The fish and wildlife management agencies signed off on the dams with the expectation that the effects of the dams would be mitigated by the construction of fish ladders and hatcheries, resulting in continued abundant salmon for harvest. Paralleling the string of dams on rivers around the Northwest are now dozens of salmon hatcheries that pour millions of smolts into the rivers each year.

It is now clear that none of the technological fixes, starting with providing passage for adults moving upstream and including hatcheries, has been completely successful in maintaining the salmon runs. In the Columbia, on average, only about a million salmon, 80 percent of them hatchery fish, return to the Columbia each year, less than 10 percent of historic abundance. Three quarters of the original 200 Columbia River natural salmon stocks are either extinct or in decline. Only three stocks (Hanford Reach fall chinook, Lewis River fall chinook, and Wenatchee Lake sockeye) are currently anywhere near their historic abundance.

Although in some areas hatcheries have successfully produced abundant fish for harvest, particularly in good ocean conditions, this accomplishment has come with a price. Hatcheries are successful only with heavy doses of antibiotics and other drugs and slow manipulation of genetics over generations to breed in characteristics of fish that survive well as juveniles in a crowded captive environment. These are not necessarily the attributes that contribute to the long-term resilience of fish that must migrate downstream, survive in the ocean, and then make their way over dams back to the hatchery. Despite the occasional successes of the massive hatchery program, hatcheries have been unable to replace the numbers of salmon lost to dams and habitat destruction. The truly successful artificial production programs have been in Canada, Chile, and Norway, where salmon are raised in pens through their whole life cycle and harvested directly without ever having been released into the wild. These create other environmental problems, however, from pollution to escape of farmed fish into the wild.

WILD FISH

Hatcheries are under attack. Even if the hatchery program worked to produce abundant salmon, it is wild fish that have the stronger advocates today. Hatchery fish are believed to compete for food with wild fish in the stream and estuary and can infect other fish with hatchery-bred diseases. Not all hatchery salmon are harvested or return to the hatchery; some stray into the rivers and spawn with wild fish, raising concerns about genetic contamination of the wild fish, particularly when the hatchery fish originate from stocks of a faraway river basin.

In addition, hatcheries find they need infusions of wild fish to ensure against genetic inbreeding. Recreational fishers believe that wild fish provide a better fight when hooked. Gourmets claim wild fish have better texture and flavor. These have all added up to a strong constituency for preserving abundant runs of wild fish. More public support for conservation of wild stocks comes from the public's concern for conservation of wildness. An adult salmon reared in a concrete holding tank before going to sea is just not the same as a salmon that was born in gravel and spent its early life struggling to survive in a flowing stream. The wildness of the stream-bred salmon sets it apart. People's feelings of connection with nature have become focused on wild salmon and the spirit of creation that they embody.

At the time the hatchery programs were conceived in the 1950s and 1960s, we as a people shared a belief that technology would deliver answers that were superior to nature. Physicians touted infant formula as superior nutrition to mothers' breast milk. We believed that synthetic fibers would soon produce better clothing than the old options of cotton, wool, and silk. Just as we could produce better fruit, vegetables, and livestock, technology surely could produce a better salmon than the ones that had to depend on nature for survival.

Today, we comprehend more of the complex balance of natural processes and our own role in nature. We understand how difficult it is to produce a product, live or synthetic, that duplicates, let alone is superior to, the qualities that have developed through eons of evolutionary change. Our irrational side, too, is at work, making connection with the wild creature that has such a remarkable life history. We appreciate the value of wildness and we seek to preserve it.

THE COLUMBIA RIVER

In the Columbia Basin, the natural salmon ecosystem has been so radically altered by the dams that scientists cannot agree on the root causes of the salmon's decline. Is it problems in the reservoirs: too much time to be eaten by predators, or not enough food, or too little flow to get them to the ocean in timing with their physiological changes? Is it problems in passing the dams? Do the fish bypass systems cause more problems than they solve? Does barging juvenile salmon downstream cause too much stress to the fish? Do they lose the imprinting of the route home by being carried downstream? Or have the dams, with their unnatural flow regimes and capturing of nutrients and sediments, altered even the condition of the estuary and the ocean at the river mouth to the point where fish are vulnerable to starvation and predators?

These are difficult questions to answer, because there are so many variables to analyze in an ecosystem as complicated as the Columbia River. It is difficult to follow a six-inch fish in the river and nearly impossible in the ocean because of the limitations of even state-of-the-art electronic tracking. It is almost impossible to see what is causing a young salmon to die.

Some scientists postulate that the Columbia River problems are so intractable that only the breaching of some dams can save the salmon. Does the Pacific Northwest love the salmon so much that it would unbuild some of the prized Columbia River hydropower system? While it may seem doubtful that the political will would be present for such a radical step, this option continues to be discussed as the ultimate solution if the Columbia River salmon are to be rescued.

THINGS LOOK DIFFERENT IN THE WATERSHEDS

On the ocean coasts of the Pacific Northwest, salmon runs have declined almost as much as on the Columbia. Here it is clearly not dams that have decimated the salmon runs but a combination of over-harvest of adult fish and the destruction of freshwater habitat.

One example is the coho salmon of the Oregon coast. Coho hatch in the winter and then spend over a year in freshwater, using side channels, beaver ponds, and flooded fields for refuge from the high water. During summer drought, they look for the coolest water in the stream, often in the holes below obstructions in the mainstem of the river, where a spring might support a colony of young salmon. In their second spring they migrate to the ocean. In their second fall at sea, coho return to their natal stream, searching for clean gravel in low gradient creeks. Coho's tendency to migrate in shallow ocean water near shore makes them particularly easy to catch in hook-and-line ocean fisheries. For decades, coho were the staple of the charter boat and commercial fishery operating out of Oregon coastal ports.

Because juvenile coho stay in freshwater so long and use so much of the available habitat, they are vulnerable to any degree of habitat destruction taking place in the watershed. Unless the stream has enough complexity to provide calm water refuges from high flows, a winter flood will blast them out to sea and a premature death. Sedimentation that fills in the deep holes will make it harder for the fish to find cool water in the hot summer. Removal of bank vegetation will cut off at the source the food chain on which the salmon depend.

The salmon recovery efforts that are taking place in the Northwest are based on the perception that everything that happens in a watershed affects the salmon. Besides the efforts to improve passage around dams, the emphasis is on restoration of habitat conditions, including creating some limited disturbances, that would allow the salmon to thrive once again. This is not a simple task, for the conditions that caused the decline of the salmon are complex and not always well understood. More significantly, human factors must often be overcome before the conditions in the watershed can begin to be addressed.

Beginning in the early 1990s, citizens in a few areas tired of the environmental conflict that had shattered their communities for the last decade. The battles over federal forest policy that reached an apex with the lawsuits over protection of the northern spotted owl separated neighbor from neighbor all over the rural Northwest.

Lack of stream structure, lack of shade, wasteful water withdrawal, silt from logging roads, contamination from farm chemicals or livestock, road culverts which block salmon's access to spawning streams, livestock in the streams, erosion from gravel pits, erosion from agriculture lands, and so forth, all cause conditions inhospitable to salmon.

No one of these problems usually ruins a salmon stream by itself, but together they make most watersheds far less hospitable to salmon. No state-run program could identify all these problems, stream mile by stream mile, let alone organize the effort to address each one. That is the strength of the watershed-based efforts, which address the factors that limit salmon production in the watershed.

Many rural landowners in the West are suspicious of any efforts made on behalf of the environment. They do not look kindly on government personnel or "do-gooders" on their land, scrutinizing and potentially criticizing their operations. It is the genius of the watershed restoration effort that it is local people, who have witnessed the decline of the species, talking to local people that brings about cooperation.

The Northwest salmon recovery effort relies heavily on these local watershed restoration efforts. There is scientific dispute as to how much these efforts can contribute to salmon recovery, particularly while much logging, farming, and land development goes on as before. However, the most significant positive result for salmon from these local efforts may be the development of community ownership of their salmon resource. Local community members have decided that salmon are important to them, not necessarily for harvest, but as an indicator of wildness and the health of the nature around them. All over the Northwest it is local efforts that are working and sacrificing for salmon preservation and restoration. The local community will exert peer pressure on a landowner who does not take care of habitat. If the present efforts do not bring about salmon recovery, the local people will look for other solutions that will. Technical and financial assistance to local efforts from the state and federal governments and then getting out of the way have been more productive than the old methods of imposing a new regulatory scheme on wary local landowners.

WHITHER SALMON?

It is easy to be pessimistic about the future of Pacific Northwest salmon. Decimated by dams and injured habitat, the once resilient wild salmon face decline and even extinction in many areas. The mild climate and open spaces of the Pacific Northwest, as well as its reputation for community spirit, are attracting population at a faster rate than all but a few areas of the United States. More people means more habitat destruction and fewer places for salmon to live and thrive.

Human beings over centuries have tended to prefer the same habitat as the salmon. The bottoms of valleys along the rivers and streams were the first areas settled and are still preferred areas for agriculture and urban development. The strategies used for preservation of other species like the spotted owl, the wolf, and the grizzly bear—setting aside tracts of undeveloped land remote from most human settlement—will not work to preserve the salmon. The destruction of the salmon is taking place literally right in northwesterners' backyards.

The engine of Pacific Northwest economic development—the Columbia River hydropower system—is at the heart of the most difficult salmon problem. This prized engineering masterpiece has come at the expense of once magnificent salmon runs that nourished generations of aboriginal settlers and then enriched the Europeans who succeeded them. On top of all that Indians have sacrificed, the loss to their culture from the death of the salmon is incalculable. That this animal, which ranged the far oceans and then came a thousand miles upstream to reproduce, now teeters on the brink of extinction is an almost unthinkable injury to the spirit of both Indians and non-Indians alike.

The largest question is whether the human populace can accept the limitations on incremental damage to habitat, no matter how insignificant it may seem at the time compared to the economic benefits. When local people value salmon as a community asset, there is reason for optimism that they will make the right choices.

Salmon have been as much a part of the Pacific Northwest as the tall, dense forests and snow-capped volcanoes. The people of the Northwest value the connection to nature that life here can afford them, including the contact still with wildness—untouched wilderness, rivers foaming with rapids, and almost all the wildlife species that were here when the Europeans arrived. The salmon is at the heart of this Pacific Northwest wild heritage. If we let the wild salmon slide into extinction, something of the unique spiritual quality of this landscape will go with them. ◙

The Endangered Species Act

THIRTY-EIGHT YEARS ON THE ARK

Jeff Curtis and Bob Davison

THE Endangered Species Act (ESA), the current version of which was passed in 1973, has achieved iconic significance. To those concerned about the environment, it is at the pinnacle of environmental laws—the 800-pound gorilla of a law that puts species conservation above development concerns. To developers and property rights advocates, the ESA is often viewed as a tool radical environmentalists use to achieve political goals. This article is an attempt by two conservationists who have worked with the law over more than three decades to provide a practical explanation of why the law was enacted, how the law works, and why it is important. We also will examine why the ESA, of all environmental laws, has become so controversial and why there are continued calls for its revision.

Years of amendments, both proposed and enacted, and the labors of a generation of members of Congress and congressional staff have, for the most part, managed to enhance rather than diminish the original vision of the ESA. That vision was driven by a concern over the loss of some of the country's most notable species.

In 1973, there were 109 species listed as endangered under the precursors to the current ESA. The bald eagle, brown pelican, and peregrine falcon were all in danger of extinction from eggshell thinning caused by pesticides, particularly DDT. The American alligator was threatened by overexploitation for its hide and loss of habitat. The continued existence of wolves and grizzly bears in the 48 conterminous states was in doubt as a result of programs to protect livestock and the expansion of development into wilderness areas. House of Representatives ESA sponsor John Dingell would declare that the "existing laws are sound, as far as they go, but later events have shown that they do not go far enough."

In its explanation and justification of the ESA legislation, the House Merchant Marine and Fisheries Committee found: "From all evidence available to us, it appears that the pace of disappearance of species is accelerating." An Interior Department assistant secretary told the committee, "The truth in this is apparent when one realizes that half of the recorded extinctions of mammals over the past 2,000 years have occurred in the most recent 50-year period."

Much of what was said and written about the need for the ESA in 1973 expressed concern over the risk that might lie in extinction. The House Merchant Marine and Fisheries Committee wrote:

> As we homogenize the habitats in which these plants and animals evolved, and as we increase the pressure for products that they are in a position to supply (usually unwillingly) we threaten their— and our own—genetic heritage. The value of this genetic heritage is, quite literally, incalculable. . . .
>
> From the most narrow possible point of view, it is in the best interests of mankind to minimize the losses of genetic variations. The reason is simple: they are potential resources. They are keys to puzzles which we cannot solve, and may provide answers to questions which we have not yet learned to ask.

As the Senate considered passage of its own ESA legislation, a much younger Senator Pete Domenici of New Mexico declared: "Man has been the culprit in bringing certain species to the point of extinction; it would be a double indictment against humanity to ignore the present situation and allow the destruction of our resource of wildlife to continue."

Noting that "sheer self-interest impels us to be cautious," Congress, with unusual foresight, constructed a law that had at its heart "the institutionalization of that caution." It is likely one of the earliest legislative expressions of what is now referred to as the "precautionary principle." This principle essentially states that precautionary actions should be taken to address human and environmental threats even if it is not possible to demonstrate scientifically any link between cause and effect.

It may surprise many that the rationale and language used to articulate the need for passage of the ESA over 38 years ago is nearly the same as that used today to argue for its continued strength. Perhaps all that has changed is that there are more examples on which to draw of species facing extinction (more than ten times as many) and of specific benefits that may be foreclosed to humans by the impending loss of this genetic material.

A SIMPLE LAW OF FAR-REACHING PROPORTIONS

The ESA that emerged in 1973 is relatively short and sweet, as federal laws go, and it has remained that way. Other stalwart environmental laws, such as the Clean Water Act and Clean Air Act, are more than five times as lengthy. But the simplicity of the ESA has proven visionary and far-reaching.

The act establishes a broad goal and expansive definitions of what it protects. It then sets up a process to determine whether an animal or plant species is either in danger of becoming extinct (endangered) or likely to become endangered (threatened). Those species found to be threatened or endangered are added to the list of species that are protected under the ESA. Once a species is listed, two key types of protection follow: it is illegal for anyone to kill or harm an individual animal or plant of a listed species, and all federal agencies are required to ensure that they don't fund or do anything that would be likely to put the continued existence of a listed species in jeopardy or adversely modify habitat critical to that species.

The broad purpose for the ESA has proven to be far ahead of its time by focusing not just on the conservation of all endangered and threatened plant and animal species, but more importantly on the conservation of "the ecosystems upon which they depend." As our knowledge of ecological systems has expanded, so has our understanding and appreciation of the wisdom in this purpose.

The broad purpose of the ESA is given meaning by the scope of its provisions. The species that were made eligible for listing, for example, include any member of the plant or animal kingdom, except insects that are pests and pose an "overwhelming and overriding risk" to humans. The 1,371 currently listed U.S. species and populations range from the Oregon silverspot butterfly, fat pocketbook clam, and California red-legged frog to the coho salmon, whooping crane, and blue whale. Only bacteria and viruses need not apply.

The original drafters of the ESA broadened the law's scope even further by expanding the traditional taxonomic definition of species to include "any subspecies of fish or wildlife or plants, and any distinct population segment of any species of vertebrate fish and wildlife that interbreeds when mature." In deciding to provide for listing of subspecies and geographically discrete fish and wildlife populations, Congress chose to protect animals that are in trouble in part of their range, but healthy in other areas. In particular, they chose to require protection of bald eagles, wolves, and grizzly bears in the lower 48 states even though there were, and still are, healthy populations of these species in Alaska. Perhaps they did so because, as the conservationist Aldo Leopold said, "Relegating grizzlies to Alaska is like relegating happiness to heaven; one may never get there."

Soon after the passage of ESA in 1973, Congress was embroiled over the controversy involving the Tellico Dam and the snail darter, a three-inch fish that was stopping completion of the dam. (The only fish story, some wag noted, where the size of the fish kept getting smaller.) During the debates, many in Congress made the argument that when they voted for passage of the 1973 act, they had intended to protect animals such as the bald eagle and the gray wolf, but they certainly would have never voted to protect such an insignificant species as the snail darter.

However, since the snail darter controversy, Congress has had multiple opportunities to limit the coverage of the act to what biologists have termed "charismatic megafauna" (large, attractive animals) and has not done so. In fact, when Congress last amended the law in 1988, it went the other direction, directing that priorities for recovery plans should be based on need and "without regard to taxonomic classification." This is due, in large part, to the expanding science of conservation biology and the consistent efforts of conservation groups and the federal agencies to educate Congress on the interconnectedness of species in the environment and the value of species diversity to human concerns.

LISTING AND CRITICAL HABITAT DESIGNATION: A PROMISE REINFORCED AND ONE UNFULFILLED

The shape of the current process for determining whether to list a species owes much to the poor judgment of former Secretary of the Interior James Watt. In the early days of the Reagan administration, Secretary Watt virtually shut down the listing of species, regardless of their imperiled status.

(The average annual number of listings dropped from 33 in 1976 through 1979 to just 9 from 1980 to 1983.) Watt also insisted that listing decisions be subject to economic analysis by the Office of Management and Budget, which presumably could veto listings that would have negative economic consequences. Congress responded by establishing a process that forced the agencies to respond to petitions from individuals and to make findings on those petitions within strict timeframes. Congress also reinforced the ESA to make crystal clear that listing decisions are to be based solely on the best available scientific information.

Unlike the almost unlimited discretion the government had regarding the listing process before Watt, the current listing process is largely petition driven. As a result, the average annual number of listings from 1983 through 2001 increased six-fold to 54. Private citizens or groups submit petitions to list animals or plants. The listing agencies, the U.S. Fish and Wildlife Service (FWS) and National Marine Fisheries Service (NMFS), must respond within 90 days with a finding as to whether there is enough information in the petition to move forward with the listing process. A year after the petition is filed the agency must decide whether or not to propose that the species be listed. Finally, two years after a petition is filed, the agencies must make their final decisions. As tightly as this process was drawn, it proved to be no match for the Interior Department of President George W. Bush, which managed to list even fewer species than Secretary Watt—an average of fewer than eight species per year.

FWS and NMFS also are required to designate "critical habitat" for the species in question at the time of listing, or at most one year later, if doing so is practicable. All federal agencies, in turn, are barred from taking actions that would result in the destruction or adverse modification of designated habitats. Although the listing decision itself is shielded from economics, the designation of critical habitat is not. The theory behind this distinction, which frankly makes more political than scientific sense (and for which one of the authors of this article admits partial responsibility), is that there may be some choices in designating habitat for a species and the listing agencies should choose the habitat that causes the least economic harm.

In practice, over most of the ESA's history the agencies resisted designating critical habitat. (Only 601 of the 1,371 listed species and populations have critical habitat designated as of December 2010.) In 1986, regulations were issued that limited the ability of critical habitat designation to provide protection beyond that already provided by the requirement that federal agencies avoid jeopardizing a listed species' existence. Since at least that time, there has been a kind of twisted logic at the root of this agency resistance to designation of areas as critical habitat. They have reasoned that if there is little value to species protection that can be gained through critical habitat designation, then given its cost and controversy, it should be given low priority notwithstanding the legal requirement that it be done.

In the last decade, however, two federal courts have invalidated the 1986 FWS and NMFS interpretation of the ESA because, as the Ninth Circuit Court of Appeals pointed out in 2004,

> Congress said that destruction or adverse modification could occur when sufficient critical habitat is lost so as to threaten a species' recovery even if there remains sufficient critical habitat for the species' survival. The regulation, by contrast, finds that adverse modification to critical habitat can only occur when there is so much critical habitat lost that a species' very survival is threatened.

Six years after the Ninth Circuit ruling and nearly a decade after the Fifth Circuit invalidated the same regulatory definition of what it means to destroy or adversely modify critical habitat, the regulation remains on the books. Interior Secretary Alberto Salazar and company, like their predecessors, are believed to be at work on a long overdue change to give back meaning to the ESA imperative of recovery.

FEDERAL AGENCY CONSULTATION
AND THE MAGIC LANGUAGE OF SECTION 7

Once a species has been listed as either threatened or endangered, the full force of the ESA is brought to bear to halt and reverse the trend toward extinction. A primary means of achieving this goal is found in the "magic language" of the Act's section 7, memorized by a generation of lawyers and the cause of the vast majority of lawsuits and controversy surrounding the ESA. Section 7 states that federal agencies "must insure that all actions authorized, funded or carried out are not likely to jeopardize the continued existence of an endangered or threatened species or adversely modify habitat critical to it." As the Supreme Court, in deciding *TVA v. Hill* (the Tellico Dam/snail darter case) said, "One would be hard pressed to find a statutory provision whose terms were any plainer than those in section 7 of the Endangered Species Act."

The responsibility for making sure that projects or activities are not approved, funded, or carried out if they jeopardize a listed species' existence belongs with each and every federal agency. It is a remarkable statement of the preference for species survival over other government activities. As the Supreme Court has said, it "reveals a conscious decision by Congress to give endangered species priority over the 'primary missions' of federal agencies."

While the federal agencies that propose actions are the responsible parties for "insuring" that their actions are not likely to jeopardize species, they must "consult" with the fish and wildlife agencies—FWS and NMFS—on those actions. The process, though in practice often complex and controversial, is conceptually simple. The agency responsible for the project discovers that a project may affect a listed species. It then must consult with FWS or NMFS, depending on the species. The agencies look at the proposed action and, based on the best science available, issue a "biological opinion" with either a "jeopardy" or a "no jeopardy" finding. Jeopardy opinions must, if possible, contain "reasonable and prudent alternatives" suggested by the consulting agencies that recommend economically feasible modifications that would both preserve the species and minimize the economic impacts of allowing the action to go forward.

In 1982 Congress provided that FWS and NMFS could issue "incidental take statements" for projects that received favorable biological opinions. This allows some harm, including death, to come to individual animals resulting from the project as long as the project does not jeopardize the existence of the species. Although incidental take statements must be accompanied by "reasonable and prudent measures" to minimize the amount of take, at times these statements can be startling, as is the case of the biological opinion on the Columbia River Hydropower System, which allows a "take" of 88 percent of juvenile Snake River fall Chinook that pass through the hydropower system.

The consultation procedure is the key mechanism by which the ESA results in economically feasible modifications of development proposals in order to prevent extinction of species. While the highly visible ESA controversies, such as the Klamath or the Snake River dams, draw considerable attention, what is remarkable about the act is how few projects have actually been stopped and how much flexibility the agencies have been able to find in the language of the law. Over the history of the act, only about one out of every 3,500 federal actions fails to go forward as a result of ESA requirements. The remainder proceed with little conflict, often with minor adjustments to projects that cost little but provide breathing room for imperiled species.

If the recommended project would jeopardize a species' existence and modifications are not reasonable—are not economically feasible—then an exemption can be sought from the requirements of the ESA. This exemption process, which is known by one of the most evocative phrases of environmental law, "God Squad," allows economically important activities to go forward, even if the agency actions are certain to cause extinction of a species. In 1978, when the Tellico Dam/snail darter conflict was at its height, Congress was in the process of reauthorizing the ESA. Rather than establish a precedent for exempting specific projects from the act, Congress established a process whereby a panel of six cabinet level officers and a representative from the state in which the project was located could exempt projects from the act if, among other requirements, the "benefits of such action clearly outweigh the benefits of alternative courses of actions consistent with conserving the species and its critical habitat, and such action is in the public interest."

The following year, after numerous votes and with the full weight of the minority leader of the Senate, Howard Baker of Tennessee, Congress finally overrode the act and ordered completion of the dam. In more than a quarter century since the God Squad was created, it has been convened only twice since Tellico Dam. The only project that it fully exempted was Greyrocks Dam in Wyoming, and that exemption in 1979 was the result of an agreement between conservationists and agency officials to conserve the endangered whooping crane. In 1992, the God Squad exempted thirteen of forty-four timber sales that were found likely to jeopardize the northern spotted owl in Oregon, but those sales never went forward and the Bureau of Land Management subsequently withdrew the exemption application.

PREVENTING HARM TO ENDANGERED SPECIES ON STATE AND PRIVATE LANDS

The ESA's other primary means of achieving its goal to bring species back to the point at which its protections are no longer necessary is by imposing duties on individuals rather than government agencies. As individuals,

none of us can "take" a listed species. In the parlance of the ESA, the prohibition on "take" means that we can't harm, harass, hunt, pursue, wound,
capture, collect, or even attempt to do any of these things. By 1975 regulation the term "harm" was defined to include environmental modification
or degradation, and four years later, in *Palila v. Hawaii Department of Land
and Natural Resources*, a federal court found that Hawaii's maintenance of
feral sheep and goat herds for hunting violated this rule by destroying the
woodland habitat of the Palila, an endangered bird. In confirming that
the ESA barred harm caused by habitat modification, the court's decision
presented a difficult issue that surfaced when Congress reauthorized the
ESA in 1982. Having decided that federal agencies that received favorable
biological opinions could "incidentally" take listed species, Congress was
faced with the fact that the take prohibition was absolute for individuals
and there was no mechanism for incidental take of species on nonfederal
projects. The result was the development of an exemption to take for those
who develop "habitat conservation plans," or HCPs.

HCPs are intended to minimize take of listed species caused incidentally by nonfederal activities and provide measures to mitigate the effects
of that take and ensure that it does not appreciably reduce the likelihood of
survival and recovery of these species. Private landowners, corporations,
or state or local governments who clear land, cut timber, or alter habitats
in some other way that might incidentally harm a listed species must get
an incidental take permit by developing a HCP. As of December 2010, 709
HCPs were approved, covering tens of millions of acres of nonfederal lands
and protecting hundreds of endangered or threatened species.

HCPs have worked well for protecting species from incidental take in
cases involving large corporate landholders, states, and municipalities,
particularly where natural habitats are almost completely eradicated, as
often results from construction of subdivisions and shopping centers.
With smaller private landowners engaged in production of agricultural
commodities or timber the story has been different. As ESA expert and
now Interior Department official Michael Bean has said, one of the ESA's
clear weaknesses is that "it has not promoted a happy marriage" between
its goals and the goals of these smaller landowners; "more often, it has
prompted the sort of bitter acrimony more typical of a nasty divorce."
But despite what many view as an unyielding law, presidential adminis-
trations responsible for carrying out the ESA during the last decade have
crafted new regulatory approaches to allay fears about the regulatory con-

sequences of having listed species on their land and to encourage the con-servation of these species.

Key among these approaches are the "no surprises" and "safe harbors" policies, which provide regulatory assurances to encourage conservation of listed species on private lands. The "no surprises" rule assures private landowners that they will not incur any additional mitigation require-ments beyond those they agreed to in their HCPs, even if protected spe-cies take a turn for the worse. In other words, if more needs to be done to prevent a species from sliding closer to the brink of extinction, the fed-eral government will get that done by some means other than going back to private landowners and requiring them to do more. The "safe harbor" rule encourages voluntary management by private landowners to provide a net benefit for listed species for some period of time, and thus promote recovery on their lands by giving assurances to the landowners that no additional regulatory restrictions will be imposed in the future if the lands are returned to a predetermined baseline condition.

ESA AND THE KLAMATH BASIN: THE INTERPLAY OF STRENGTHS AND WEAKNESSES

Nevertheless, while implementation of the ESA has continued to evolve, particularly in the area of conservation on private lands, many argue the need for these regulatory approaches and a multitude of other changes to be incorporated into the law. Indeed, the ESA has been the subject of nearly continuous calls for changes in its provisions.

The authors are among those who believe the ESA certainly could be improved by additional amendments, but we also maintain that many blame the act for things that are not the fault of the law. The criticism showered on the ESA has more to do with its being the only law with firm standards that fundamentally are substantive, not procedural, than it has to do with any flaws in the act. It has more to do with the act's forcing change. Few of us particularly care for change, and even fewer of us like to be forced to change. This dislike of change applies to the refusal by many to embrace experiment and change in the ESA. And it applies equally well to those who focus almost solely on ESA shortcomings as though that were the source of our natural resource conflicts over the last 20 years.

Too much of our focus is on the controversies surrounding the ESA. Too little of our attention is on how effectively we are protecting our environment and ensuring sustainable levels of development under the myriad of other laws that supposedly have those goals as their purpose. Our failure to manage ecosystems, to prevent the component parts of these systems from becoming threatened or endangered, is not a failure of the ESA. To say that it is, is a form of blaming the victim.

The controversy in the Klamath River basin in Oregon and California is a perfect, if tragic, illustration of both the strengths and weaknesses of the ESA. Once a bountiful natural system producing large runs of salmon and steelhead and providing habitat for millions of migratory birds, the basin has been replumbed to provide for agriculture and electric power. The Bureau of Reclamation's Klamath Project diverted massive amounts of water for agriculture. Wetlands in the upper basin were drained for cattle operations. Hydroelectric dams on the mainstem of the river blocked passage for anadromous runs of salmon that once spawned above Klamath Lake. Dams and water diversions on the Shasta, Scott, and Trinity Rivers, key tributaries to the lower Klamath River, destroyed and degraded habitats for salmon. Throughout the basin, agricultural runoff, exacerbated by the drainage of wetlands, pollutes both Klamath Lake and the river below.

As a result, indigenous fish in the upper basin, unfortunately called Lost River and shortnose suckers by non-Indians but known as Kuptu and C'wam to the Klamath Indian tribe, have been pushed to the brink of extinction. Coho salmon and steelhead in the lower basin, much of their habitat blocked by dams and much of the flow reduced by water diversion projects in the Upper Klamath Basin and the Shasta, Scott, and Trinity sub-basins, have been listed as threatened. The Kuptu and C'wam and the salmon are the subject of treaties signed with the Native American tribes in the nineteenth century. In short, the fact that the Klamath ecosystem is severely stressed cannot be denied.

The causes for the demise of the Klamath ecosystem are many, but the operation of federal and state laws and the failure of other legal mechanisms to arrest a decline several decades in the making lie at the heart of the problem. The Klamath Act, which established the Klamath Project a century ago, is a single-purpose law, and that purpose is irrigation. Klamath irrigators, backed by the administration of George W. Bush, argued that the law required that water be delivered to their fields even during drought years, regardless of the impact on the indigenous fish in Klamath Lake or the salmon in the river below. Oregon and California water laws, based on the mid-nineteenth-century doctrine of prior appropriation, allowed irrigators in the upper Klamath Basin and California's Scott River to obtain water rights to virtually all of the water in these tributaries. Between 80 and 90 percent of the Trinity River flow into the lower Klamath River has been diverted to the thirsty farms and cities to the south.

Other laws that we expect to protect the environment have failed to prevent the ecological disaster. The Clean Water Act has been largely ineffective in dealing with agricultural runoff. The National Environmental Policy Act (NEPA) is largely powerless against decisions made a century ago, long before its passage. Until the Kuptu and C'wam were listed in 1989, there was little in the way of substantive law to stop the ecological destruction of the basin. With the coming of the ESA, federal and state agencies were forced to begin the painful process of addressing the impacts of a century of unrestrained development of the natural resources of the Klamath ecosystem. Conflicts between the federal project and the ESA simmered until the drought year of 2001, when the federal government shut off water to part of the Klamath Project to provide water for the Kuptu and C'wam in Klamath Lake and the coho in the lower river. The ensuing conflict, with acts of civil disobedience by farmers and threats of violence, led many politicians to call for the "reform" of the ESA. In 2002, the Bureau of Reclamation, relying on a draft National Research Council report that questioned the link between flow levels and fish survival, and relying on legal theories that there is no flexibility in the operation of the Klamath project, provided full water deliveries to the project irrigators at the expense of the Kuptu and C'wam and the salmon downstream.

In the fall of 2002, chinook salmon, returning from the ocean to begin their spawning journey, encountered a river that had too little water, and the water that was in the river was too warm. Jammed together in narrow channels, the salmon succumbed to a common fish disease, appropriately nicknamed ich, that raced through the population. Over 33,000 fish died. While the Klamath chinook are not listed, they are extremely important to tribal fisheries as well as to non-Indian recreational and commercial fishers.

Coho salmon, which are protected under the ESA, were also affected, but fortunately their run timing brought most of them into the river after rains and cooler weather had improved conditions. During the period of the die-off, over half of the Klamath River was being diverted onto the agricultural lands that are part of the Klamath Reclamation Project. In statements that strained credulity, officials from NMFS and FWS stated that it was premature to say that the lack of water was the cause of the die-off and that further study was needed to determine the true causes of the disaster. There is considerable irony in the calls for reform of the ESA in the wake of the Klamath conflict. If there is any consensus in the scientific community, it is that the Klamath system is severely stressed and that changes need to be made to bring the system back into some semblance of ecological balance. To extend the old analogy of endangered species being like canaries in the coal mines, blaming the ESA for the conflict in the Klamath would be like the miners blaming the canary for the lack of oxygen. It is killing the messenger rather than heeding the message.

It is also ironic that the ESA, which has been substantially amended several times in its 38-year history, is the subject for calls for reform when there are other laws that have never been seriously reexamined. Given a situation like that in the Klamath, shouldn't we take a hard look at the century-old Reclamation Act or even more archaic nineteenth-century state water laws? How do we respond to those who say that the ESA needs to be changed to make it more flexible? If there are no alternative means of carrying out an action that won't jeopardize a species' existence, then seeking greater flexibility in application of the law is just another way of asking to increase the likelihood of extinction. The question posed essentially is, "Are we absolutely sure that the species will go extinct if we allow some action?" While the congressional sponsors of the ESA stated that "sheer self-interest impels us to be cautious," more selfish interests now urge us to put the burden of risk entirely on the species. This is the pressure to abandon stewardship entirely.

USING "SOUND SCIENCE" AND OTHER TROJAN HORSES TO WEAKEN THE ESA

Of the many guises adopted by those who seek to weaken the effect of the ESA on their interests, the most reasonable seeming and, therefore, the most insidious appears in the form of a call for basing decisions under the act on "sound science." The ESA already requires decisions to be made on the basis of the best available scientific information. The call for decisions to be based on "sound science" is an effort to weaken the ESA by requiring absolute proof of significant harm to a species before any restrictions are placed on any economic activity. It is in fact a reversal of the "institutionalization of caution" that the ESA's authors established over 38 years ago, which requires that those implementing the ESA err on the side of the species when uncertainty exists. The problem is that it rarely will be possible to demonstrate fully and scientifically a causal connection between habitat modification and species survival. We know, for example, that fish need water. But how little can they get by with and for how long? That can depend on a myriad of other environmental conditions. What is the temperature of the water? For salmon, what were the ocean conditions that they experienced? Were there diseases present in the fish population? Given enough activities that destroy and degrade habitat, at some point there will be a crash, but "sound science" proponents argue that each activity considered should go forward unless it can be shown unequivocally to be the activity that will cause the crash. At which point it's too late.

Another possible change in the act, either through legislation or administrative changes, could be a blurring of the distinction between wild salmon and salmon produced in hatcheries. Hatchery fish have different life histories from wild fish (hatchery fish are spawned in plastic buckets, incubated in trays, and raised in concrete raceways), and there is now considerable scientific evidence that hatchery fish pose a threat to wild fish. If hatchery fish and wild fish are treated the same for purposes of the ESA, then habitat protections can be relaxed as hatchery fish can be produced without relying on the natural environment. While this is obviously contrary to the intent of the ESA to protect species and the habitats on which they depend, property rights groups have made this issue one of their top priorities.

The effectiveness of the ESA ultimately depends upon the commitment of the federal agencies to enforce its provisions. While the ESA, as has been amply demonstrated, provides multiple opportunities for litigation by interests from the entire spectrum of political advocates, much depends on the commitment of the federal agencies charged with implementing the Act, the FWS and NMFS and, more importantly, agencies like the Corps of Engineers and the Forest Service that carry out actions that can affect endangered species. In the coming years, will the "take" provisions be enforced against timber companies that destroy spotted owl habitat? Will the Bureau of Reclamation claim, as they have in the Klamath, that it has no discretion under the law to provide water for listed fish species? That same rationale has been used to withhold water from Bureau of Reclamation projects for the Rio Grande silvery minnow. Will federal agencies, in fact, find ways to circumvent the hard choices that the ESA forces?

The Supreme Court has said the ESA represents "the most comprehensive legislation for the preservation of endangered species ever enacted by any nation." But in the end, our commitment to species conservation must go beyond the ESA. Precious few species have been recovered, and the ESA has often succeeded in maintaining species and their habitat only at threshold levels. Often underfunded, with the agencies that administer the ESA and the act itself often under attack, species conservation cannot be carried on the back of one law. Letting our level of natural resource stewardship so often devolve to merely trying to avoid species extinctions surely represents the lowest level of stewardship imaginable. We need, instead, to devote more effort toward ensuring that the laws governing the management of our public lands and our nation's waters make the ESA a rarely used, last resort rather than the only barrier to loss of the nation's biological heritage.

AUTHORS' NOTE

We still believe that the ESA, because of its strong substantive standards, carries too much of the burden for protecting against environmental damage that should be shouldered by other environmental laws. This is even more true today as fish, wildlife, and plants try to survive the effects of global warming. The most obvious example is the polar bear, which was recently placed on the list of threatened species specifically because global warming is drastically reducing the sea ice habitat of the bears. Despite its strong standards, the ESA cannot limit coal-fired plants in China or deforestation in Brazil; nor is it likely to force higher fuel efficiency standards in the U.S. or even successfully prevent oil pollution of Alaska's Beaufort Sea. Only comprehensive efforts to address global warming and spur renewable energy, coupled with more vigorous use of our nation's environmental pollution and land management laws, offer any real hope of helping the ESA prevent species extinctions in the increasingly complex, uncertain, and variable world of a changing climate.

What is somewhat hopeful is that the strong standards in the act have also provided impetus for some truly significant actions. We wrote about the dire situation in the Klamath Basin as an example of the ESA carrying the burden for harms that should be addressed by other laws. Since we wrote the article, a coalition of Native American Tribes, environmental and fishing groups, agricultural interests, and the energy company Pacificorp have reached a tentative agreement on managing the water levels in the Klamath Basin and the Klamath River and to remove four sizable dams on the Klamath River. Despite numerous attempts to circumvent the act by the George W. Bush Administration, including the personal involvement of Vice President Richard Cheney, the Basin residents decided it was in their own self-interest to enter serious negotiations.

The ESA cannot prevent the pollution of our heat-trapping emissions from destroying habitat for the polar bear and other species, but as the Klamath demonstrates, the law's strong standards can give species a fighting chance at surviving a warming climate by forcing us to look very hard at ways of reducing the threatening consequences of our other activities. In the end, of course, even with our best efforts at making species resilient to the impacts of global warming, the ESA may only succeed in buying a species like the polar bear more time before the inevitable. That bargain, familiar to us all in our own lives, sure beats the alternative. And in the process of buying the polar bear time, the ESA makes the impending ecological disaster of global warming, and the impact on the human environment, more real. A large white bear as the ultimate canary in the global coal mine? Perhaps. Let's hope this messenger is too difficult for us to ignore. ◙

NIGHT LIGHTS

Robert Sack

. . . the pillar of cloud by day and the pillar of fire by night
did not depart from before the people.

—Exodus 13:22

FOR many people, especially children, a glowing nightlight dispels
the demons of the dark and makes it easier to fall sleep. Perhaps we
humans are born with an instinctual fear of the dark. After all, once upon
a time, nocturnal predators stalked us. Hunter-gatherers, who live in the
open, often keep a fire (a kind of nightlight) burning through the night for
security as much as warmth. When our ancestors moved indoors, their oil
lamps, candles, and hearth replaced the open fire, but these more numerous sources of light were nevertheless tiny pinpoints in the otherwise
immense darkness of the night. Except for the moon, the sky was pitch
black, and stars shone with an intensity and splendor so compelling, they
were thought to rule men's lives.

And then came electricity! Edison switched on the lights and not only
dispelled much of the dread of the night, but freed us to work and play 24
hours a day. Tonight, our city will generate a pillar of light from a hundred high-rise buildings, thousands of parking lots, rows and rows of
streetlights, flashing billboards, sprawling shopping centers, and endless

streams of headlights. The light will flood skyward and reflect off the dust and particles, obscuring the heavens. The urban corona will be seen from 50 miles away.

The city nightscape has an undeniable beauty, but it obscures the beauty that lies beyond. When the Northeast region of the U.S. blew a fuse and blacked out, many people were suddenly surprised and delighted (despite the inconvenience) to see the Milky Way for the first time in their lives. Except for this kind of blackout, our own galaxy is invisible from two-thirds of American homes.

It is remarkable that, in an era that has emphasized the importance of the environment, so little attention has been paid to the unnecessary, expensive, and intrusive uses of artificial light. However, that may be changing. The pollution of the night sky is now getting some serious atten-tion. Besides blocking our view of the Milky Way, what's the problem?

For me, it begins with a personal annoyance. I recently moved to a remodeled house that is unfortunately situated between two very bright mercury vapor streetlights. At night, crisscrossing beams of bluish light that resemble floodlights in a prison yard illuminate my living room. I presume the streetlights were installed to discourage criminals, but I sus-pect they could just as well make it easier to spot a good entry point for a break-in. In fact, a number of studies have shown very little anti-crime benefit from streetlights. They can produce a false sense of security as well as being ugly, intrusive, and unnecessary.

More importantly, overly bright nightlights can be hard on wildlife. Animals have evolved to adapt to a light and dark cycle, and artificial light disrupts their biological rhythms. Nocturnal species are especially sensi-tive to light—more so than humans. For example, in Florida, bright lights near the beach discourage female turtles from coming ashore to nest. If they do lay eggs, the hatchlings may crawl the wrong way, toward the house lights, instead of the ocean. Bright lights can also confuse migrating species. When flying through a brightly lit urban area, migrating birds can become disoriented and may crash into brilliantly lit broadcast towers or buildings, or circle them until they drop from exhaustion.

Because bright artificial light is so ubiquitous, it is difficult to know if there are any detrimental effects on sleep. An interesting study conducted at the National Institute of Mental Health showed that placing normal subjects in total darkness for 14 hours each night, mimicking the winter experience of our pre-Edisonian ancestors, significantly altered their sleep patterns. Sleep occurred in two main bouts, early and late in the night, with an extended period of reverie in between. It took subjects a while to get used to, but eventually they considered it rather pleasant and certainly refreshing.

Based on our research regarding the human circadian system, my colleague Alfred Lewy and I concluded that the effects of bright light exposure on people were not much different from the effects on most other species. Moreover, in a study in which we had patients with winter depression sit by a bright light for two hours in the evening before going to bed, sleep-onset insomnia was a common side effect. (The best treatment for winter depression is bright light exposure, first thing in the morning.)

Whatever its effect on human biology, unnecessary and inefficient lighting also wastes energy. About a billion dollars a year is spent blasting photons skyward into the universe. The 175-watt mercury vapor lights, so common on our streets, are cheap to install, but are highly inefficient and waste energy over the long run.

Bad lighting can produce glare that actually makes the environment more confusing, rather than less. The American Automobile Association cites glare as a contributing cause of traffic accidents.

Astronomers yearn for dark skies. Only about 1 percent of the American (and European) night sky is unaffected by light pollution. Because of skyglow, the 100-inch telescope on Mount Wilson, near Los Angeles (where Edward Hubble discovered the expanding universe), is no longer useful for deep sky observations. A new telescope facility installed by Reed College in Portland has been sited far from the city and is operated remotely by a website connection.

What's to be done? Near Tucson, Arizona, there are two large observatories that would be blinded by the usual urban glow, except for the region's "dark skies" ordinance. All outdoor lights in the Tucson area must be directed downward—it's not just a good idea, it's the law! Streetlights are shielded. House lights must be low to the ground. If you have a chance to visit Tucson, look upward; you can see the stars!

Other measures that can darken the skies include timers that automatically shut off certain lights for the late hours of the night; for example, between midnight and sunrise. Mercury vapor lights can be outlawed, especially where they "trespass" into a neighbor's property.

Locally, the city of Sandy, Oregon, has instituted "dark skies ordinances," but they apply only to new construction, so the impact will be slow in coming. But it's a start.

I am getting Portland General Electric to put a shield on the streetlights outside my house. Eventually, I hope to persuade my neighborhood association to petition for new streetlights that are low to the ground and point down. Who knows, maybe someday I will glimpse the Milky Way through the skylight in my bedroom as I am dozing off to sleep. ◙

Energy

The Power of Wind, Sun, and Falling Water

Angus Duncan

PAST AS PROLOGUE

Fɪʀsᴛ a little ancient history: I graduated from Medford High School, down in southern Oregon, in 1964. That dates me back to when there was only one high school in town and one high school football team, the Black Tornado. Our guys always tore up the Southern Oregon conference—that's how I remember it, at least. I added my two cents from up in the bleachers.

In 1964 our electricity came from COPCO—an inelegant acronym even then—the California-Oregon Power Company, which later became Pacific Power and Light.

If this isn't enough to date me, in 1964 we drew something like 95 percent of our power as a region from a renewable resource: falling water. "Renewable" mostly meant "low cost" and "reliable" back then, without any environmental flavoring. We had the lowest power rates in the country, rates that had been declining (in real dollars) since Bonneville and Grand Coulee dams were placed into service in the early 1940s. We had a regional aluminum industry that had been recruited to the Northwest to sop up what then seemed an inexhaustible supply of hydropower, and to make airplanes for the war effort. These plants stayed around for the next several decades, providing economic growth and family-wage jobs while alternately supporting and manipulating the Bonneville Power Administration (BPA) and the power system to their advantage always, and to ours often enough.

In 1964, Columbia River salmon runs still seemed strong and no source of concern, although we now know they were propped up by hatchery numbers and 20 years of wetter-than-average rainfall and runoff.

The Northwest economy yo-yoed up and down through these years, tracking fluctuations in interest rates, the housing market, and timber prices. The hydropower system ballasted our economy, delivering abundant power at predictable, stable, and generally declining rates. Over the last sixty years the dams have proven to be our second best public power investment (energy conservation is tops; more on that later).

Back in 1964, if we had claimed these virtues—low power rates, abundant salmon runs, good-paying industrial jobs—as intrinsic to a renewable energy-based system, we'd have gotten back blank stares.

Forty years later, our regional power supply is 50 percent dependent on nonrenewable hydrocarbons—the coal and gas plants we built when we ran out of sites for new dams (hydropower now serves less than half the region's electricity use, and its share continues to dwindle).

To old reliability problems like tree branches falling on power lines, we have added new ones. We have a nationally interconnected, exceedingly complex, and often congested transmission grid that has suffered major multi-state outages, east and west, in the last two decades. Our investments in that grid system dropped 60 percent nationally from 1975 to 2000.

As we've become more dependent on Montana coal and Alberta gas, we've also become hostage to global commodities markets, not to mention California price spikes and Enron market manipulations. Many Northwest consumers are now paying electricity rates that look downright Californian, while large slices of Northwest wind are shipped to San Francisco and Los Angeles. Regional businesses trying to plan next year's operating budgets, and the next decade's capital investments, can only guess at their future energy costs.

Where Bonneville and Grand Coulee once put Depression-marooned workers into paying jobs that built the region's electricity infrastructure, now our energy dollars go north and east to buy coal and gas, and will soon travel overseas to pay for imported liquefied natural gas (LNG).

Before, our energy dollars circulated regionally, paying workers' wages, buying building materials, creating housing and communities where local goods and services were bought and sold. Today many of those same dollars and jobs are headed out of the region or overseas.

MORE BAD NEWS

Those exported dollars buy us not only coal, oil, and gas but also the political instability that comes with a top-heavy fossil fuel dependency. The largest known reserves of international oil are in Saudi Arabia, Iraq, and Russia. The largest known reserves of natural gas are in Russia, Iran, and Qatar. The world's largest exporter of LNG is third-world, politically risky Indonesia. The countries atop those pools of oil and gas are nobody's idea of the kind of steady, reliable, cost-predictable energy suppliers our economy needs.

We've suffered major global interruptions in our oil supplies in 1973 and again in 1979. Now we're fighting two full-scale middle-eastern wars. We have ever more enemies with the means to strike us where we are most vulnerable, smack in our energy dependency. And, ironically, we are bankrolling them with our petro-dollars.

Then there are the unanticipated consequences of our hydrocarbon habit: global warming and climate disruption. Most Americans who are not still holding out for a flat earth acknowledge that climate is a problem of the first magnitude, with ultimate consequences that may give true and final meaning to the word "calamity." A confidential 2004 Pentagon study, describing the potential consequences of abrupt climate change ("disruption and conflict . . . endemic features of life"), argues that it "should be elevated beyond a scientific debate to a U.S. national security concern."

Closer to home, a 2004 "consensus statement" issued by 49 scientists from Oregon State University, University of Washington, and other institutions offered a look at the likely effects of climate change in the Pacific Northwest. Substantial reduction in snowpack by 2050 is "highly certain." Sea-level rising with significant coastal erosion, "very certain." Earlier snowmelt, decreased summer river flows, higher temperatures, and other water quality issues that will stress fish runs and intensify competition for late summer water, all likely.

Other effects supported by the science include northward migration of tropical diseases, longer and more intense allergy seasons, drier forests, more—and more intense—forest fires, and general disruption in the ecosystems that support Oregon's plant and animal species.

BETTER NEWS

There's also better news to report. In 2004, some thirty new coal plants were being proposed across the western states, poised to ship their power to urban areas west and east, and their carbon emissions skyward. Today most of these plants and plans have been abandoned. From Montana to Texas, utilities are acknowledging the pressure of approaching carbon regulation and are backing away from new coal.

That said, the embedded national fuel of choice for generating electricity is still conventional coal (49 percent of U.S. power generated in 2008). Technology fixes to coal that would lower carbon emissions, such as gasification and carbon sequestration, remain promised but undelivered.

In the Pacific Northwest our largest source of new electric generation is gas. This is good news, and bad: good because high efficiency gas plants produce half the carbon emissions per kilowatt hour (kWh) of coal, and bad, because we will still be adding to overall emissions. We have to *cut* regional emissions by about 30 percent in the next ten years to meet state goals in Oregon and Washington. We have to accomplish this while providing a growing population with homes, jobs, mobility, health care, and the other goods, services, and amenities that make up our economy and communities. We're projected to have 12 percent more people in the region by 2020. If we are fueling this growth with new gas-fired generation atop a base of aging coal plants, emissions don't shrink; they grow.

More mixed news: on the one hand, per capita consumption of gasoline across the region has *declined* in the last ten years to the lowest level since 1966. We've gone from above the national average to 9 percent below. But this is cold comfort when per capita reductions are almost exactly offset by population growth—the reality of the last decade and the prediction for the next ten years to continue to 2020.

In Oregon, transportation accounts for around 40 percent of greenhouse gas emissions. In Washington it's about 45 percent. We don't meet our greenhouse gas reduction goals if the best we can do is level off.

"CHANGE WE CAN BELIEVE IN"

In both the utility and transportation worlds, the forces of far-reaching change are gathering. Out in the Columbia Gorge, ranks of sky-scraping wind turbines are churning out energy at market costs that compare favorably with gas- and coal-fired generation. If the operating life of these turbines is 30 years or more as anticipated, and capital costs are amortized over a customary 20-year term, real (inflation adjusted) costs can actually go down over time.

With stable, predictable, and probably declining real costs, wind power starts to look a lot like the region's hydropower base. It should.

Over the same period, fossil fuel costs are generally expected to increase steadily, with occasional dazzling episodes of destabilizing price spikes. That's before we add in carbon costs, which we must.

When I first worked in the wind industry—this was out on the untamed California frontier, away back in the 1980s—the actual cost of wind power, excluding tax credits and other subsidies, was around 25¢ per kWh. Today it's more like 6¢ to 8¢/kWh (including the costs to store and retrieve the power so it's there when consumers need it). That's competitive with gas-fired generation at today's gas costs. And wind costs have continued to decline—by about 15 percent with each doubling of installed capacity.

Globally, new wind capacity has grown 10 percent annually since 2006. The 8,000 megawatts (MW) installed across the U.S. in 2009 equaled 40 percent of all new generation placed into service last year.

In the Pacific Northwest wind capacity clocks in at around 3,000 MW by the end of 2009, or about 8 percent of our installed capacity. For reference, it would take roughly 4,000 MW of wind turbines operating at a 30 percent average capacity factor to meet the energy needs of the City of Seattle. That's real, measurable change.

It's also enough new wind that the region is now being pressed to plan new transmission lines and explore new energy storage technologies. Our hydropower reservoirs do not have sufficient capacity to store and retrieve the expected new wind generation. This issue will be compounded when we begin importing wind power from Montana, Wyoming, and the Dakotas where the country's greatest wind resource exists. The challenge will be integrating not 3,000 MW but more like 30,000 MW if we are to make our carbon reduction targets.

GOOD DAY, SUNSHINE

Now that utility planners can no longer dismiss wind as too costly, solar has stepped into wind's shoes. The 2008 cost of power from solar photovoltaic (PV) systems (again excluding incentives) is approximately 25¢/kWh . . . or about what wind cost 30 years ago.

There's every expectation that solar costs will decline on a curve as steep as that of wind, or steeper. This is because the productivity and economics of wind, as with hydropower, are very sensitive to site selection.

Wind requires a sometimes elusive combination of wind resource, topography, near access to transmission, and avoidance of environmental complications. In contrast, solar energy is ubiquitous, a site can be as near as the nearest school roof, interconnection is local and uncomplicated, and there are few environmental conflicts (but very large solar PV and thermal plants can pose siting and integration challenges similar to those of large windfarms).

Solar has two other advantages that are only now starting to be exploited. First, solar panels are far easier to mass-produce than wind turbines. Second, solar can be designed into building architecture, displacing costs for facades or roof shingles. Solar windows and even solar fabrics are in development.

How far away is cost-effective photovoltaic generation? Probably not as far as wind was twenty years ago.

STEPPING UP THE PACE OF CHANGE

The pace of renewable development could be accelerated by the federal government and the states fully engaging the public policy tools at their disposal. Some states leverage new renewables with tax credits or state investment funds. Oregon, Washington, and other states have adopted a Renewable Portfolio Standard for their utilities—a specified share of their loads to be served from new renewables—that is stimulating the development of hundreds of additional megawatts in remarkably short order.

Carbon counting is another policy option. In the absence of federal action, the Northeast and West Coast states are tracking greenhouse gas emissions and creating a schedule for required reductions within— at least—the utility sector. Tax incentives, public investments, and other tools are being tested for use in managing industrial, transportation, waste management, and other emissions sources.

Short of a carbon cap, perhaps the most influential tool available to the federal government for driving down greenhouse gas emissions is a procurement strategy that gives points for low carbon content. Such an approach at a national level can incent innovation and new carbon-light products to meet the government's needs while rapidly driving the costs of these goods and services downward. These products then spill over into consumer markets, transforming them. There's historical precedent for this effect. In the 1950s the Defense Department specified that small, efficient, durable transistors would replace older, less reliable vacuum tubes in new weapon systems designs. Within ten years the cost of transistors dropped from $20 per unit to 25¢. The policy opened up new technical applications that led to today's microprocessors.

A comparable Defense procurement policy on solar photovoltaics, driven by a growing military need for secure energy resources to supply bases and weapons systems, could have equally startling effects on commercial supply, demand, and price of this technology.

Two more critical questions: Is there enough wind and solar out there to make a dent in our fossil fuel dependency? What about other renewable technologies?

Answering in reverse order, geothermal, ocean, and hydroelectric resources are unlikely to be consequential at the needed scale. All are site-specific, and each project will have an environmental footprint that will limit wide deployment. Large-scale hydro is flat out of usable sites. But where there is a fit between site and resource, certainly these technologies should be deployed.

Biomass is potentially a large and highly adaptable contributor, able to make use of a range of fuels and conversion processes (combustion, aerobic and anaerobic digestion, pyrolysis), producing usable energy in different forms (electricity; heat; solid, liquid, and gaseous biofuels), and able to be dispatched to match demand. On the down side, the fuel may be distributed lightly across a wide expanse of territory (e.g., timber; grass) and is often low in energy intensity (BTUs by unit of weight or volume). Biomass generation that relies on fuels such as wood waste or manure can become hostage to price and demand fluctuations in markets for wood products or milk, making project finance difficult and reliability suspect. Solve these problems and biomass can be another substantial contributor to low carbon power supply.

Wind, solar, and energy efficiency are the real near-term competitors for new energy resources to displace fossil fuels. For wind to be a major player, supplying upward of 30 percent of U.S. power needs, will require additional technology and operational efficiencies. It will need ways to store energy generated when demand is low, then ship it when demand rises even if the wind has died down. It will need new long-line transmission to the east and west from sites in the high plains states. It will need the costs of carbon emissions to be reflected in energy markets, raising the cost of competing coal- and gas-generated power.

Solar needs similar carbon cost and storage fixes, but not new transmission at the same scale (except for some promising large central station solar thermal technologies that may be distant from urban loads). For solar the greater challenge is to improve "capture" efficiencies (how much of the sun's energy can be converted to electricity), reduce fabrication costs, and diversify applications. Eventually every properly exposed square foot of a building's skin should be a candidate for solar roofing, siding, or window treatments.

To wind, solar, and the niche renewables add energy efficiency and enough gas to bind the ingredients together. That, for much of the U.S. and the world, is the recipe for our carbon-constrained times.

"GENERATING" ENERGY EFFICIENCY

Energy efficiency requires its own brief digression. Since 1980 it has been treated in the Northwest as an energy resource comparable to new sources of generation. In that time we've captured over 3,900 average megawatts (aMW)* of annual electricity savings (think nine coal plants, or four Seattles) at average costs one-third what new gas generation would have required. Our savings equaled $1.6 billion in 2007 alone. Most of those savings stayed in the region, keeping businesses operating and people employed.

In the next 20 years we can almost double these savings—garnering nearly 6,000 aMW at an average cost that's one-third or less than the least costly new fossil fuel plant (according to the Northwest Conservation and Power Council planners). There are additional savings from efficiencies where natural gas is used directly for space and water heating. Serious national action on carbon would amp these figures up again. McKinsey and Co. has identified building and appliance energy efficiency opportunities sufficient to reduce the nation's greenhouse gas emissions by 12 percent—or nearly a billion tons annually—that would also save consumers money.

---

*   An average megawatt is a unit of energy measurement equal to 1000 kilowatts of electricity being generated every hour over a year's time. No power plants operate every hour of the year, so this measurement allows productivity comparisons over a wide range of energy technologies.

So how promising is all this, taken together? Promising enough that we are now—in 2010—discussing early shutdown of Oregon's only in-state coal plant and replacing it with efficiency, wind, and gas. A successful shutdown, one that benefits ratepayers, shareholders, and the public alike, will validate the carbon reduction goals and strategies that Oregon and its neighbors have undertaken.

That's what's needed. Not just meeting load growth with efficiency savings and renewables, but shutting down coal plants with them.

WHAT ABOUT THOSE TRANSPORTATION EMISSIONS?

In Oregon about 40 percent of our CO_2 emissions come from moving ourselves and our goods and services around. Here, too, the progress is uneven but not without promise.

On the one hand, Oregon and Washington are laboring to replace the I-5 bridge over the Columbia River with a new structure projected to relieve congestion and reduce emissions from vehicle crossings . . . compared to a "business-as-usual" trajectory. The preferred design also would include a new light rail line, more buses, and more bicycles.

That design anticipates that automobile crossings—mostly single occupant vehicles—will grow from today's 140,000 or so to 178,000 by 2030. That's a marginal improvement over the projected business-as-usual case of 184,000 crossings daily if we keep the current bridge. But none of these figures—not the business-as-usual case or the transit-assisted levels or even today's auto use levels—meets the state's greenhouse gas reduction targets. Not unless we magically replace nearly every auto engine rumbling across the river with an electric vehicle (EV) by 2020. Not even the most ardent electric car advocate believes this will happen.

Metro, the Portland area's regional government, with its well-deserved international reputation for progressive land use and transportation policies, offered a Regional Transportation Plan (RTP) in 2009 that had Vehicle Miles Traveled and greenhouse gas emissions rising in lockstep with population growth.

It doesn't scan. The Metro plan doesn't meet the most forgiving carbon sniff test. Indeed, Metro and the Oregon Department of Transportation both acknowledge the inconsistency between transportation plans and emissions reduction targets. It's just that we are all too able to put climate goals in one part of our brain and wall it off from the immediate, the practical, the day-to-day business-as-usual decisions that have to be made. The consequence is that the carbon hill we have to climb grows steeper with each business-as-usual choice.

The flip side of this record plays better. The I-5 corridor from Eugene to Seattle is about to become a national test bed for electric vehicles. By the end of 2010, more than 4,000 public EV recharging stations will be deployed in communities and at rest areas along this corridor. At least four different electric car models will be marketed commercially here, maybe more. Portland's record for most Prius buyers per capita nationally sealed its selection as a test market.

Regional utilities are gearing up to incorporate EVs into their planning scenarios and are bringing Smart Grid technologies and efficiencies into their aging transmission and distribution systems. They plan to recruit your hot water heater and dishwasher into service as "distributed storage" units for the electric grid, something that has been a technological gleam in the eye for decades. Now it's about to sweep up your plugged-in EV into the bargain.

As whiz-bang techno-solutions go, this one is encouraging but not sufficient. No modeling, under even very aggressive technological assumptions, gets us to our greenhouse gas goals without transit, car-sharing, bicycles, and cities redesigned to rely in substantial measure upon them.

Business-as-usual thinking stands between us and the only future in which we, and the planet, prosper.

HOW DO WE GET FROM HERE TO THERE?

Where's "there," exactly?

It's not a "greenhouse gas emissions per capita" or "per GDP" goal. It's not a percent of generation from new renewables or energy efficiency.

"There" is when the sum of our choices is an energy system that meets our environmental goals, above all our greenhouse gas reduction goals, while creating clean energy jobs and laying the foundation for widely distributed economic prosperity.

And we get to "there" by matching private sector innovation and initiative to the right set of public policy goals, regulations, and incentives.

We get there by adding public investment to private capital in amounts that reflect the societal value of clean, carbon-free energy. We devise regulatory signals that reflect public values and the long-term public good. We shouldn't make it any more complicated than the decision to begin moving earth and pouring concrete for Grand Coulee Dam. *Déjà* FDR all over again.

Decide what we wish to accomplish, weigh and assign priorities, assemble and invest the capital. If some current consumption must be deferred—the Humvee you might be pining for, or my daily double mocha, or, to be less flippant, overgenerous tax cuts for the wealthy *and* the middle class—it can be deferred.

We can tax consumption of fossil fuels, or emissions of greenhouse gases, with accommodations for low-income consumers.

Why do we need public intervention if a technology like wind is already cost-competitive with fossil fuels? First, because competing fossil fuel plants already have their own substantial public subsidies. These need to be cleared away, or offset to level the playing field. Second, as wind projects move from sites with stronger winds and easier access to transmission to more difficult ones, public intervention will be needed to maintain the pace of technical and site development. This is critical if we are to develop the enormous wind resource in the high plains states where transmission access is a daunting barrier and energy storage capacity nonexistent. Third, there are the other essential renewable technologies, solar and biomass especially, that require the nurturing pull of public policy to emerge as mature, competitive options.

President Carter was widely ridiculed for calling his national energy program the "moral equivalent of war." But that's just saying that national emergencies sometimes need to trump short-term considerations. The United States didn't do a cost analysis to decide *whether* to respond to the Depression with government-created jobs (although such analyses are helpful in deciding which programs produce the most jobs). We used government funds to put people to work building projects like dams.

Roosevelt's response, the day after Pearl Harbor, wasn't to mobilize the analysts to calculate whether to return fire. Overriding national priorities trump narrower concerns.

Roosevelt's British counterpart, Winston Churchill, observed: "Sometimes doing your best is not enough. Sometimes you must do what is required."

Of course neither Churchill nor Roosevelt could spend their national treasure without regard to cost-effectiveness, cash flow, or carefully thought out priorities. They didn't have that much treasure, and neither do we.

If even the middle-ground outcomes of global warming are experienced, we have a national emergency, and we don't have the resources to spend our way out of trouble. Alaska is contemplating relocating a single Indian village at the mouth of the Yukon River, exposed to rising sea levels and to violent storms and winds as its once-protective ice shelf has retreated. The estimated cost for one village relocation is $100 million.

But we do have the resources to transform our energy system to one that emits greenhouse gases no faster than the land and oceans can absorb them. The swifter and smarter companies, states, and nations will make a bundle by delivering that transformation, then selling the technologies and services they developed to their more dull-witted competitors.

In the process we'll generate jobs for the people of the Northwest. A University of California/Berkeley study estimates that renewable energy development generates three jobs for every one that would come from sticking to fossil fuels. Other research supports this finding.

Still other studies, from Department of Energy research labs and the Union of Concerned Scientists, suggest the front-end costs of meeting 20 percent of the nation's electricity appetite with renewables would return net savings in the tens to hundreds of billions of dollars by 2020.

Most credible analyses say we can meet our national greenhouse gas reduction goals, using strategies like those discussed here, for a net cost of around 1 percent of gross domestic product, or about $140 billion annually. That's still not chump change. But just increasing the fuel economy of our existing auto fleet from 25 mpg to 40 mpg would allow us to reduce oil imports by a billion barrels annually; at today's oil price of $80 per barrel, these savings alone get us $80 billion a year, well over half way there.

We can save energy, greenhouse gas emissions, and dollars doing more of what we've been doing for the last 20 years. The Pacific Northwest invested $2.3 billion dollars in electric energy efficiency from 1991 to 2002. We recover that entire investment, in energy cost savings, on average once every 24 months.

The world market for solar equipment, $30 billion in 2008, is projected to grow to $80 billion by 2018. Unless we decide we want a share of this growing market and make our research and production investments accordingly, Americans will be buying their solar components from Japan and Germany as we do today.

Global demand for wind turbines is projected to grow from $50 billion in 2008 to $140 billion in 2018. Today, with the exception of General Electric, most of the wind turbines available in global markets are German, Danish, Spanish, and Japanese. Chinese designs are in the wings, supported by capital investments in clean energy at nearly twice U.S. levels.

Does Denmark have some unique capability or advantage that we do not? No! We don't have to cede these markets. American solar and wind resources, and potential American demand for the power they can generate, dwarf the same advantages available to most other countries. We have the innovative skills, the technical capabilities, and the access to capital to dominate these markets.

But just as a company can't sit on its investment in steam technology when the internal combustion engine beckons, so we can't hunker down with our outdated technologies and dwindling fuel supplies beneath a thickening blanket of greenhouse gases and hope the future will simply be a replay of our memorable past.

The future we need to be investing in, to be innovating and legislating and striving for, is one that resembles, more than anything else, that storied year for renewable energy and high school football in southern Oregon, 1964. ◙

SUNSHINE
—for Caroline

Scot Siegel

Daddy, I like it when the sun
interrupts us...

Oh, yes . . . Yes, like when it
burns through fog, splashing leaves,
and touches the side of your face
warm as your mother's kiss?

No, dad, just the sun
all by itself—
      no kiss
      no flame
      no leaves

Just the sun's sudden rays
pouring down
right here
right now

on you and me

Good Driver!

James Opie

PASSING through steeply descending terrain amid dramatic peaks in the Hindu Kush Mountains, south of Mazar-i-Sharif in northern Afghanistan, with treacherous cliffs dropping abruptly only yards to our left, my driver and I saw before us a disturbing scene of near disaster. A public bus had crashed into an enormous rock on the right-hand side of the road. Disarrayed clusters of passengers surrounded the bus, but no one appeared to be hurt. My driver slowed to a crawl, for fear of hitting passengers who spilled out onto the road, begging for rides. As we drew abreast of the accident, my driver and I saw that the entire front end of the bus had been crushed against a house-sized boulder. Immediately my driver exclaimed, "Good driver! Good driver!"

We regained speed and drove another kilometer or so before I spoke. "You said, 'Good driver.' Would you tell me what is so good about crashing a bus full of people into a rock?"

"You not understand," he said. "Driver lose brakes. Bus will crash. It must! But where? Driver has to decide. Not easy to decide in such situation. Easy to wait, and wait. Not easy to do difficult thing and crash up here. Easy to delay, later and later, until bus goes too fast! If he crash here, maybe some people hurt. No one die. Other way," he pointed down the mountain, "everyone die. Everyone!" He hesitated a moment and then repeated: "Very good driver!"

We were silent for the remainder of the trip south to Kabul. The driver must have spent some of this time organizing his thoughts. Sitting together in his car in front of my hotel, he saw fit to shape our shared experience into a broader lesson.

"You young man," he said. "Not yet realize, sometimes in life is better to crash when damage not too much. Sometimes you wait and wait. Damage very great! Price of delay too high! Must know when to crash."

He looked at me intently, for a rather long time, as if his eyes could carry this lesson to a place within me that words alone could not penetrate. We sat quietly. The sound of his breathing mixed with my own. The future felt suspended, as lightly as the specks of dust hanging weightlessly in the air between us. ◙

SECOND THOUGHTS ABOUT
RAIL TRANSIT IN AMERICA

Emory Bundy

R AIL has a nostalgic grip on the public imagination. It made a nation of the United States, joining disparate, far-flung communities into a coherent body. It transformed disconnected hamlets and modest cities with an infrastructure suited to a continental power, linking farm and city, state to state, the Atlantic seaboard to the Pacific. Not only could people move faster than ever before, and in much better style, but freight of all kinds could be shipped across the land. Rail was the first truly Big Business of the U.S., with a dominating influence on enterprise and politics.

As George H. Douglas enthused in his historical treatise, *All Aboard! The Railroad in American Life* (1992),"Ralph Waldo Emerson likened the railroad to a magician's rod—it had transformed America into a great industrial nation with merely one wave. In 1820 the United States was a disjoined nation composed of lonely and self-sufficient farmers. . . . It welded the nation together, creating an American outlook, an American point of view."

While England started the train, in short order the U.S. developed the world's most elaborate, advanced rail network. The extent and superiority of the North's railroad system helped it win the Civil War and maintain the Union. In large measure it opened the West. It facilitated commercial development. It was an essential instrument in transforming Jefferson's nation of yeoman farmers into an industrial powerhouse. Heading into World War II, the railroad system was a critical force undergirding "the arsenal of democracy," adroitly moving the massive components of war materiel, then troops and civilians.

Overlooked these days by those who imagine that rail service equates with concentrated populations in the cities and walkable neighborhoods, and undercuts the viability of the suburbs, is the elemental fact that the railroads created the suburbs. They provided the way for people to live in bucolic settings and commute to work in the cities. In substantial measure the railroads also created the small towns dotting the landscape, most of them plopped down in empty spaces along the tracks, often empty spaces owned by the railroads.

The railroads, beneficiaries of enormous grants of land in return for extending their lines westward, dispatched many hundreds of agents to foreign countries in order to entice people to immigrate to the U.S. As George H. Douglas related, "the railroads moved with a zealousness and a ferocity that is probably unmatched in American history. . . . [They used] 'fairyland pamphlets' . . . grossly exaggerating the quality of life on the frontier. . . . Only cruel and backbreaking labor could wrench a comfortable and hearty livelihood from this stubborn prairie."

While many became disheartened and returned home, and others perished, the inducements were dramatically successful in swelling the U.S. population. The legions who hung on provided the market for the railroad-owned lands, and added to the market for its transport services.

While passenger rail is fun, romantic, and historic, for longer trips it is terribly expensive and slow, compared with other contemporary options. In its 1906 schedule, for example, the Excursion Special offered by the Acheson, Topeka, and Santa Fe Railway was a one-way coach trip from Chicago to California for $33. Adjusting for inflation, that's $792 today. A century ago it was virtually the only viable way to make the trip, but today a coach seat on United Airlines, Chicago to California, can be obtained for only $119, less than one-sixth as much. Plus, UAL's passengers don't have to spend two long nights sleeping in their seats. Few people take trains such long distances anymore. Some do so for the nostalgic pleasure of the venture, just as some take their kids for short excursions on historic railways like the Georgetown Loop. But not many, and not often.

When today's passenger rail works well, as with the modest distances covered by the Boston to Washington Metro Link, serving fairly dense concentrations of settlement, well and good. That service travels at reasonably good speeds, is able to deliver its patrons to downtown centers, rather than outlying air terminals, and it's cost-effective. The home-to-destination trip by Metro Link can compete in both trip time and price. But when passenger rail can't compete, which is the normal condition in the spacious and fairly lightly settled United States, it ought not to be propped up with lavish public subsidies. What does "when it works" mean? When the use of the service is at a meaningful scale, and the extent of the subsidies isn't ruinous.

The matter of urban transit, especially the cost of rail transit, was recently addressed with a breath of fresh air by the head of the Federal Transit Administration, Peter Rogoff. At a conference before transit managers he delivered an address titled "Next Stop: A National Summit on the Future of Transit," using forthright language uncharacteristic of Department of Transportation officials, of either political party. He reported that in a recent, thorough study, the FTA found a $78 billion backlog of deferred maintenance that threatens the ability of transit to perform its mission safely. Basic operations are in peril, and passengers are at growing risk of bodily harm. He enumerated recent examples of near-tragedies.

Some could have equaled or exceeded the tragic death in 2009 of nine passengers traveling on Metro D.C.'s aging rail equipment. As the *Washington Post* recounted at the time, "Had there been enough money at the right time, Metro could well have replaced or substantially refitted the 30-year-old rail car that ran amok, as the [National Transportation] safety board recommended five years ago after another fatal Metro accident."

Of the backlog of deferred maintenance borne by the nation's modest number of rail and large number of bus transit systems, Rogoff said, fully $50 billion of the $78 billion is due to seven rail transit systems. Seven. And the administrator wasn't talking about bringing the systems into "pristine condition"—merely to a marginal "good repair" standard of 2.5 on a scale of 5.

"Clearly, unless we can bring the nation's transit systems into a state of good repair, we won't get the riders we need to cut oil consumption and greenhouse gases, the sustainability of our transit systems will be in jeopardy; and the economic vitality of our cities will be undermined. . . . "

Rogoff called for removing the barriers between what public transit is, and what it should be. That includes having "the guts to say 'no' when everyone around the table wants you to say 'yes.'" He then laid it on the line and called for "telling truth to power," saying:

Rail systems are extremely expensive. . . . busways are cheap.
A little honesty about the differences between bus and rail can have
some profound effects. . . . Communities deciding between bus and rail
investments need to stare those numbers in the face. Some communities
might be tempted to pay the extra cost for shiny new rails now. But they
need to be mindful of the costs they are teeing up for future generations. . . .

Are we at risk of just helping communities dig a deeper hole for our
children and our grandchildren?

Indeed, that's exactly what we've been doing. FTA Administrator
Rogoff's commentary is a breathtaking turn-around for an agency that
abandoned any pretense of cost-effectiveness as a standard for project
funding. That move eased its promotion of rail transit projects.

Several contemporary examples illustrate the merits of Rogoff's warnings:

BART, Bay Area Rapid Transit, introduced four decades ago, was the
first American rail transit system to be built in modern times. Its twin
missions were to provide high-quality, efficient transit service and to curb
urban sprawl. It has failed on both counts. Its failure has been unusually
well-documented, as it's been a recurrent object of scrutiny by the University of California's Transportation Center, such as its landmark study,
"Middle Age Sprawl: BART and Urban Development" (Spring 1999).

Recently it was acknowledged by the region's Metropolitan Transportation Commission (MTC) that, in the past decade, costs of Bay Area transit
have doubled, while ridership increased by only seven percent.

In recent years 11 public votes have been approved for more transit rev-
enue, some, as in 2004, adding billions of dollars. Yet money is scarce,
ridership is almost stagnant, fares are being raised, and service is being cut
back. MTC finally has admitted the obvious: Bay Area transit, as it currently operates, is unsustainable. But the agency still resists announcing
forthrightly that a ranking cause is the history of overlaying well-subsi-
dized bus transit with prodigiously subsidized rail transit systems, rapidly
diminishing productivity.

In Washington D.C., the splendid, modern D.C. Metro rail system was
paid for primarily by very generous, one-time capital grants from the federal government, Maryland, and Virginia. The hefty sales tax accepted by
the D.C. population was supposed to supplement fare revenues in order to

operate the system and build necessary capital reserve funds. But capital costs were higher than predicted, operating costs are much higher, ridership fell short, so farebox revenues were much lower. Capital reserves are starved, there's practically no money to sustain capital equipment as it ages, and the agency struggles just to stay afloat. Also, D.C. starves its bus system, the fifth most-used in the nation, in a losing battle to protect the solvency of its rail system.

D.C. Metro started rail service 34 years ago, and many components are wearing down and wearing out. It needs $11.4 billion to refurbish and replace rolling stock, communication systems, elevators and escalators, and the like, and make necessary system improvements. In addition to the recent loss of nine lives, there are recurrent near misses, also due to rail equipment malfunctions. D.C. Metro needs a new round of funding from all the original parties, comparable to the original grants and taxes—federal government, Maryland, Virginia, and D.C. taxpayers. Recently some D.C. area congressional leaders angled for a congressional earmark mandating that the federal government chip in $150 million per year for ten years, providing that the three local jurisdictions match it with annual subsidies of $50 million apiece. The federal grant was designed to leverage pressure on the local jurisdictions, though, unable to print money, they're in more of a financial pickle than the federal government.

But even if that ten-year, $3 billion package materializes, it will be far from sufficient to address the current $11 billion backlog. Worse, when pressure for more money succeeds, it's only a matter of time before the need for the next massive rail bail-out accumulates, as costs consistently outstrip revenues.

In 1980, the Los Angeles Metropolitan Transit Authority won a half-cent sales tax to underwrite the development of 11 rail transit lines. But rail cost overruns triggered cutbacks in bus service and fare increases, so LAMTA served fewer patrons than it had before, while accumulating billions in long-term debt. By 1990, only three of the 11 rail transit lines were complete or nearly so. Another half-cent sales tax was voted in to finish the job. By 2009, five of the 11 lines still were not finished, and the agency was again in financial distress, so a third half-cent sales tax was enacted. That brought the tax rate to triple that originally proposed, and the target completion for the original 11 lines is as far in the future as ever.

Now the mayor of Los Angeles is lobbying the federal government to guarantee multi-billion dollar construction bonds, putting Uncle Sam on the hook if the city can't pay them off. He also proposes that the federal government subsidize 70 percent of the interest charges. That way U.S. taxpayers can speed the completion of L.A.'s unsustainable rail transit projects and help create public works jobs. If the mayor succeeds, his counterparts all over the country will want their access to the trough, too. Meanwhile, the great City of Angels is on the edge of bankruptcy.

With transit tax revenues in L.A. disproportionately directed to rail, transit market share has dropped as costs have soared. Ridership hit a highwater mark in 1985, just before the diversion of money from bus to rail started. Even in the face of all the diversions, the more efficient L.A. buses still carry 80 percent of MTA's patrons.

Denver is in an earlier stage of a comparable experience. In 2004 the transit agency persuaded voters to pass a large, 0.4 percent sales tax, to expand its FasTracks light rail system by six lines. In 2009 it notified the public it must double the taxes in order to do what it promised in 2004. If it doesn't get the additional money, many of the communities that were promised rail service, and are being taxed for it, won't get it. That's the pitch: Double your taxes or you won't get what you're already paying for.

Seattle, and the Central Puget Sound region it dominates, provides a notorious record of rail transit profligacy. Since the mid-1960s there has been a recurrent effort to launch rail transit. After a succession of failures, in 1996 voters granted taxing authority for the Sound Move Ten Year Regional Transit System Plan. The plan provided for a 21-mile "starter rail," a test drive for a regional 125-mile light rail network, an 82-mile commuter rail line, plus some express buses. In ten years there were to be at least 52.2 million annual boardings, about 175,000 per day (in a region with about 35 million daily trips), at a cost of $5 billion. Then, having proven what a good idea it was with quality execution, more taxes could be proposed to complete the entire system by 2020.

After 13 years, a major portion of the transit agency's 21-mile Central Link light rail centerpiece was completed, and carries about 20,000 rides per day, rather less than the promised 125,000. In 2009, the average cost of each boarding was $9.30, considerably higher than that projected. Fares, which were to pay for 53 percent of the operating costs, covered only 11 percent. Though the system is far from complete, with the most costly six miles ahead, it already has absorbed considerably more than the proffered $2.3 billion. The Central Link starter rail should be finished by 2020; the final cost will approach $6 billion.

Sounder commuter rail is on a similar trajectory. It was supposed to be complete and fully operating in 2002, but that won't occur until 2012, at best. Operating costs are higher than projected; ridership is lower.

Now Sound Transit receives 30 percent of the entire transportation budgets of the three-county Central Puget Sound region, for transit, roads, highways, bridges, and ferries. But it serves only a fraction of one percent of the region's daily trips. Its costly light rail and commuter rail operations, the primary objectives of its spending, carry fewer than one-tenth of one percent of the daily trips. Its express buses cost far less, carry far more passengers, and are much more cost-effective.

It is recurrently claimed that customers strongly prefer trains to buses. Perhaps they would, if the trips were comparably convenient, but usually they're not, because trains are so inflexible in their routes, and so limited in their reach. For example, three times as many daily commuters from downtown Everett and Tacoma to downtown Seattle go by Regional Express buses, in preference to parallel routes by Sounder commuter rail. Why? Largely because the buses travel through downtown Seattle, dropping off and picking up passengers in the financial and commercial center of the city. Sounder reaches a solitary station south of Pioneer Square, and its patrons need to navigate the rest of their way to work as best they can, whether by bus, taxi, or foot. So, while Sounder is vastly more expensive for the region's and the nation's taxpayers, commuters are much more strongly inclined to travel by bus, given the opportunity.

To counter the implications of superior bus performance, the rationale turns to the claim that rail transit is permanent, and its permanence assures "transit-oriented development," walkable communities where people can live close by. They will walk or maybe bike to the station and commute to work, and their other desired destinations, by rail. They can reduce or even eliminate their driving and dispose of a family car or two.

Reality is at odds with that pretension. As evidence, Sound Transit madly builds massive parking lots and parking structures at its Sounder stations—because it is acutely aware that if people don't drive to its stations it will have very few patrons. There is a parking space for virtually every commuter; it's rare to spot anyone approaching a Sounder station on foot. Sound Transit clearly recognizes that it is not making a transition to centers of transit-oriented development, as it has budgeted hundreds of millions of dollars for thousands of additional parking spaces to be developed over the next two decades.

The patrons using Sounder are subsidized 95 percent: a $3 fare entitles the passenger to a $60 per boarding trip. Roughly one-fourth of the $60 is the operating cost subsidy, and the balance is the per-trip annualized capital development subsidy. So yes, so long as the public sector is willing to lavish so much money (in excess of $20,000 per year per commuter) on a tiny number of privileged travelers, they can continue to ride their gravy trains. But times, comprehension, and attitudes can change.

In his recent address, FTA Administrator Peter Rogoff warned that officials opting to develop rail transit "need to be mindful of the costs they are teeing up for future generations. . . . If you can't afford your current [rail] footprint, does expanding that underfunded footprint really advance the president's goals for cutting oil use and greenhouse gases? Does it really advance our economic goals in any sustainable way?"

So how will Sound Transit carry on when its money is exhausted? Just like Los Angeles, Washington, D.C., Denver, etc.: more taxes, huge bailouts, and then higher fares and service reductions. As equipment ages and safety becomes an issue, repeat the process.

But the remarks of Administrator Peter Rogoff could signal a change in the game. If the federal government emphasizes good maintenance of existing services, and resists squandering money on costly, unproductive expansion projects, priorities may change.

As Ken Orski, a veteran transportation expert, close observer of national transportation policy and publisher of *Innovation Briefs,* wrote, when reporting on Peter Rogoff's extraordinary remarks and the study that triggered them:

> Fiscal realities can do wonders to bring federal officials down to earth. . . .
> Forget about massive capacity expansion; focus on getting the most out of
> the assets already in place by maintaining them in a state of good repair.
> To critics of the DOT's new posture—and there will be some—a good
> answer could be: It's just a different way of looking at what it means to be
> pro-transit. ◙

IV

How Do We Use
What We Know?

If you show people the problems and you show them the solutions
they will be moved to act.
— Bill Gates, At *Live8* (July 2, 2005)

Science and Public Policy

The Twain Must Meet

William D. Ruckelshaus

People think and complain a lot about government, but practically no one complains or thinks much about science, even though arguably science has more impact on our lives, for good or ill, than does government. Maybe it's because science seems to be an aspect of nature itself, like mountains and seas. No one gets exercised about mountains being high or seas being wet. Or maybe it's because government casts an unflattering light on the human condition; government is us, and we often don't like what we see. The historian Barbara Tuchman once observed that as you look through the long course of history, at all the civilizations that have come and gone, you find that despite their great differences in culture and achievement, whatever different things they did best, they did the same thing worst, and that was government. You look at a historic culture that's perfectly competent in art, in commerce, in architecture, and if you were to ask them how they govern themselves, you would get something like, "we give absolute power to a dimwit because he's the oldest son of the homicidal maniac who used to be in charge."

Things are somewhat better nowadays, of course, since it's generally agreed that choosing leaders democratically is superior to relying on a genetic lottery, but there is still something to many people deeply dissatisfying about government, especially about remote national government, and especially about the way that national government deals with natural resource and environmental protection issues. How can this be? Despite what people think, we are not in general ruled by dimwits anymore. We are the most advanced scientific nation in the world. Thousands of highly skilled and dedicated people are struggling with these environmental and natural resource issues every day. Why can't we do better?

Well, I think we probably can, but in order to do so we are going to have to change the way science and public policy are brought together to address these problems.

Let's start with how we got here. Originally, it was some authority—a Caesar, a monarch, a noble—that determined what was good and what was true. Then came the period we refer to as the Enlightenment. Science arose to determine what was true, and when people wanted to pursue the good collectively, they came to accept that democratic forms of government were worth a try. Modern science and modern democracy are both children of the Enlightenment, but there's always been something of a sibling rivalry in their relationship. That's because among the good things it produced, the Enlightenment also brought forth one of the most toxic ideas in human intellectual history, that being the notion that a bunch of smart people could figure out a political system that could answer every human need, a system that had the authority of science behind it. Naturally, when people came to realize how really wonderful such systems were, they would democratically choose them, but in the meantime, they could legitimately be imposed on the people, by force. After all, who can argue with scientific truth? As we know, the monstrous political systems that convulsed the century just past were one result. As we also know, democracy is a perilous game, and its occasional failure is no surprise. In fact, in the opinion of practically every political thinker in the Western tradition, from Plato on down, democracy leads inevitably to anarchy and anarchy to despotism.

We were more fortunate in our own country, largely because the democratic instinct is so strong here and because our society is so solidly grounded in the rule of law. In turn, the law is grounded in the assumption that ordinary people can make the often complex judgments necessary to an ordered state. Thus we have juries, and legislatures. But law is also presumed by some to be based on reason. Oliver Wendell Holmes said it was based on experience. William Blackstone, before Holmes, said, "if the law is not rational, it is not the law." Now, science is the epitome of reason. As the decisions that a democracy must make become more complex than deciding whether the guy robbed the bank or who should pay taxes and how much, science increasingly comes into the house of law, into the house of democracy, and starts throwing her weight around. This has to be some-what uncomfortable, because science is not democratic. Scientific issues are not decided by vote. If all the scientists in the world believe one thing to be true, and a single scientist demonstrates that it's not true according to the protocols of the scientific method, then all those scientists have got to change their minds. This has actually happened from time to time in the history of science, and the people who have shown all their peers to be wrong are hailed as heroes. Everybody thought the planets had to move in circles, and Kepler showed their orbits were ellipses. Everybody thought time and space were absolute, until Einstein showed they were relative. Everybody thought the genetic material had to be a protein, but Oswald Avery demonstrated that it was really DNA.

This has been going on for a while, so that democratic policymakers have become used to turning to scientists for answers, often, it has to be said, in a grudging way. They want the scientists to come in, give them a simple answer, and leave. But it doesn't work that way. To understand why, we have to take a closer look at the nature of science and what scientists actually do.

Science works primarily by analysis, the breaking down of complex problems into smaller ones. The goal is to develop a problem that's sus-ceptible to an experiment or an observational regime involving a relatively small number of variables. If the variables are controlled or easily deter-mined, then the scientist can be accurate and precise. We know exactly where the planet Mercury will be twenty-five years and a day from now, and what happens when we mix two chemicals together under specified temperature and pressure.

Science is also statistical. That is, scientists typically don't say that something is true, but only that something is true subject to specified lev-els of uncertainty. For experimental data, scientists like the uncertainty to be down around the one percent level, which means that you'd expect to see your data resulting from chance alone only one in a hundred times. It is important to understand that this is not what policymakers usually mean by uncertainty. Policymakers are paid to make decisions on scant data, and often they are in circumstances where a decision simply must be made. In those situations an 85 percent chance of being right may look pretty good. But they are not going to get that kind of estimate from a sci-entist as science. Scientists are paid to say this is what we know under the statistical rules governing science, and this is what we don't know. They're not really supposed to guess. If they do, their opinions are no more valuable than those of any informed and educated citizen.

What separates actual science from the opinions of people who happen to be scientists is an elaborate process of peer review and publication. Science is literally that which is published in peer-reviewed journals. Unfortunately for the policymaker, this is always a moving target. Dr. Smith publishes a result, and Dr. Jones publishes a conflicting result. Smith replies with a letter to the journal and additional data. Then Dr. Brown weighs in with a paper that demonstrates that both Smith and Jones are right in some respects and wrong in others. Over time, the truth comes out. Yes, the planets really do revolve around the sun in elliptical orbits, and everything really is made of atoms. But time is just what the policymaker often does not have. They need answers today, or in any case before Smith, Jones & Brown can work things out.

So policymakers are often in the position of asking scientists to be unscientific, thus obviating any logic to be found in consulting scientists at all. They do this for two reasons. First, because science has a reputation for the pursuit of truth without fear or favor. In contentious policy wrangles they may be seen as neutral referees. Second, nothing in our intellectual culture matches the prestige of science. Scientists sent men to the moon, scientists have cured some of the worst plagues of humanity—surely they can tell us whether or not to build this little dam.

But often they cannot, and especially not when things like dams are involved. There is no policy area more fraught with problems involving the inclusion of science than environmental protection and resource management. And it's easy to see why this is the case. We saw that science is most precise when variables are few and well controlled. But the environment has a vast number of variables, and they are nearly impossible to control. That means that environmental questions are very hard to answer through controlled experiments. We can collect data and do computer simulations, of course, but these are subject to criticism by political groups offended by their results. It's always possible to claim that something crucial was left out, because something crucial is so often left out. Yes, it is possible to develop a consensus about a particular scientific issue—global warming for example—but this consensus is never going to be as convincing as the consensus that the planets rotate around the sun. The environment is just too complex, and moreover, in environmental science we start to push up against the limits of what can be known about the world. Complexity at a certain level introduces us to the universe of chaos: we know pretty much what causes lightning, for example, but we will never be able to predict where it will strike.

And environmental science is particularly hard-pressed to answer questions of just the type that policymakers most want to ask, questions like "what will happen to some endangered animal if we do thus and so?" Or, "what is the safe level of a certain pollutant?" To these and similar questions, science can only give uncertain answers. But saying that an answer must be uncertain is not the same as professing total ignorance. We know a lot, and that knowledge should be used to enlighten decisions. Unfortunately, we have historically lacked an institutional theater in which science and policymaking can come together efficiently and produce more light than heat.

In order to understand why this is so, we now must take a look at the origins of the legal institutions that we've devised to protect the environment and manage natural resources. There are three distinct streams of development in our legal institutional history. The first of these is the common law and the tort process. It was an early discovery that airborne pollution causes damage to life and property. People so damaged naturally sought relief in the courts, and here judges discovered a problem. A polluting factory is not a mere nuisance; it is the source of economic livelihood for its community, and judges have to live in communities, too. So beginning in the 1950s, some courts began turning to formal science advisory boards to determine whether there was a level of pollution below which damage could not be found. One of the first of these cases was decided in the Pacific Northwest, when a farmer sued smelter and refinery operators for crop damage. In that case and in many others, courts and their science advisors found that there was a safe level of pollution, below which damage claims would not be entertained by the courts. The farmer lost. It's often forgotten, especially by dedicated government bashers, that the first environmental standards established by courts were a blessing to industry, or at least the lesser of evils, the idea being that putting in pollution controls is cheaper and more predictable than losing a lawsuit.

Standards were also being established through the second stream of development, which was public health, by far the oldest source of environmental law. Governments have been legislating to protect the public health since antiquity, and until the middle of the last century such controls had been local in origin and impact. But air and water pollution, which respect no geographic or political boundaries, required national standards, and these were established, together with the administrative apparatus for issuing detailed regulations and enforcing them. Eventually, almost all of these programs were combined into the Environmental Protection Agency. The EPA has appointed various science advisory boards, which have labored mightily over the past thirty years to develop a sound scientific basis for federal regulations. It has not been easy. The federal regulatory process is painfully slow, and its products are invariably challenged, most often for the science on which they're based. The affected parties can hire scientists, too, whereupon we are treated to the unedifying spectacle of scientists duking it out in a courtroom, any pretense to neutrality quite abandoned.

Finally, we have the vast system of governmental control and ownership that is designed to protect the American landscape and conserve our natural resources. This was largely a late nineteenth-century development, stirred by the observation that if things were left entirely to private interests, the national resources would be despoiled and wasted and its priceless scenery ruined. In short order came the national park system, the national forests, the Bureau of Land Management, the federal water projects, and decades later the Endangered Species Act. The political philosophy behind all of these programs was that national resources belonged to all the people of the nation, not just the people who happened to live in the vicinity and might derive their livings from them; and further, that the people living near them—largely westerners—could not be trusted to manage the resources. That was the job of scientifically trained experts, who had no economic stake in the resources and could therefore be trusted to manage them for the good of all Americans, present and future. This arrangement was, and remains, profoundly undemocratic. If scientists are considered natural philosophers, which is what they were once called, then the natural resource regime in the western United States is very close to the philosopher kingdom prescribed by Plato, and yearned after ever since by people for whom democracy is too messy and prone to corruption. Thomas Jefferson had their number when he wrote to the effect that if you think the people not enlightened enough to use their powers wisely, the solution is not to remove or restrict those powers, but to enlighten the people.

This we have not done. When I said just now that we have no efficient theater in which science and policymaking can come together, I really meant that we have no regular means of popular enlightenment, a place

where democratic powers can be exercised in concert with the application of the best scientific understanding. What we have instead are the
courts, with their dueling experts and sometimes confused judges; the legislatures, with those same dueling experts and contending interest groups;
and the press. The press is where if 300 of the world's greatest scientists
swear that black is black, some enterprising reporter in search of "balance"
will locate the lone scholar willing to testify that black is white. I exagger-
ate, of course, because these questions are hardly ever simple, and there
is legitimate disagreement in the halls of science. But there has to be a
better way. What we're doing now is not working. We are still losing too
much of our environment. We are not effectively managing our resources.
Everyone is angry with the federal government and discounts its scientific
expertise. Why is this so hard?

When we confront a seemingly intractable problem in human affairs,
it's well to look toward basic human frailty for an origin, and here we find
what I believe is the psychological basis for our situation, what we might
call the mutual corruption of science and policymaking. Let's look at the
policymaker first. Occasionally, we have a situation in which the policymaker has already made the decision for political or ideological reasons
and is simply using science as a fig leaf. That's typically when you get
claims that my science is good science and your science is bad. Everyone is
for good science. (So far I have met no one who favors bad science.) More
commonly, the policymaker genuinely doesn't know what to do, but has to
make the decision and wants a little cover. Policymakers don't like to get
people mad at them if they can help it. Making a tough decision based on
your values is probably the hardest thing to do in public life. Half the people think your values are cockeyed, and most of the other half thinks that
you made the decision because some interest group or others got to you.
That leaves your family and a few personal friends to testify how noble you
really are, which is not a lot of solace or votes. How much easier and safer
it is to declare that science has made the decision! Our science advisory
board has told us that green frogs will rain from the sky unless we replace
the dam, and while I am personally much more in favor of a tax break or
free ice cream, we will have to follow the dictates of reason.

Now, because avoiding direct responsibility for such decisions is so
pleasant, policymakers will often chivvy scientists into stepping outside
the legitimate bounds of science and ask questions that science cannot
answer, either because the data and the theoretical understanding are

insufficient, or because the question is not scientific at all. A question like "What should the ABC Valley look like?" is not a scientific question. Science can tell us what the valley looked like 500 years ago, and can suggest what it will look like in 50 years if current uses continue, but science doesn't do "shoulds." To get around this, policymakers often erect general concepts like "pristine," "sustainable," "natural," and "wilderness." Then scientists find themselves, knowingly or not, trying to establish measurable indicators of such policy-based concepts. There is nothing wrong with this *per se*, but it's an error to think that it's scientific or value-free. Finally, science is useful to policymakers who would rather not make a controversial decision at all. "We're studying the problem" is a fine old perennial.

The analog of the policymaker who uses science to disguise or delay a values-based decision is the scientist who departs from science and starts dabbling in policymaking. Scientists are citizens like everyone else and have the right to weigh in on environmental or any other issues. The problems start when scientists are brought in to render specific scientific assistance and instead give what amounts to policy advice. I recall some years ago an occasion where I was supposed to introduce a panel of distinguished scientists to the president of the United States to tell him what was known about acid rain. The evening before the meeting I got together with the scientists over dinner and explained that they were only supposed to talk about the facts and not try to tell the president what to do. And they all said they understood and agreed. The next day, of course, no sooner had they sat down in the Roosevelt Room of the White House than they were pouring out advice about how to run everything from controlling acid rain (the policy issue involved) to restoring damaged statuary in Rome. It's the truth. All to President Ronald Reagan's complete and understandable befuddlement. Because of their performance, the control of acid rain (what they wanted) was postponed for about six years.

Their conduct was only human, but it was not helpful. Government agencies therefore spend a lot of time and effort trying to keep science advice in the strict sense separate from policymaking. At EPA we made a lot out of the difference between risk assessment and risk management. Risk assessment was supposed to be a scientific activity that presented a pure estimate of how much risk was posed to health or the environment by the use of some chemical or the generation of some pollutant. Then the scientists were supposed to drop this on the desk of the policymaker and slip away, and the policymaker was supposed to balance this risk against other social concerns, like economic costs or impacts on employment or agency priorities, and make a balanced decision. In practice, it's not so easy to separate the assessment from the management side—there's no Chinese wall, because the assumptions you make in conditions of high scientific uncertainty are going to influence the outcome of the study and the levels of risk you describe. These assumptions can and will be challenged as improper intrusions of management concerns into the supposedly "pure" scientific study.

The end result of this inter-corruption is that science is delegitimized in the public eye. Anyone who does not like the policy implications of a scientific study can decry it as bad or junk science. Rationality tends to drain from the system, to be replaced by raw politics based in part on demonization: the pointy-headed Washington bureaucrats or the irresponsible, land-grabbing despoilers, or the granola-worshipping tree huggers. Science, which is in its essence a program for reaching agreement about the nature of the world, then, becomes a mere adjunct to politics. Contending groups review the same literature and by selective interpretation announce that "science shows" whatever suits their chosen policy. In this process the extremes tend to dominate, and so we see a face-off between environmentalists claiming the planet is on its last legs and cornucopian economists who think everything is just fine, or would be if those environmentalists would just shut up.

At the same time, lacking a basis in good information, policymaking is paralyzed. Among the technical agencies, we observe the growth of what's been called the "conspiracy of optimism." That's when the U.S. Forest Service, for example, promises to each of its constituencies the fullest realization of its values: to the timber interests as much wood as you want, to the recreation interests as much fishing and hunting as you want, to the conservationists as many trees as you want, and to Congress a program that makes money doing all those things. What you end up with, however, is an agency that pleases no one and loses money at the same time.

Well, it's easy to throw up our hands at this point and say that science is science and politics is politics and never the twain shall meet. But the twain must meet in some more productive and creative way, or else we will continue to fail in resource management, particularly here in the West. The consequences of failure are not good, and not just for America. If we cannot, with all our knowledge and political stability and wealth, figure out how to manage our own natural resources for the present and for future generations, how can we expect people in the rest of the world to do it? We need our solutions to serve as a democratic example—and that is still the best way to lead. Otherwise, we are going to lose huge swathes of the natural world.

How could we do it better? First, we have to admit that we side with Jefferson and against Plato. It should never happen that an elite body of experts is going to be allowed to make natural resource decisions in this country. In the end these are always going to be democratic decisions; the real question is how to make them the best possible democratic decisions, and include as much rational analysis and technical expertise as we can.

Given that, we have no option but to devise ways of enlightening democratic processes directly, with the contributions of scientists. Is this really possible, when we read studies that say 40 percent of Americans don't believe in evolution, and interviews that suggest that many of our fellow citizens have ideas about the natural world more characteristic of the first millennium than the second or the third? It gives one pause. On the other hand, my own experience tells me that when ordinary people and policymakers from a particular locality get together to make decisions about resources in their place, they can come up with solutions that the experts haven't thought of. Given the right stimulus, and with the stakes high enough, people can learn enough to make good and technically competent decisions

I think three things are required for this to happen. First, the scientific analysis has to be transparent. By that I mean that the decisionmakers have to understand the origins of the scientific advice and what assumptions have gone into generating the results. Everyone has to understand what part of the decision is based on data, and what part on values. It is usually recommended that the science part of the process be formally separate from the policymaking part, so that the scientists drop their findings on the policymaker's desk as if they were delivering a pizza. I'm not sure this is workable for reasons I've already discussed. We should always strive to know what's science and what isn't, but the best way to do that is through continual feedback between the scientists and the people who need to make decisions based on the scientists' work. What we don't want is the familiar complaint from policymakers that the scientists have produced useless studies, and from the scientists that the policymakers are misusing their science.

Next, I think there has to be a frank admission of uncertainty and a commitment on the part of policymakers not to use uncertainty as an excuse for inaction. Natural resource and environmental decisions are always going to be made under conditions of uncertainty, and that will throw the values of the policymakers into high relief. In an uncertain world, do you want to err on the side of public health protection? On the side of endangered species? On the side of self-sufficient energy generation? On the side of present prosperity? On the side of posterity? Each of these is reasonable, and science has nothing to say about which to choose. Policymakers need to make the decision and make it clear on what basis it is made and not blame the uncertainty.

Finally, I think we have to address how the question of scale affects how science integrates with policymaking on natural resource decisions. The political context for such integration is not a hopeful one. For generations, experts lodged in federal resource management agencies have tried to impose resource decisions on localities, justifying such actions on two counts: first, that the resources belonged to all Americans, not just those who happened to live in those regions, and second, that they were the experts. Who can argue with expertise? The late Scott Matheson, when he was the governor of Utah, summed up this situation by saying that the feds considered that since the West was virtually uninhabited, the people who lived there constituted a new class of citizen, the virtual uninhabitants, who did not have a full set of democratic rights. The anger that this attitude provoked made it easy for western politicians to run against the federal government, with the result that the states containing most of the resources under federal authority came to be represented by a solid phalanx of politicians whose primary political character was resistance to federal authority.

Of course, in politics as in physics any reaction provokes a reaction that is equal and opposite, and so there developed powerful national lobbies supporting federal authority. Environmental and conservation interests deplored the western resistance as land-grabbing exploiters dependent on federal largesse but ungratefully unwilling to abide by the rules devised to protect resources on behalf of all Americans. The westerners, they claimed, had but one hypocritical cry, which was, "Get out, but give us more money."

This is a recipe for political gridlock. The western conservatives win all the elections but can't govern in their own backyard, and the conservationists, having won many early battles, such as the Clean Air Act and the Clean Water Act, can now block any major adjustments in Congress. What has emerged from this wasteland and the frustration it spawned, remarkably enough, is a new process called resolution by collaboration. These processes arise when interest groups and government agencies at all levels with a stake in some local issue come together to solve problems that no single one of them could solve alone. Donald Snow of the Northern Lights Institute in Montana described these groupings as "coalitions of the unalike." They typically include all stakeholders—farmers; ranchers; federal, state, tribal, and local officials; business and environmental representatives—bringing together people who rarely meet regularly across a table, and might not choose to do so if there were any alternative. Essentially, people in the West have found that if you set out to solve problems on a local scale—a watershed, say, or a river basin—you can achieve concrete solutions to problems that would be intractable if you had to depend only on a national regulatory program.

Scientific or technical analysis is critical to the success of such groups, and it has an effect that it typically does not have when it tries to address enormous problems that are national in scope. Something really interesting happens when you get analytic information fed directly into a group that has both an intimate understanding of a particular landscape and a keen interest in what happens to it. Nothing does a scientist more good than having to explain things from first principles, without the typical jargon of the trade. Nothing does a group of citizens with disparate backgrounds and conflicting interests more good than coming together around an analytic, technically accurate picture of their home place. This has to be what Jefferson meant when he talked about enlightening the people. Over and over again we have seen real change occur in these groups. Trust grows, as does confidence in the creative powers of ordinary people. In short, I think that this is probably the only way that we are going to bring our twain together.

I am hopeful that we have the basis for a new American institution, one that builds on the technical and democratic strengths of our nation and region. It's significant that collaborative processes such as this are native to the American West. As the author Wallace Stegner wrote, "Angry as one may be at what heedless men have done to a noble habitat, one cannot be pessimistic about the West. This is the native home of hope. When it fully learns that cooperation, not rugged individualism, is the quality that most characterizes and preserves it, then it will have achieved itself and outlived its origins. Then it has a chance to create a society to match its scenery." ◙

Lessons from the Land for Protection in the Sea

The Need for a New Ocean Ethic

Jane Lubchenco with Renee Davis-Born and Brooke Simler

Updated by Kirsten Grorud-Colvert

I STILL suffer from withdrawal. I recently returned from one of the great wild places on Earth, Kruger National Park in South Africa. It took days for me to begin to adjust to being out of the park. The long withdrawal was in sharp contrast to the almost instantaneous transition I experienced upon entering the park. I quickly grew accustomed to consciously (and, as I discovered later, subconsciously) searching for telltale signs of elephants, rhinos, lions, chameleons, baboons, hornbills, rollers, and the delightful plethora of other wild creatures that inhabit this spectacular place.

Frequently reinforced by the intense pleasure of observing fascinating behaviors or exotic wildlife, I quickly began to discriminate certain shapes, colors, or movement that signaled something distinct from the background of acacias, grasses, marula trees, the occasional baobabs, and other fixed features of this landscape. Days were a delicious state of alertness as I reveled in the abundance and diversity of the South African savanna: leopards, Cape buffalo, water monitor lizards, zebra, impala, hammerkop, drongo, duiker, and more. The sounds of nocturnal African wildlife, going about the business of foraging, interacting, and surviving, quickly became my evening lullaby. Kruger felt alive, teeming with life and ripe with potential.

Later, upon leaving the park, I found myself still searching the landscape for hippos, secretary birds, bateleur eagles, giraffes, kudu, warthogs, and crocodiles ... even though I knew full well my search was in vain. The contrast between inside and outside Kruger was dramatic, visceral, and long lasting.

A delicious habit dies hard but provokes thought and discussion. As I shared these Kruger experiences and their aftermath with my colleagues Renee and Brooke, we realized that the intensity of my withdrawal was strong testimony to the importance of protected areas around the world— on land and in the oceans. Wild places like Kruger provide not only enriching and inspiring experiences but myriad other benefits. Unless people consciously protect them, wild places and wildlife slowly disappear.

Recognition of this threat of disappearance prompted the establishment of parks on every continent. The concepts of "land conservation" and the "land ethic" articulated in earlier centuries by Teddy Roosevelt, John Muir, and Aldo Leopold have been embraced by many to acknowledge the responsibility of humans for good stewardship of the land and protection of the plants, animals, and microbes that live together and interact. Parks and wilderness areas are one expression of this land ethic.

As a marine biologist, I am fully aware that this same ethic has not yet been extended to the sea. Protection comparable to that afforded by parks does not exist for most ecosystems and wildlife in the oceans. The need for safe havens for fishes, corals, sponges, tube worms, seaweeds, shrimps, and seals has not been obvious to many people. What lessons have we learned from terrestrial parks and their history that might inform our thinking about ocean protection? What is happening in oceans that merits thinking about them in new ways? What might good ocean stewardship look like? What is the equivalent of parks in the ocean? How do these global concerns affect those of us in the Pacific Northwest? I address each of these questions in turn.

LESSONS FROM THE LAND:
KRUGER AND U.S. NATIONAL PARKS

South Africa's Kruger National Park is widely regarded as the shining emerald in the world's crown jewels of national parks. Many consider it one of the most wild, diverse, and spectacular places on Earth. Kruger's huge size and history of science-based management make it unusual. At two million hectares, Kruger is roughly equivalent to Yellowstone, Everglades, and Grand Canyon national parks rolled into one. Kruger boasts some of the richest diversity on the planet. In addition to the spectacular tourist bait, the so-called "Big Five"—elephants, lions, leopards, rhinos, and buffaloes—the park contains an impressive number of described species: 336 species of trees, 49 species of fishes, 34 species of amphibians, 114 reptilian species, 507 bird species, and 147 species of mammals. In addition, there are large numbers of insects, other invertebrates, fungi, lower plants, microbes, and other life that are less well known but important nonetheless.

Kruger National Park has not always been this bountiful. In fact, the impetus for protecting the area was a noticeable decline in many animals. By the late 1800s wildlife populations had declined precipitously due to hunting for sport and, to a lesser degree, subsistence. By the turn of the twentieth century, the vast swath of land eventually designated as Kruger National Park was home to fewer than a dozen elephants and only three black rhinoceros. The white rhinoceros had been locally extirpated.

Citizens, sport hunters, and public officials demanded that areas be protected from hunting, not with the goal of conservation *per se*, but rather to provide a safe haven for breeding wildlife and to ensure future hunting opportunities. In 1898 President Paul Kruger established the Sabi Game Reserve. In subsequent years South Africans kept a watchful eye on the nascent national park system that was expanding in the United States.

In 1926 the South African government passed the National Parks Act, combining the Sabi Game Reserve with other protected areas to create Kruger National Park. Today approximately 8,000 elephants, 300 black rhinoceros, and 2,000 white rhinoceros plus an astounding variety of other animals and plants inhabit the park—strong testimony to the protection it has afforded wildlife. Above and beyond the protection of biodiversity, the park provides a wealth of other benefits that derive from the functioning of the intact ecosystems within the park. Kruger's resounding success can be attributed to a combination of foresight, good enforcement, high quality academic scientific research informing park policies, and, more recently, a serious commitment to adaptive, ecosystem-based management and attention to benefits provided by the park to all of the people in the country.

Closer to home, the history of U.S. national parks and wilderness areas tells a story not unlike the early days of Kruger. Wanton killing of buffalo, antelope, and other great animals across America in the 1800s sparked the creation of the first national parks. In a recent speech, Theodore Roosevelt

IV, descendant of President Theodore Roosevelt, one of our nation's fiercest leaders in the protection of natural areas, captured the sense of the time:

> It was the devastation to wildlife on the American plains which President Theodore Roosevelt witnessed during his ranching and hunting days that inspired his own conservation ethos. On a hunting trip to the Badlands in 1883, he found the buffalo herds small and scattered. Just four years later, on another trip, there simply were no bison, no beaver, no antelope, no grizzlies, and no wapiti.
>
> Theodore Roosevelt realized then that we were pushing species beyond their ability to recover—that the yields taken from the land were no longer sustainable and would ultimately hurt our nation. His actions, and those of other concerned citizens—mostly hunters, by the way— helped to turn the tide and preserve places and species for the rest of us.

In 1916, President Woodrow Wilson approved legislation that created the National Park Service. This agency was charged "to conserve the scenery and the natural and historic objects and the wildlife therein and to provide for the enjoyment of the same in such manner and by such means as will leave them unimpaired for the enjoyment of future generations." Building on this land ethic, Congress later passed the Wilderness Act of 1964. This law expands the park concept to wilderness, "in contrast with those areas where man and his own works dominate the landscape, as an area where the earth and its community of life are untrammeled by man, where man himself is a visitor who does not remain," and requires that a wilderness area be managed to preserve "its primeval character and influence." Today the national Wilderness Preservation System encompasses nearly 650 wilderness areas (including some parks)—comprising 106 million acres, an equivalent to nearly 5 percent of all the land in the U.S.—for the benefit and enjoyment of Americans. Our nation's commitment to the protection of terrestrial areas is clear and strong.

SEA CHANGES: THE NEED FOR BETTER PROTECTION

The need to protect wildlife and habitats on land was recognized during earlier centuries. A comparable need for protection in the oceans is now emerging as three interrelated conclusions are becoming obvious: oceans are important, oceans are threatened, and oceans are not well protected.

These conclusions lay the groundwork for a new ocean ethic—a serious commitment to protecting and restoring the abundance of life in oceans.

Oceans are undoubtedly important, and not just to marine ecologists like me. They cover 70 percent of our planet and encompass 99 percent of the inhabitable three-dimensional space for life on Earth. Oceans provide a wealth of benefits in the form of food, fiber, medicines, pharmaceuticals, blueprints for new materials, a storehouse of knowledge, the recycling of nutrients, detoxification of pollutants, partial regulation of the water cycle, partial climate regulation, regulation of gases in the atmosphere, and the provision of spectacular places for recreation, tourism, inspiration, and enjoyment—essentials we call "ecosystem goods and services." These goods and services are collectively provided by an impressive diversity of ecosystems: coral reefs, kelp forests, mangroves, salt marshes, mud flats, estuaries, rocky shores, sandy beaches, sea mounts, continental shelves, abyssal plains, open oceans. Each ecosystem harbors a complex assemblage of species that interact with each other and the specific physical and chemical environment of the place. The services are byproducts of the functioning of intact ecosystems. We are only now beginning to appreciate the importance of these different ecosystems, the diversity of their inhabitants, the goods and services they provide—and indeed the importance of oceans in general to our health, prosperity, and well-being.

Unfortunately, oceans are under threat. For eons, humans believed that oceans were so vast and bountiful that they were impervious to human influences. Now, however, we are confronted by a multitude of symptoms of serious degradation. Alarm bells are sounding. Globally, the frequency of each of the following has increased significantly over the last century:

crashes of important fisheries due to overfishing, bycatch, habitat destruction, disruption of ocean food webs because of removal of top predators, and pollution;

destruction of habitat due to coastal zone development, certain fishing practices such as bottom trawling, and aquaculture;

appearance of large areas of low or no oxygen (so-called "dead zones") at the mouths of rivers draining large agricultural areas or concentrated animal feedlot operations, due to nutrient pollution, primarily too much nitrogen from fertilizers and animal wastes;

outbreaks of red tides and harmful algal blooms as consequences
of nutrient pollution and spread of non-native species by transport
in ballast water;

bleaching of corals, likely a reflection of increased ocean water
temperatures due to global warming;

invasions of non-native species due to transport by ballast water in
ships, aquaculture, and aquarium trade;

appearance of new diseases, possibly associated with global warming; and

mass mortalities of marine mammals and invertebrates due to oil
spills, introduction of disease, and various kinds of pollution.

The fact that these symptoms are increasing in frequency reflects the
increases in a wide variety of land-based and ocean-based human activities, compounded by a lack of understanding that actions in one place can
trigger consequences elsewhere. (Who would have thought, for example,
that increased use of fertilizers in the Midwest could trigger dead zones in
the Gulf of Mexico that are now the size of Massachusetts?) The cumulative effects of these activities are increasingly disrupting ocean ecosystems
to the extent that they cannot continue to provide the goods and services
that society expects and needs. A broad spectrum of human activities is
unintentionally but most definitely changing the chemistry, biology, ecology, and physical structure of oceans, especially in coastal areas.

We are witnessing serious declines in ocean wildlife like the declines
of the great herds in the U.S. or in Kruger. In his recent speech, Theodore
Roosevelt IV asserted that humans do not yet appreciate the gravity of
our impact on oceans: "We may be seeing the last great buffalo hunt taking place in the world's seas." The best documentation of this trend comes
from economically important species (fisheries) or large and charismatic
ones (turtles, for example).

A 2008 report by the United Nations Food and Agriculture Organiza-
tion underscores this change: fifty years ago, only 5 percent of major marine
fisheries were categorized as "fully exploited, over exploited, or depleted";
today nearly 80 percent of the global fisheries are in these categories. From

5 percent to 80 percent in fifty years! Successively more and more fisheries are in serious trouble. In U.S. waters, the National Marine Fisheries
Service reports that more than one-third of the known fish stocks have
declined more than 70 percent between 1970 and 2000. Of equal concern is
the fact that there is not enough information to evaluate the status of over
half of the 531 fished species in U.S. waters that were reported to Congress
in 2008. Of the stocks where the status is known, one in four is currently
overfished.

Numerous unfished species are also in decline, often as an unintended
consequence of fishing activities. Fish, birds, turtles, and marine mammals
are often captured accidentally, as "bycatch," and simply tossed back into
the sea dead or dying. The United Nations Food and Agriculture Organi-
zation estimated global marine bycatch at around 44 billion pounds or 23
percent of the overall global catch in 2008. For some species, this uninten-
tional mortality can be devastating. Of the six sea turtles species (green,
Kemp's ridley, olive ridley, hawksbill, loggerhead, and leatherback) found
in U.S. waters, for example, all are designated as threatened or endangered
under the Endangered Species Act.

The conclusion is inescapable: oceans and their wildlife are insufficiently protected. U.S. federal and state governments have recognized the
need to protect marine life and ocean water quality. A variety of legislative acts and executive orders have attempted protection, but collectively
they are proving to be seriously inadequate. Two examples illustrate this
point. The Magnuson–Stevens Fishery Conservation and Management
Act, enacted in 1976, clearly lays out the objective of maintaining catches
at a level that will ensure future fishing opportunities, yet that goal has not
been achieved. Coastal communities and fishermen around the country
and the world are reeling from the consequences of the declines documented above and those happening even more recently.

The Marine Protection, Research, and Sanctuaries Act, passed by Congress in 1972, is intended to protect marine areas for their biodiversity,
ecological integrity, and cultural legacy. President Richard Nixon signed
the act into law 100 years after our first national park was designated to
safeguard unique places on land. Although this act articulates some conservation ideals, the level of ocean protection it calls for is drastically less
than what a national park provides on land. At the time the act was passed,
Americans viewed pollution and oil spills as the greatest threats to marine
life. As a consequence, any new drilling for gas or oil is banned in the

national sanctuaries. Other activities such as commercial and recreational fishing and ocean shipping were deemed to be of little threat and were permitted within sanctuary boundaries. In retrospect, the name "sanctuary" is a misnomer. It implies a far greater degree of protection than actually exists. The reality is that only a small fraction of our national marine sanctuaries is in fact fully protected from extractive activities (drilling, mining, and fishing). True refuges are too few.

The contrast between the fraction of area protected on land and in the ocean is striking: Whereas 5 percent of the U.S. land area is protected, in 2008 only about 1 percent of U.S. territorial waters was fully protected in no-take areas. If you consider that U.S. waters represent an area 20 percent larger than the U.S. land area, the low level of comprehensive protection is even more striking. More importantly, the rest of the 99 percent of U.S. waters is insufficiently protected, and much of it is in the process of being seriously degraded.

TIME FOR A NEW OCEAN ETHIC

To date, the U.S. approach to ocean management has been haphazard, piecemeal, and ineffective in the face of declining ocean conditions. The time is ripe for better management strategies that should reflect a new ocean ethic. The goal of this new ethic would be to protect and maintain healthy marine ecosystems—i.e., to protect and restore the abundance and diversity of life and the productivity, diversity, and resilience of ecosystems in the oceans. Only when this goal is achieved will healthy, sustainable fisheries be possible. Only when this goal is achieved will vibrant coastal communities be feasible. Only when this goal is achieved will people receive the full range of goods and services that oceans can provide. A new ocean ethic recognizes the intimate dependence of human health, prosperity, and well-being upon the existence of healthy marine ecosystems. A new ocean ethic acknowledges human responsibility for good stewardship of the oceans and the planet. A new ocean ethic provides adequate protection for habitats and species.

The framing and implementation of this ethic are formidable challenges, especially in the face of a growing population, increased migration to coastal areas, greater demand for ocean resources, the plethora of activities currently degrading oceans, and ongoing global changes such as global warming. Fortunately, a number of relevant dialogues are underway, involving the full range of stakeholders—citizens who care about

oceans, those whose livelihood depends on oceans, those who enjoy rec-
reating at the shore or on the water, those who study marine life scientifically, those whose official responsibilities are to formulate ocean policies
or implement ocean practices, and those whose primary concern is with
ethical and moral issues.

Almost a decade ago, two national commissions on oceans were established, each of which conducted thoughtful and comprehensive reviews of
U.S. practices and policies affecting oceans. Convened in July of 2000, the
Pew Oceans Commission was an independent group of American leaders
conducting a national dialogue on the policies needed to restore and protect living marine resources in U.S. waters. I had the pleasure of serving on
the Pew Commission. The Commission on Ocean Policy was established
by congressional act and first met in 2001. I accepted the invitation to serve
on the Pew Oceans Commission because I have personally witnessed the
destruction of unbelievably spectacular undersea oases, because I believe
that scientific knowledge should be available to guide our understanding
of problems and possible solutions, and because I sense that there is a continuous need for crafting of innovative solutions.

In a new decade, the discussion continues to move forward with the
new Interagency Ocean Policy Task Force, established via a memorandum
signed by President Barack Obama on June 12, 2009, in response to a growing understanding of the need for comprehensive ocean management. This
task force recently proposed a national ocean policy that would develop a
strong, cohesive, and effective system to manage our oceans, coasts, and
Great Lakes. This would provide a framework for Marine Spatial Planning,
which is a public process of analyzing and allocating all human activities in marine areas to achieve ecological, economic, and social goals. The
framework offers a strategy for improved stewardship and an integrated
approach to management that emphasizes stakeholder input.

The task force has held public hearings, seeking advice from experts
and the general public to frame broad recommendations to the nation. It
is my hope that our country will continue to rise to the challenge of framing a new ocean ethic and defining the changes necessary to accomplish it;
then that citizens and our leaders will help make the necessary changes a
reality. Parallel dialogues must continue at the international, regional, and
local levels as well.

As we look toward the future and seek to preserve our country's ocean
wilderness, a comprehensive suite of changes is clearly in order; no single

silver bullet exists. Among the broad sweep of new institutions, mechanisms, and tools that are under discussion, those that focus on science-
based, ecosystem-based management appear particularly promising.
Smart coastal development, reduction of nutrient and other kinds of pollution, more effective fisheries management, and environmentally sustainable aquaculture are all key elements of the new ethic. One specific tool
stands out as effective, long-lasting, and useful in helping to achieve better
protection for ocean ecosystems and wildlife: marine reserves.

ONE STEP TOWARD REALIZING THE OCEAN ETHIC:
MARINE RESERVES

Tools that afford ecosystem-based protection and promote an ocean ethic
are within reach. Marine reserves—areas of the sea that are fully protected
from extractive, additive, and ecologically destructive activities—are being
discussed with increasing frequency by scientists, policymakers, resource
managers, ocean users, and conservationists as one of the most promising
new tools. Sometimes called "ecological reserves," "fully protected marine
reserves," "wilderness areas," or "no-take areas," they are the best way to
protect habitats and ecosystems, provide havens for biodiversity and, in
some cases, help recharge depleted fisheries. Within a reserve, all life is
protected through prohibitions on dumping, mining, drilling, fishing, and
the removal or disturbance of any living or nonliving thing, except as necessary for monitoring or research to evaluate reserve effectiveness. These
areas may host nonextractive activities such as diving, snorkeling, and
education as long as they are not damaging to the wildlife or ecosystem. It
is the long-lasting and complete protection from damaging activities that
enables reserves to offer a unique host of benefits.

The primary objectives of a reserve are to protect habitats, restore populations of species, and ensure the persistence of healthy marine ecosystems
in an area. Reserves are not a new concept; some have been in existence
for decades. Globally, however, reserves protect less than 0.08 of a percent
of the ocean surface as of 2007. Scientists monitoring the performance of
reserves throughout the world find dramatic and consistent changes inside
reserves. Well-enforced reserves result in relatively large, rapid, and long-
lasting increases in population sizes, number of species, and productivity of marine plants and animals. Long-term protection from destructive
activities allows organisms to survive and accumulate in greater sizes and

numbers. Reserves protect habitat against human activities, such as the unintended consequences of destructive fishing gear.

Not surprisingly, animals left undisturbed in a reserve typically grow to larger sizes than animals outside the reserve. The importance of this outcome cannot be overemphasized: large marine fish and invertebrates produce enormous numbers of offspring. Even a small increase in the size of a crab, lobster, sea urchin, anemone, or fish results in a tremendous increase in the number of young produced. A major result of all these biological changes is simply a lot more animals inside and outside the reserve.

Large populations, along with large individuals, may also influence areas outside a reserve. Adults and juveniles from a reserve may swim or crawl into neighboring areas. This is called "spillover." Larvae or other young produced in a reserve may be carried by currents to seed surrounding waters. This process is termed "export." Studies show that spillover and export enable marine reserves to act as source areas that can replenish nearby populations. Reserves can thus function as both parks (protecting species within their boundaries) and natural hatcheries or nurseries (exporting young and adults to areas outside the reserve).

It is likely that reserves will be useful in replenishing some depleted fisheries, but not all. Regardless of this potential, reserves should not be conceived as replacements for adequate fishery management outside the reserve. In fact, reserves and good fishery management should be understood to be complementary to one another. Good fishery management cannot replace reserves—it cannot adequately protect habitats and species from the full spectrum of destructive activities. Likewise, reserves cannot accomplish all of the goals of good fishery management. Both are essential to the ocean ethic.

The creation and protection of diverse, bountiful marine ecosystems make sense from a stewardship perspective. Why, then, if reserves produce such clear and convincing results, are there not more of them? Four reasons seem paramount. (1) Oceans have historically been viewed as open to all. Restrictions on any use are vigorously resisted, with assertions that citizens have the right to use oceans as they always have. (2) The dramatic degradation in oceans (described above and providing rationale for better protection) is not obvious to enough people. (3) Concern about short-term losses (in areas available to be fished) is more strongly voiced than are the merits of long-term benefits (to conservation, fishery improvement, and maintenance of healthy marine ecosystems). (4) Fishery management is in transition, having only recently embraced the concept of ecosystem-based fishery management, and some argue that simply getting fishery management right will suffice.

There is increasing appreciation for the argument that oceans should be viewed and regulated as a public trust. Doing so will require changes. The litany of symptoms of degradation cited above is testimony to the fact that this public trust has been violated, that current uses have resulted in the tragedy of the commons. Setting aside important and unique areas and maintaining the essential functioning of healthy marine ecosystems will be vital components in restoring oceans to function as a public trust.

Not all concepts of land conservation are directly applicable to ocean conservation. Kruger is successful in part because it is huge. Large marine reserves may not be the most effective way to provide conservation and fishery enhancement goals. In 1998, an international team of marine scientists at the National Center for Ecological Analysis and Synthesis in Santa Barbara, California, concurred that the establishment of networks of smaller reserves would be more effective in accomplishing all goals than a single large reserve. Since that time, numerous scientific publications have illustrated the potential benefits of marine reserve networks. A network of marine reserves is a series of reserves within a large ecoregion that are connected via larval dispersal or juvenile or adult migration. Examples of ecoregions include the Gulf of Maine, the Gulf of Mexico, or the California Current System (off Washington, Oregon, and California). Within such areas, there are vast numbers of different configurations for networks, all of which could function effectively to protect and restore the ecosystem. Reserves within a network would be linked together through oceanographic processes and the movement of animals and plants.

Creating a network of small or moderately sized reserves can be an effective way of conserving species and replenishing populations, while minimizing the amount of area off limits to fishing or other extractive uses. Where, how many, and what size these reserves should be demands an examination of the particular area, its organisms and habitats, and the ecological and oceanographic processes occurring there. The reserves should be sized and spaced such that they are small enough to allow animals to travel beyond the reserve boundaries and near enough to allow reserves to replenish each other with larvae, juveniles, and adults. Varying the sizes and spacing of the reserves in a network can protect species with different characteristics. Because of the wide variation in dispersal distances among species, fluctuations in ocean currents, and other factors, one of the most effective strategies for protecting multiple species is to establish a network of reserves of different sizes that are located in habitat areas of interest.

Because any of a number of configurations of reserves within a network could likely function effectively, there is ample opportunity for public choice and involvement in selecting the combination of places that will suit a number of different social and economic goals. Cutting-edge data emerging from areas such as the Channel Islands and the mainland coast of California as well as the Great Barrier Reef show that established networks of reserves planned by local officials, scientists, and stakeholders can be successful at achieving their goals of preserving ocean species and habitats. As planning conversations about marine protected areas now continue in places such as the state of Washington, the United Kingdom, and east Australia, these data will prove critical for designing the most effective networks of reserves and other protected areas.

THE OCEAN ETHIC IN OREGON

Closer to my home, Oregonians are widely known for their strong and sincere commitment to land stewardship. But how does ocean stewardship measure up in Oregon, where management and protection of the terrestrial environment is the cornerstone of the state's culture, and where the coast and ocean are valued as local treasures?

Those of us who live in Oregon recognize it as one of the nation's best-kept secrets. We appreciate our good fortune to possess a dramatic, dynamic, and sparsely populated state—whether in eastern Oregon, in the Willamette Valley, or along the coast. Oregon has made progressive strides in natural resource management, including land use planning, waste reduction, and protection of our rivers, forests, beaches, deserts, and alpine areas. The land ethic is strong and evident.

Oregonians also have a powerful relationship with the coast and ocean. The state boasts progressive coastal land management through maintenance of beach access, comprehensive plans for managing rocky shores and estuaries, a stellar state park system, and the effective use of urban-growth boundaries. Despite Oregon's admirable track record with coastal planning and the perception that the coast is both ecologically and economically healthy, the fact is the ocean off Oregon is far from pristine and untouched. Management of Oregon's ocean does not receive the same amount of attention as management of Oregon lands. Consideration of an ocean ethic is indeed timely for Oregon.

Oregon relies on its marine environment for many reasons. Coastal activities such as commercial fishing and tourism are vital to Oregon's economy and coastal communities. According to statistics from the state's economic agencies, commercial fishing and processing of fish and shellfish landed in Oregon generated $264 million in income in 2003. In 2004, an estimated $514 million was generated for coastal communities from tourist expenditures. Oregonians understand that a stunning and unspoiled natural coast and ocean are crucially important to the state's draw as a tourist destination.

Oregon's marine environment is exhibiting signs of crisis. Two issues in particular—fishery declines and invasive species—have dominated the headlines over the past decade. In 2000, the U.S. Department of Commerce declared a federal disaster in the West Coast groundfish fishery. At the time, nearly half of the groundfish species assessed were overfished. More recently, the West Coast salmon disaster declared in 2008 was extended into 2009 for California and Oregon, leading to management that reduces commercial salmon fishing off southern Oregon and California to near zero. A total of $53.1 million in disaster funds is projected for aid to fishing communities. The Pacific Fishery Management Council, the regional body charged with managing fisheries in federal waters (3–200 nautical miles offshore) off the coasts of Washington, Oregon, and California, continues its work to rebuild the seven out of 30 assessed stocks that are currently overfished. But this is shadowed by the lack of information on 62 of the 92 groundfish species that the council manages. Oregon has also been the victim of many kinds of invasive species. Multiple studies document that over 100 non-native species—including European green crab, Atlantic marsh grass, and the purple varnish clam—have invaded Oregon's estuaries. These exotic species threaten diversity by competing with native species and altering habitats and ecosystem processes.

Additionally, the ecological legacy of earlier human activities is not clear. For example, in the 1700s and 1800s, Steller's sea cow and the sea otter were extirpated, with unknown consequences. In the early to mid 1900s, most of the estuarine salt marshes on the Oregon coast were lost through diking or filling. Our coast and ocean may be beautiful, but they are far from pristine.

A number of additional threats are emerging. The 2000 census showed that Oregon's population grew rapidly during the late 1980s and throughout the 1990s. Between 2000 and 2008, the state's population grew from 3,421,437 people to an estimated 3,790,060. At the current rate, Oregon is growing faster than the rest of the country, with some central Oregon counties growing up to four times faster than the national average. Growth in coastal areas is increasing quickly as well. Lincoln County—home of Newport, the Oregon Coast Aquarium, and Oregon State University's Hatfield Marine Science Center—watched its population grow 73 percent from 1970 to 2000. In anticipation of the 2010 national census, Oregon's population is projected to continue increasing at a rate faster than the national average. This growth brings additional demands for development, food production, recreation, and transportation of goods. Oceans, including Oregon's state waters, will undoubtedly feel the pressure of these demands.

Oregon now is in the middle of a historic opportunity to make significant advances in addressing existing and potential risks facing its marine environment. In July 2000, Governor John Kitzhaber charged the State of Oregon Ocean Policy Advisory Council (OPAC)—an advisory group established in 1991 to provide coordinated policy advice to the governor and state agencies—to assess marine reserves and how they might apply to Oregon's coastal and ocean waters. In 2008, OPAC, representative of Oregon citizens, made its initial recommendation to the governor with input from state residents. As a result of the community-based nomination process, two marine reserves will be established in June 2011—one at Redfish Rocks near Port Orford and one at Otter Rock near Depoe Bay. In addition, local communities will continue to discuss the potential for marine reserves near Cape Falcon, Cascade Head, Cape Perpetua, and Cape Arago. How Oregon responds to the question of marine reserves will demonstrate the strength of Oregon's ocean ethic.

Marine reserves have strong potential to help Oregon achieve one of its lauded and progressive statewide goals for planning: Goal 19, Ocean Resources. Goal 19 asserts an Ocean Stewardship Area, within which Oregon has clear economic and ecological interest in the conservation of ocean resources. This area includes the state's Territorial Sea, the continental margin seaward to the toe of the continental slope, and adjacent ocean areas. This mandated goal requires that the state of Oregon "conserve marine resources and ecological functions for the purpose of providing long-term ecological, economic, and social value and benefits to future generations." The state's ability to realize this goal, which highlights the need for holistic, ecosystem-based management of the ocean, would be greatly enhanced through the use of networks of marine reserves.

Other states are watching. For example, a Marine Protected Areas Working Group in Washington has recently completed a comprehensive review of the state's marine protected areas and has provided recommendations for improving their use. Of the 127 marine protected areas in Washington, none are completely protected from extraction as marine reserves. If Oregon—long considered a leader in natural resource stewardship in this country—does not take full advantage of what marine reserves can offer, what can we expect from other states in regards to ocean stewardship? What will this mean for our national commitment to marine reserves . . . to an ocean ethic?

EMBRACING AN OCEAN ETHIC

A century ago, Americans recognized the threats to spectacular and diverse places and the species inhabiting them, and resolved to protect these areas under the auspices of the National Park and later the Wilderness system. Around the same time, South Africans saw the value of taking a new approach to species recovery and natural resource management by designating what has become Kruger National Park. We are now poised to do the same with the seas.

My fervent hope is that we will be successful. I look forward to the day when you or I could slip below the surface, enter a marine reserve, and encounter a spectacular array of huge lingcod, canary rockfish, and dark-blotched rockfish, immense delicate anemones waving their tentacles, colorful tube worms feeding on tiny particles of food, brilliant sponges being fed upon by sea lemon nudibranchs, arborescent bryozoa harboring amphipods and ribbon worms, bright cup corals, ancient sea fans, and a wide array of worms slithering in and out of the sediment or tightly secured to the rock. We could easily become enthralled with the playful antics of harbor seals and sea lions cavorting or feeding, watch the furtive movements and methodical feeding of Dungeness crabs, observe a predaceous sea star stalk giant red sea urchins in slow motion, or marvel at the intricacies of the mating displays of shrimp. Walls of gigantic rock scallops interspersed with yellow, red, and green sponges, carpets of meter-long mussels, fields of ethereal sea pens, and clouds of darting fishes would be common. Forests of bull kelp would harbor shorter iridescent seaweeds, sea braid, and sea ferns that in turn would be fed upon by gumboot chitons, blue top snails, kelp crabs, and rough keyhole limpets. Algae, invertebrates, fishes, marine mammals, and seabirds would appear in dense profusion.

We would be struck with the immediate difference inside and outside the reserve, but also the greater abundance outside compared to earlier days before the reserve existed. We would know that this abundance and diversity of marine organisms signaled a healthy ecosystem that was protecting biodiversity, providing useful knowledge, seeding fisheries, supporting a diverse array of plants, microbes, herbivores, filter feeders, and predators—all essential to the provision of the full range of goods and services. We would be inspired to guarantee adequate protection from possible sources of degradation outside the reserve. We would welcome the existence of adequate upstream and downstream reserves that would function in an effective network to ensure persistence of each reserve. We would be reassured that the legacy of healthy marine ecosystems would continue into the future for the benefit and enjoyment of our children and grandchildren. And we would appreciate the foresight of those who understood the importance of protecting these treasures. ◙

Peace on the River

THE KLAMATH BASIN SETTLEMENT

Edward W. Sheets

I T was the largest crowd that anyone could remember in the Oregon Capitol; it filled the rotunda, the stairs, and balcony. After an invocation by Jeff Mitchell, the lead negotiator for the Klamath Tribes, Oregon Governor Ted Kulongoski began the ceremony by saying: "The word historic is often overused, but today we're going to sign two agreements that by everyone's definition are historic; the Klamath Basin Restoration Agreement and the Klamath Hydroelectric Settlement Agreement."

California Governor Arnold Schwarzenegger followed Kulongoski: "This historic agreement will result in the largest dam removal and river restoration project in modern history. This is a $1.5 billion project; $450 million will be paid for by the two states, by California and Oregon, for the removal of those dams, and $1 billion-plus will be paid for and invested by the federal government in order to restore this great river."

The former actor incorporated a couple of lines from his movies, saying "*Hasta la vista* to the dams on the Klamath River. . . . I can see it already, that the salmon are screaming, 'I'll be back.'"

On a more serious note, Schwarzenegger added: "And I hope that the rest of the country looks at this as a model, because there are many hundreds and hundreds if not thousands of projects that are being held up right now because those forces cannot come together and can't come to an agreement. So I urge everyone all over the country to look for that sweet spot, just like we did, and you can do it. As I've always said, protecting the environment and protecting our economy can go hand in hand, and here is a perfect example."

Secretary of the Interior Ken Salazar also called the process a model for resolving complex disputes throughout the country, providing "an unprecedented opportunity to undertake the largest river restoration project in the world. Equally as important as that great achievement will be, is the manner in which these agreements came together. They came together from sharp conflict to the cooperation that gave them their birth. Last night and today, as I have met with many of the people who have worked on this agreement, what I heard was their words, and those words tell the story. The words are about struggle, hard work, courage, partnership, and commitment."

These leaders, together with the under secretary of the Department of Commerce, Jane Lubchenco; the CEO of PacifiCorp, Greg Able; the chairmen of the Karuk, Klamath, and Yurok tribes; elected officials from Humboldt and Klamath counties and representatives from irrigation districts; and conservation and fishing groups came together to sign the Klamath Basin agreements. As this article goes to press, 45 organizations have signed on as parties.

The two agreements address the myriad issues and actions that are needed to restore one of the few rivers on the West Coast that has the potential to produce significant populations of salmon. The agreements include: 1) fisheries restoration, reintroduction, and monitoring and adaptive management programs; 2) innovative programs to increase Upper Klamath Lake levels where suckers are protected under the Endangered Species Act (ESA) and river flows for salmon that are also listed under the ESA, and for water supplies to two National Wildlife Refuges; 3) creative strategies to develop renewable resources to provide affordable electricity for the pumps that move water through the Klamath Reclamation Project and the refuges and return water to the Klamath River; 4) development of plans to address drought conditions and climate change; 5) programs to improve the stability and viability of agricultural and tribal communities; 6) a detailed process for the potential removal of four dams on the Klamath River; and 7) an agreement on the interim operations of the dams until they are removed.

Until recently, no one thought a comprehensive solution for the Klamath Basin was possible. For the last decade, major conflicts have raged through the basin, and 2001 was a terrible water year for farmers and fish. Low water levels in Upper Klamath Lake forced the U.S. Bureau of Reclamation to shut off water to farmers in the Klamath Reclamation Project to protect ESA-listed suckers, idling 200,000 acres of land. Farmers and local business suffered significant economic losses. Local farmers mounted numerous protests, and tensions among irrigators, federal agencies, Indian tribes with fishing rights in the Klamath Basin, and conservation and fishing groups ran high.

In the spring of 2002 water was restored to the farmers in the project; later that summer, high water temperatures caused a large fish die off—an estimated 33,000 salmon died. In 2006, weak salmon runs in the Klamath River forced the closure of all commercial salmon fishing on the West Coast, prompting Congress to provide economic emergency funding to fishermen that totaled $60 million.

Finally, PacifiCorp, the power company that owned four dams on the Klamath River, was going through a contentious process to renew licenses for the dams from the Federal Energy Regulatory Commission. Under that process, PacifiCorp's customers were facing significant costs for the installation of fish ladders and screens to provide safe passage so salmon could migrate past the dams; also, some groups and various state and federal agencies were urging the removal of the dams.

How did the people in the Klamath Basin move from one of the most contentious water fights in the United States to a broad-based agreement? Are there lessons that would help resolve other major natural resource issues? The themes that Secretary Salazar heard in his conversations with people in the Klamath Basin tell the story.

It started with courage. A number of people came to the conclusion that things were so bad that there had to be a better way. The protests and litigation created a lot of heat and cost time and money, but had not produced more water or more fish. Several leaders for the tribes and irrigation districts stuck their necks out and started talking to each other. As these leaders got to know and trust each other, in addition to talking, they started listening. These conversations gave them a better understanding of other communities' interests and values and their hopes and fears.

The real courage came when these leaders started looking for common ground. They concluded that any solution had to work for all of the communities in the basin. The tribes wanted their fishing restored, but did not want to put their neighbors out of business. The farmers and ranchers needed water, but also wanted the fish to survive. A recital in the Restoration Agreement summarizes it well: "The Parties have negotiated this

Agreement to achieve peace on the river and end conflict that has persisted related to the Klamath Reclamation Project."

When the draft of the Restoration Agreement was released for public review, Greg Addington, the director of the Klamath Water Users Association, said: "The result of the negotiations is a series of compromises and proposed commitments between farmers, tribes, conservationists, counties, and state and federal agencies aimed at keeping all of the Klamath's rural communities economically and ecologically viable." Troy Fletcher, the lead negotiator of the Yurok Tribe, added: "This spirit of trust, respect, and compromise is unprecedented in the Klamath Basin. This agreement will provide a path to restore fish populations and strengthen our commitment to work with each other."

The parties realized that any agreement would need support from all of the key interests in the basin. Most of these interests were already participating in the Federal Energy Regulatory Commission relicensing process for the PacifiCorp dams. As various groups discussed what to do with the dams, they also identified other actions that were needed to restore fisheries and provide more certainty for irrigators.

There were originally 28 organizations in the process to develop a framework that outlined the key elements of a settlement. Two conservation groups were not willing to accept several provisions in the framework; after several months working on ways to address their concerns, the 26 other parties decided to proceed without them. They formed the Klamath Settlement Group and hired a neutral facilitator. The facilitator helped them develop protocols, a confidentiality agreement, and a process for the negotiations. In April of 2007, the group began the long and arduous negotiations to draft the Restoration Agreement.

The parties recognized that there were mutual gains that were achievable only through settlement. To achieve these gains, negotiators had to find ways to address the critical needs of the parties. In many cases, the negotiations developed creative solutions that brought additional benefits to the table. In other cases, the parties were forced to compromise, and none of the parties got everything they wanted. This was distasteful and hard to swallow, but required to achieve the overall benefits.

Some of the innovative approaches developed for the Klamath Basin may have applications for other settlements.

The federal and state fisheries agencies, tribes, and conservation and fishing groups needed actions to improve the survival of fish in Upper

Klamath Lake and the Klamath River. The agreement includes commitments to improve habitat and water quality. It also includes a number of measures to increase the amount of water available for fish and additional storage so the water can be used when the fish need it the most. This required agreements by irrigators in the Klamath Reclamation Project to reduce their historic use, especially during dry years, and for irrigators that were not part of the federal project to agree to implement a voluntary water use retirement program.

Irrigators were seeking certainty about water supplies and pumping costs. Under the agreements, the parties will support funding to use conservation easements, forbearance agreements, conjunctive use programs, efficiency measures, land acquisitions, water acquisitions, groundwater development, groundwater substitution, and water storage to meet the water use limits for the Klamath Reclamation Project. The agreements also include provisions for the Bureau of Reclamation to become a customer of the Bonneville Power Administration to purchase federal power, and the parties will support funding for the construction of renewable resources to provide affordable electricity pumping costs.

To increase the certainty for irrigators, the Karuk, Klamath, and Yurok tribes have given interim assurances that they will not seek additional water, beyond the limits in the agreement, from the Klamath Reclamation Project. These assurances would become permanent once a number of specific provisions, including removal of the four dams, are fully implemented.

The potential removal of the dams also created uncertainty for farmers and ranchers; they were concerned that there would be additional regulatory requirements when salmon started returning to areas that have been blocked for nearly a century. The agreement includes provisions to develop and implement habitat conservation plans and other techniques available under the ESA so adequate protections will be in place when the salmon return.

The negotiations were based on science. As the negotiators worked to find common ground, the package of restoration measures was analyzed by federal, state, and tribal biologists to ensure that it was sufficient. The U.S. Fish and Wildlife Service developed a detailed analysis of the measures in the draft Restoration Agreement and Hydroelectric Settlement and concluded that the agreements would benefit the species listed under the ESA and "achieve the Agreement's stated goal of restoring the 'natural sustainability of fisheries and full participation in harvest opportunities, as well as the overall ecosystem health of the Klamath River Basin.'"

The 26 organizations released a draft of the Klamath Basin Restoration Agreement in January of 2008 for public review and comment. The groups then turned their attention to discussions with PacifiCorp.

A major issue that had to be resolved for the success of a restoration effort was the future of four dams on the Klamath River: Iron Gate, J.C. Boyle, Copco 1, and Copco 2. These dams inundate 58 miles of the river and block fish access to more than 300 miles of habitat above the dams.

PacifiCorp's priorities were to protect its customers in terms of costs and liability. Other parties wanted to ensure that removing the dams would be safe, that adverse impacts would be mitigated, and that dam removal would provide real benefits.

After lengthy negotiations, the Hydroelectric Settlement laid out the process for additional studies, environmental review, and a decision by the secretary of the Interior regarding whether removal of the dams 1) would advance restoration of the salmon in the Klamath Basin; and 2) was in the public interest, which included consideration of potential impacts on affected local communities and tribes.

The timing of dam removal also required innovative approaches. California and Oregon agreed to seek funding from a ratepayer surcharge that would provide up to $200 million (up to $184 million from PacifiCorp's Oregon consumers and up to $16 million from customers in California), and the parties agreed to limit Pacific Power customers' costs to a surcharge of less than two percent. The funding cap was the minimum of the estimated costs that ratepayers would likely incur for installing fish ladders and screens to get a new license for the dams. California also agreed to seek funding from state bonds to provide $250 million. The schedule for regulatory review, permitting, and funding resulted in a target date of 2020 for dam removal.

Another key to success was commitment. Leaders from federal and state governments, tribes, irrigation organizations, counties, and conservation and fishing groups committed to participate in the process and also provided the people and resources to see the negotiations through to conclusion.

At the federal level, the effort started with a commitment by former Secretary of the Interior Dirk Kempthorne. As governor of Idaho, he had participated in a successful effort to craft a water settlement for the Snake

River and wanted to replicate that experience. Secretary Salazar continued the commitment to the process when President Obama's administration took office in 2009. A federal team coordinated among agencies to ensure a single federal position. The team included a number of organizations within the Department of the Interior, including the secretary's office; the solicitor's office; the bureaus of Indian Affairs, Reclamation, and Land Management; and the Fish and Wildlife Service. It also included representatives from the Department of Justice, the National Marine Fisheries Service, and the Forest Service.

The governors of California and Oregon also committed to the process and appointed top officials to represent the states. State fish and wildlife, environmental, and water agencies also committed staff to participate in the negotiations. Other organizations also dedicated the necessary policy, legal, and technical resources to participate in a sustained negotiations process.

PacifiCorp had participated in settlement talks for several years during the relicensing process. When this new approach was developed, the company committed top-level executives to the negotiation process and also provided legal and technical expertise at every step of the way.

This policy-level commitment of resources by all the organizations was essential because the amount of work that went into these agreements was extraordinary. The two documents, including appendices, total 573 pages. There were difficult issues that had to be resolved on almost every page. The process to develop the agreements required 24 meetings of all the organizations; these meetings typically lasted two or three days and were attended by 50 to 100 people. There were also eight full group conference calls with 40 to 50 people participating.

Much of the work was delegated to small groups to work through each issue. There were more than 570 drafting committee and other small group meetings and conference calls to prepare specific provisions or resolve issues; some of these calls involved a few people for an hour or two, most involved 10 to 25 people for three or four hours, a number of drafting committee calls had more than 25 people and lasted six to eight hours. There were also many other meetings and calls among the parties. In addition to the hard work, this complex process required stamina, patience, and a good sense of humor.

The final key to success was professional assistance to shepherd the negotiations. The parties hired a neutral facilitator to develop the process, schedule and chair meetings and conference calls, and identify and track follow-up actions. It is often difficult for the parties in a negotiation to recognize potential areas of agreement, offer compromise language, or keep track of all of the outstanding issues. A neutral facilitator or mediator can work with the parties to help find common ground on an issue—a neutral can often hear areas of agreement and help shape acceptable language. It is also important to have someone keep the process moving; parties can get fixated on an issue and need someone to push for resolution and then move to the next set of issues.

If such a diverse group can come to a settlement on one of the most contentious set of issues in the nation, there are lessons to be learned. First, it requires leaders with the courage to recognize that the status quo is not sustainable and a willingness to reach out to others to explore solutions. Second, the parties that are essential to implementing a solution have to be willing to find common ground. Third, the parties have to commit the policy-level attention, time, and resources to see the process through. Finally, resolving complex disputes requires creativity, stamina, and a lot of patience and can often benefit from professional facilitation or mediation.

Governor Kulongoski summed it up at the signing ceremony: "To each of Oregon's partners I say you have shown the way. Conflict is not inevitable and solutions are not unreachable. All that is needed is good faith among neighbors, fair dealing, hard work and an abiding commitment to future generations. That is exactly what you have done." ▣

On Judicial Activism

Diarmuid F. O'Scannlain

No constitutional office of the United States is bestowed by the formal approval of fewer people than federal judge. The president, with a bare majority of the Senate, may appoint to the position anyone he chooses. The entire process requires the concurrence of a mere fifty-two individuals. Picking a judge may seem easy, but its consequences can be complex and surprising indeed.

Under Article III of the Constitution, which establishes the judicial branch of the United States government, a federal judge serves during "good Behaviour." By tradition, this means life tenure, unless impeached for "high Crimes and Misdemeanors" by a majority of the House of Representatives and convicted by at least two thirds of the Senate. Although thousands of men and women have served as federal judges over the course of the nation's history, fewer than ten have been expelled from office. Fewer than twenty have even been impeached. As a practical matter, federal judges are rarely called to answer for their performance on the job.

As difficult as they are to remove, federal judges are equally difficult to demote. Article III explicitly prohibits the diminishment of a judge's salary while in office, no matter how errant—or delinquent or unpopular—his or her decisions may be. On the whole, judges are easily the most independent constitutional officers.

How can it be that such government officials enjoy substantial power yet effectively answer neither to the people nor to Congress? The very touchstone of a democratic republic, after all, is that the exercise of power reflects the will of the people as inferred from electoral results. Could it be argued that federal judges are delegates of elected officials and, therefore, indirectly delegates or agents of the people? This argument is based on the notion that the procedure for appointing judges resembles a sort of delegation. An individual is screened and selected (by the president) to perform a specific task (judging). The analogy between judges and delegates does not seem particularly apt, however. An agent is generally conceived of as acting on the behalf of, or pursuant to the direction of, his master.

A judge, however, is not expected to act on any person's behalf or pursuant to anyone's direction. Indeed, he must do precisely the opposite in his official role, spurning not only personal affinities but all communication outside of the courtroom. Even if we were to conceive of a judge as a peculiar kind of agent, one that is charged with acting without concern for his master, the judge-as-agent could be brought to heel by his master when he is derelict in his duties, however they are framed. That is, the judge would be subject to effective oversight. Nevertheless, it is exactly the lack of oversight that makes the judicial office remarkable. If judges fit easily into the framework of the democratic republic, it is not because they are indirectly representative of the popular will.

In my view, judges fit into our democratic framework not because they choose to exercise their power in popular ways but because they do not actually exercise personal power at all. Alexander Hamilton captured this idea succinctly with his observation that federal judges have neither force nor will, only judgment. Unlike executing the law, which is the president's role, or making the law, which is the Congress's, judging is a passive process. A judge confronts the law as it is written and the facts as they have been placed in evidence. His power may be great over the parties before him, but almost none of it—if exercised properly—can be exerted to advance a judge's own objectives. It is to guarantee this neutrality that he is given independence.

Consider a criminal case. Congress enacts a statute that makes certain conduct a crime and provides a punishment. Someone violates that law. The attorney general, who is the president's appointee, then prosecutes. Only upon the confluence of these events does the judge become involved. With the government and the defendant before him, the judge evaluates whether the specific acts committed by the defendant fall within the ambit of the statute. Whereas the Congress had broad latitude in formulating the substance of the statute, and the president and his officers had significant discretion in their selection of targets and enforcement strategies, the judge has almost no discretion over the course and outcome of the prosecution. If the law has been correctly enforced against the defendant, the judge must announce the defendant's conviction; conversely, if the law has not been correctly enforced against the defendant, the judge must acquit.

The role of the judge is thus limited to determining whether the law has been enforced "correctly." This determination is traditionally conceptualized as having two elements. First, the relevant facts must be wholly and accurately established; second, the law must be faithfully applied to the relevant facts. The skeptic will wonder how it is that the judge can be thought to be any more intrinsically "accurate" or "faithful" than the prosecutor who comes before him. That is a fair question, and it gets to the heart of the role of the judge. Those terms are meant to depict the consequences of the decision-making process rather than any metaphysical qualities of the decisions themselves. That is, judicial determinations are presumed to be accurate and faithful exactly because they are made by someone acting solely as a judge: a person who is new to the dispute (and thus without any vested interest in the outcome) is drawing conclusions through due process of law in the context of an open and adversarial presentation (in contrast to a one-sided investigation), and is independent (not answerable to the president or Congress).

This presumption, it should be emphasized, does not rest on some unsubstantiated premise that judicial decisions are by their nature good decisions. That is to say, the argument is not that a decision is "good" because it is made by someone who acts like a judge; rather, a decision is "good" because it is made within an accuracy-enhancing procedure, and judicial decisions also tend to be "good" because that same procedure is the one that judges use. The Supreme Court has expressly acknowledged that the marginal improvement secured by this procedure can have constitutional significance even in the context of decisions that are not traditionally reserved to judges. In the 1970 case of *Goldberg v. Kelly*, the Supreme Court concluded that a state could not constitutionally terminate benefits to a welfare recipient without an adversarial hearing. In prescribing the indispensable elements of the constitutionally mandated pre-termination proceeding, the court stated:

The fundamental requisite of due process of law is the opportunity to be heard. The hearing must be "at a meaningful time and in a meaningful manner." In the present context these principles require that a recipient have timely and adequate notice detailing the reasons for a proposed termination, and an effective opportunity to defend by confronting any adverse witnesses and by presenting his own arguments and evidence orally. These rights are important in cases such as those before us, where recipients have challenged proposed terminations as resting on incorrect or misleading factual premises or on misapplication of rules or policies to the facts of particular cases.

The Supreme Court's observations underscore the importance of several attributes that are intrinsic to judicial decision-making but typically absent from executive and legislative decision-making: a neutral arbiter, written notice to the concerned parties, confrontation of adverse witnesses, and opportunity for oral argument. Unsurprisingly, the Court found these attributes to be critical when rules are applied to "the facts of particular cases."

The constitutional underpinnings of the Supreme Court's decision in *Goldberg v. Kelly* remind us of an essential element of the judicial inquiry into whether the law has been faithfully applied. Judges must consider not just the relevant statute whose vindication the executive specifically seeks, but also the procedural and substantive provisions of law that protect individuals from governmental misconduct and overreaching. In short, judges must ensure that the statute at issue does not, in either its enactment or its enforcement, invade that sphere of constitutional liberty preserved for the individual.

Law and liberty will inevitably conflict. Every individual at his liberty may do anything he is physically capable of doing. An individual under the law, however, may do only what the law has not proscribed, and this will certainly be less than what the individual might otherwise do. Thus, an individual cannot enjoy absolute liberty under the rule of law.

In this light, the rule of law seems distinctly unattractive. Even in that most salubrious of states, the democratic republic, absolute liberty is lost—subsumed to the will of one's community. The loss of some liberty, however, can improve the value of the remainder. As Thomas Hobbes persuasively observed some three hundred and fifty years ago, too much liberty results not in happiness but in despair:

During the time men live without a common power to keep them all in awe, they are in that condition which is called war, and such a war as is of every man against every man. . . .

In such condition there is no place for industry, because the fruit thereof is uncertain: and consequently no culture of the earth; no navigation nor use of the commodities that may be imported by sea; no commodious building; no instruments of moving and removing such things as require much force; no knowledge of the face of the earth; no account of time; no arts; no letters; no society; and, which is worst of all, continual fear and danger of violent death; and the life of man solitary, poor, nasty, brutish, and short.

In the face of such a prospect, we are only too happy to surrender some of our liberty to law. We continue to wonder, however, just how much liberty we should be surrendering. Too much liberty results in life that is "nasty, brutish, and short," but, as the lives of people in the totalitarian states of the twentieth century made painfully clear, too much law is no better.

One can view the guarantees of individual rights in the Constitution as our nation's documented consensus on where to draw the limits of law. At the Founding, we viewed the Constitution and the Bill of Rights as constraining the scope of the national government almost exclusively. That government, imperious and remote, seemed more likely to capitalize upon our collective abdication of individual liberty in a way that would degrade our lives rather than enhance them. We were understandably loath to abdicate too much.

At the same time, however, we left to the states relatively unfettered authority to intrude into spheres that we now consider inviolably personal. Most states lacked provisions analogous to the federal Bill of Rights. Our consensus on the appropriate limits of the law changed, however, by the end of the Civil War. During Reconstruction, congressional Republicans sought to prevent the reemergence of the sort of oppressive state law that had been increasingly relied upon to prop up slavery in the ante-bellum South. The Republicans thus proposed and spearheaded the ratification of the Fourteenth Amendment, whose terms imposed upon the states most of the provisions of the Bill of Rights. As a result, the line between law and liberty encroached further on the power of the state and gave individual liberty a wider scope.

The constitutional compromise between law and liberty has always been subject to dispute. Many people believe that the government is much more substantially limited in what it may do than is apparent on the face of the Constitution. Others contend the opposite. Occasionally, the dispute has resulted in the revision of the Constitution, as with the Fourteenth Amendment; most of the time, however, no such revision has occurred. In discharging his duty to determine whether the law has been faithfully applied, the judge in any given case must prevent a partisan in the dispute from getting the upper hand. In short, the judge must defend the constitutional compromise between law and liberty as memorialized in the text of the Constitution itself. To alter the compromise (or to allow it to be altered) is not faithfully to apply the Constitution but to amend it—to usurp a power reposed exclusively in the people of the United States.

Preserving the constitutional compromise between law and liberty requires federal judges to defer to the legislative and executive branches on all issues properly within the realm of the law. If the text of the Constitution does not preclude the government's action, the judge must uphold it. He must do so even if the government's action is patently unfair or plainly inappropriate, for determining that something is "unfair" or "inappropriate" without an independent standard for fairness or appropriateness requires an exercise of sheer will. And the power to direct government action pursuant to one's own will is precisely the power that a judge lacks.

The judge's duty to apply the law faithfully demands that he do more than merely defer to the political branches of government when they permissibly exercise governmental power. The very concept of law requires the judge to apply it in a manner that is both predictable and uniform. Predictability ensures that everyone knows what the law is at any given point in time. Uniformity ensures that the law is applied in the same way by any judge to any party anywhere in the country.

When a judge is swayed by his own sentiment rather than considerations of deference, predictability, and uniformity, he fails by definition to apply the law faithfully. This is the essence of judicial activism. It is impossible to say with certainty in any given case that the judge's sentiments will lead him to a "bad" decision, but no one could say that they never would. Any of us would appreciate a judge's merciful departure from a draconian law. How many of us, though, would appreciate a judge's draconian departure from a merciful law? The remedy for a bad law is to change the law through legislative action, not to depart from it one way or the other in the courts. The solution, in short, is democracy—the political process—and not judicial activism.

Judicial activism is not always easily detected, because the critical elements of judicial activism either are subjective or defy clear and concrete definition. For instance, a critical consideration is the state of mind of the allegedly activist judge. Judicial activism means not the mere failure to defer to political branches or to vindicate norms of predictability and uniformity; it means only the failure to do so in order to advance another, unofficial objective. Occasionally, the fact that a judge has an ulterior motive is evident, but oftentimes it is not. We are left to infer the existence of an ulterior motive from the relative distances that separate the judge's actual decision from the decision that would have been correct and the one that would have most perfectly accorded with the judge's personal sentiments. This gives rise to another difficulty in detecting judicial activism, which is that we must establish a noncontroversial benchmark by which to evaluate how far from the "correct" decision the supposedly activist judge has strayed. Occasionally this, too, is easy—but not always. Because of the inherent difficulty in detecting judicial activism with any certainty, many activist decisions may pass without significant criticism and many others may be labeled by particularly sensitive commentators as "activist" when they are not.

Perhaps the most notorious instance of judicial activism is captured in the century-old Supreme Court case, *Rector of the Holy Trinity Church v. United States*. Congress had enacted a statute declaring that:

> it shall be unlawful . . . in any manner whatsoever, to prepay the transportation, or in any way assist or encourage the importation or migration, of any alien . . . into the United States . . . to perform labor or service of any kind.

Because the defendant church had contracted with an English clergyman to come to New York City to serve as rector, the government brought suit under this statute. Both the trial and appellate courts ruled that the church had violated the law. The Supreme Court disagreed. After observing that "this is a Christian nation," Justice Brewer reached the remarkable conclusion for the court that religious ministry could not have been the "labor or service of any kind" that Congress had intended to proscribe.

Justice Brewer plainly thought, and all of his brethren agreed, that his departure from the statute did nothing but benefit the American people. Even if it was well received at the time, the court's characterization of the country might not be so benignly received today, particularly as the basis for departing from a statute duly enacted by our democratically elected representatives.

The problem with the court's decision was that it undermined the predictability and uniformity of the law. Before the Supreme Court ruled, the statute was clear; afterward, no one could predict its true scope. Moreover, lower courts would now be free to apply whatever exemptions they, too, thought Congress might have intended, regardless of the language Congress actually enacted.

Judicial activism can have consequences that are far more profound than the unregulated immigration of nineteenth-century English rectors. When applied not simply to arcane statutes but to the United States Constitution—the foundational document of our Republic—judicial activism inevitably works a seismic shift in the balance between government and individual and has often done so on divisive questions.

Take, for example, the question of whether an individual's decision to end his own life is beyond the power of the government to regulate. After the people of the state of Washington rejected the ballot measure at the polls, several Washington residents brought suit and invited judges to give them what the legislative process would not: a governmentally enforceable right to assisted suicide. The United States Court of Appeals for the Ninth Circuit, which includes Washington and eight other western states, eventually ruled for the plaintiffs, declaring that the Constitution guaranteed each of them a "right to die."

This decision, though purportedly compelled by the federal Constitution, rested upon nothing written in that document. Eight judges of the eleven-judge panel hearing the case simply promulgated a new constitutional right, one unheard of in over two hundred years of American history. The Supreme Court, in *Washington v. Glucksberg*, recognized the Ninth Circuit's decision for the rejection of democracy that it was and unanimously reversed, but not before rivers of ink had flowed in celebration or condemnation of a judgment that seemed intrinsically more political than judicial.

Perhaps the outcome reached by the Ninth Circuit was the better policy; arguably someone who is terminally ill and wants to end his life really should not have to act alone. It is certain that many people other than the plaintiffs in the *Glucksberg* case thought so. Even if it were true, which seems rather difficult to ascertain in any objective sense, this belief does not establish that the court made the right decision, because the court was wrong to make the decision at all.

Readers who resist this conclusion need only look at the experience of the people of Oregon. Unlike their northern neighbors, a majority of Oregonians went to the polls only a couple of years later and enacted a law giving a terminally ill individual the right to physician-assisted suicide. Nevertheless, just like their northern neighbors, the people of Oregon were rebuked by a federal court declaring that they had overstepped the scope of governmental authority. In that case, entitled *Lee v. Oregon*, a federal judge held that in his view there was "no set of facts" in which Oregon's newly enacted assisted suicide law could be considered "rational." That conclusion must have come as quite a surprise to the thousands upon thousands of Oregonians who voted for the law. Surely, the conclusion must have unsettled the view of the eight Ninth Circuit judges who had previously joined together in declaring that the Constitution *guaranteed* the very right to assisted suicide that the same Constitution was now being read to preclude the people of Oregon from enacting. This uncomfortable tension was resolved when the Ninth Circuit reversed the *Lee* decision and returned the issue of assisted suicide once again to the realm of political discourse, where it belongs.

Even for someone who cares not a whit about whether an individual has the right to assistance in committing suicide, these cases underscore the problems that arise when judges purport to apply the law but fail to apply it faithfully—the problems, that is, of judicial activism. The first of these problems is, of course, that our democratic republic descends into what Thomas Jefferson famously reviled as "oligarchy." The will of one judge or a handful is substituted for the will of the popular majority—or, at the very least, the political representatives elected by and accountable to that majority. Moreover, because judges exert their will, when they do, by pronouncements applied retroactively in individual cases rather than by codified statutes or rules, the resulting "law" lacks not only democratic validity but predictability and uniformity as well. Decisions that manifest judicial activism do not, in short, amount to what we think of as "law" at all.

When it involves constitutional interpretation, judicial activism presents a unique additional problem. A judicially active interpretation of the Constitution shifts the dividing line between government power and individual liberty. That judge-made shift, unless subsequently repudiated by the Supreme Court, can be remedied only by a constitutional amendment. Ratification of such an amendment, which requires supermajorities at both federal and state levels, is arduous by design and, when undertaken, is rarely successful. The consequence of all of this is that judicial decisions redefining individual liberties distort the delicate balance of power between the branches of government. What Congress could once do by the relatively straightforward process of statutory enactment, it can thereafter do only by discharging the Herculean task of constitutional amendment.

Not only does judicial activism in whatever form hobble the political branches of government, it also undermines the judiciary itself. Courts, lacking the power to enforce their own judgments, rely on popular confidence in those judgments for their implementation. Judicial activism erodes this confidence and thereby erodes the efficacy of the judiciary as a whole. One need not look far to find the breakdown of confidence in, and resulting threat to the independence of, judicial decision-making. By far the most famous such incident occurred with the advent of the New Deal in the 1930s. Franklin Delano Roosevelt had been elected president after campaigning on the promise of federal relief from the widespread economic dislocation accompanying the Great Depression. Upon his inauguration, President Roosevelt proposed and, with the assent of the Congress, enacted into law an unprecedented program of economic reform. After the Supreme Court invalidated several popular statutes at the core of the president's program, the President pursued a plan to "pack" the Supreme Court. He proposed to increase its membership so that he could appoint enough new Justices to win a majority in future cases. The plan was never executed because, faced with this threat, the Supreme Court relented and upheld subsequent legislation. It thus appeared that the Supreme Court very nearly became the casualty of its own judicial activism.

Far from being merely a product of the exigencies of the Great Depression, political assaults on specific judicial decisions still occur. In the last presidential election, both parties' nominees openly criticized a federal trial judge in New York for his refusal to admit as evidence in a drug prosecution large amounts of cocaine seized by law enforcement officers. After President Clinton suggested on the campaign trail that the judge might resign his office, the judge reconsidered his ruling and reversed it. This incident, like the Supreme Court's about-face sixty years earlier, raises the disturbing specter of judicial decision-making by popular will, and the fear that our judges might have become little more than politicians in robes.

What lesson can we learn from these experiences? Judicial activism generates a vicious cycle: it triggers a lack of confidence in judicial decisions which triggers political meddling which reinforces a lack of confidence in judicial decisions. A politician in robes is no judge at all. Once a judge imposes his will as legislator, he loses his democratic legitimacy. No one person in a democratic society of 270 million citizens should wield legislative power if only fifty-two people have approved of him. A judge who wields power like a politician enters the political process. Having forsaken neutrality, he will soon lose his independence. The people will allow a judge to be independent only for as long as they perceive him as truly neutral—forsaking decisions based upon his own interests and biases.

Thus, judicial activism encourages political interference both in the process of judging and selection of judges. One need look no further than the battle between the White House and the Senate over judicial nominees for a glimpse of the extent to which the judicial appointments process has become politicized. Nor does the threat of political interference end after the judge is selected. A multitude of proposals have been offered in Congress to weaken the independence of the judiciary. Some take the form of constitutional amendments to impose term limits on judges; others have been nothing more sophisticated than calls for the impeachment of particular judges who have rendered unpopular decisions. These may be only harbingers of what is to come.

Fortunately, judges retain—at least for now—their independence to apply the law neutrally and faithfully. But so long as one judge indulges his own sympathies rather than following the text of the law before him, he will only make it harder for his colleagues to retain the courage to decide cases in faithful, predictable, and uniform ways. ▣

FIRE AND WATER

Kathleen Dean Moore

I HAD always thought that when I died, my children would scatter my ashes under the pines beside Davis Lake, where we have camped for twenty years. But it's all ashes there now. Wildfire flared up along the road behind the east campground. Driven by 25-mile-an-hour winds, the firestorm charged across the road and ran hard and fast through miles of lodgepole pines, torching the manzanita and exploding into the crowns of the trees. Fire crews pulled back and let it burn; what else could they do with the fire roaring around them?

For two weeks, heavy smoke and unpredictable winds closed the roads into Davis Lake. Helpless, I watched on the Internet as the fire expanded, red spots encircling the lake until the whole map was blotchy red. But as soon as fire crews cleared the trees that had fallen across the road and removed the barricades, I headed for Davis Lake, driving the Cascades Highway through a healthy forest of ponderosa pines.

Car windows down, I can smell the thick beds of pine needles, warm and sweet in the sun. Ponderosas rise from meadows of green grass, blue sagebrush, currants already turning orange. Then suddenly the color is gone. For miles in front of me, all I see is a blanket of white ash stuck through with tree trunks, broken and black, and the shadow of a raven swerving between spars. A thin line of smoke rises from a smoldering stump. I pull onto the side of the road, step out into ashes, and listen.

I had loved the sound of Davis Lake in the spring. I remember waking early one morning, years ago, under pines at the edge of the lake. As Frank and our little ones breathed quietly beside me, great blue herons flapped over the marshland, croaking. Red-breasted nuthatches called from the pines. Coots splashed in circles, and sandhill cranes clattered on the far side of the lake, leaping and flapping their wings in a clumsy dance. I remember how the frogs shouted that morning, filling the air like a cheering crowd. In a pine far down the lake, fledgling eaglets begged without ceasing, a scraping sound like pebbles against steel. I had settled deeper in my sleeping bag, warm and grateful.

But now the silence is so complete that I brush my ears to be sure I can still hear. Finally a raven calls. A single grasshopper scratches in black stubble. The wind lifts slender whirlwinds from the ashes. But without pine needles to make music of the wind, even the whirlwinds are silent. I stand with my head back and my eyes closed, trying to understand how it could be so suddenly gone—the green singing life of this place.

I'm a philosopher by trade, so I should know how to be philosophical about loss. The world is in flux, and change is the only constant. Forests are no exception; they grow and burn and grow again. I know this. Everybody knows it. Almost three thousand years ago, the Greek philosopher Heraclitus acknowledged the necessity of change: You can't step into the same river twice, he said. But why not? I want to know. Why can't what is beautiful last forever?

Everything has to change, Heraclitus answered, because all the world is fire and water in constant conflict. Fire advances and is quenched by water. Water floods and is boiled away by fire. And so people wake and sleep, live and die, the fires of their spirits steaming against the dampness of their flesh. Summer changes into winter, as sun gives way to rain. The mountains boil up from the seas, and the seas come into being and pass away. Forests are reduced to ashes, and from the ashes rise new forests, damp and shining.

How easy it is to write these words, so good in theory. But in fact, the only thing rising from the ashes today are the whirlwinds. A pickup rumbles to the side of the road. A man steps out, inhales sharply, then turns to his buddy. "Look at those huge big dirt-devils," he says. The two of them stand without speaking, watching ashes lift in thin spiraling threads and flatten against the sun.

One August evening maybe fifteen years ago, Frank and I crouched on the beach with our children, thrilled and terrified. We flinched each time lightning struck the forested ridge three miles across Davis Lake. A thunderous crack, a flash of light that turned our eyelids blue. Then a flame flickered on the ridge and a thin tendril of smoke rose into the air. Lightning struck into the forest again and again until the hillside was dotted with little flames, each with its trail of smoke, like candles on a birthday cake.

The moon rose, flaky and red. As the lightning moved slowly away over the lava ridge, flashing silently above the eastern plains, Frank tucked the children into their sleeping bags, then sat by the tent, watching across the lake. I launched a canoe onto water that pooled red around my bow. Every pull of my paddle spun off a ruddy spiral and vibrated the lake into red and purple ripples. I could smell smoke and water, damp algae on the shore. Gradually, as I rocked in my boat, black clouds drifted over the face of the moon, and water licked in the reeds. Soft rain fell, ticking on water that faded from red to gray, and one by one, those little fires went out.

Water won that round. But I knew that fire's time would come.

For eighty years, lodgepole pines have grown up thick as doghair on the flats around Davis Lake. A person deliberately laying a fire in that forest couldn't have done a better job than the trees did themselves. Pile kindling under each tree—stacks of downed branches, hard and silver and scratchy. Sprinkle the kindling with dry pine needles. Drape branches into the kindling so any ground fire is sure to climb the tree. Let the forest bake in the sun and the drying wind. Then all it takes is a spark—dry lightning, a Bic lighter, an ATV.

Lodgepole pines need to burn. It's the earliest science lesson I remember.

When I was growing up in Cleveland, somebody mailed my father a shoebox crammed with lodgepole pine cones. Although he had never seen a lodgepole forest, my father had read of these western trees in biology books and the journals of Lewis and Clark. So as my sisters and I jostled around him, he spread the cones on a cookie sheet and baked them in the oven. We watched through the oven door, marveling as the cones bloomed like roses in the heat, releasing papery seeds.

My father handed each of us a seed, and together we admired this wonder: how the cones stay on the trees for years, tight as fists, until fire warms the resin that holds them shut and they release the seeds to replant the burned-out forest—a forest made in just such a way that the very fire that destroys it will create it anew.

So I can understand the battles between water and fire, cycles of living and dying, the urgent necessity of death, all of us designed to die—just exactly that—everything we love designed to die, as the lodgepole pine forest is made to burn. I can understand this in my mind, but how will understanding ease this loss?

Davis Lake has always been a lesson in the cycles of living and dying. One year, the water in Davis Lake rises so high it floods into the trees. In a year like that, the whole valley shimmers—a gleaming bowl, alive with trout and mayflies. Another year, the water is so low that the creek winds almost a mile across a playa to the clouded eye of the shrunken lake. Fishermen call each other to find out the lake level. "Where's Davis Lake this year?" they ask. It's always a disappointment when the lake's too low to launch a boat, but the water always comes back.

Snow falls on the mountains above Davis Lake, melts, and trickles through the porous rock, making its way—maybe in a matter of months, maybe in a year—through the mountain to the springs that feed the lake. But as water pours into Davis Lake, water flows out through the lava dam and lake bed. Canoeing over shallow water, you can see the funnels, the "suck holes," my family calls them, where water spirals into cracks in the lava, like water down the drain. This terrifies me, to float above the place where water drains into prehistoric darkness and a silence unbroken and complete, as if the silence could suck a person down before she's ready to go.

You can say that it's all a natural process, that the appearances and disappearances are all the result of cycles working themselves out over time. A lodgepole pine forest isn't merely the place that shelters my tent; it's a process of growth and change—trees transforming themselves to ashes to green seedlings to barren spars to seeds on the wind. The lake isn't only a place where my children float with blue dragonflies. It's a stream of water that flows from light on the mountaintops to the long, dark caves, emerging into the blue lake and plunging into the dark again like a serpent that has no end. And what is a human life but a new arrangement of molecules that once were stars?

You can say that it's something particularly human: this tendency to misunderstand natural change as unsupportable loss. You can say that sorrow is part of the same arrogance, the same self-centeredness that leads humans to measure time by the span of their own lives, to define what is real by their own needs.

If I could step outside my own life span and purposes, then maybe I could make myself believe that the difference between a natural disaster and a natural cycle is only a matter of time. Aldo Leopold advised his readers to think like a mountain—on that timescale. A mountain wouldn't mourn the loss of a forest any more or less than a human mourns the leaves that twist off an oak in autumn.

But how can I think like a mountain? Tell me: Does a mountain feel its scree slipping to its feet, or hear sand sliding ceaselessly down its flank?

All the back roads into Davis Lake are closed by barricades and striped tape. But the assistant fire manager for the Deschutes National Forest, Gary Morehead, agrees to drive me in. I pull on the yellow, fire-resistant suit he hands me. Then he shoves his truck into gear and steers it around the first barricade.

We follow a dusty track through a landscape of black tree trunks stuck at every angle to the ashes. Here's where cats bulldozed a clearing in the forest, Gary tells me, a safety zone where firefighters could retreat if the flames turned on them. Here's where the force of the fire-generated wind snapped every tree and sent it crashing into flames. Here in the ashes of the campground is a fire ring, solid and ironic, and the bent frame of a lawn chair, tossed on its head.

The fire created a wind so fierce, Gary says, that it threw a canoe into a tree, and drove flames against it until the canoe melted over the branches. The fire vaporized two spotted owl nests; too young to fly, the young owls surely died. And the firestorm sucked the eagles' nest out of the tree.

I trudge along the edge of the lake. Where, in ashes turned violet by the ferocity of the fire, is the place where I lay on pine needles with our newborn son, pointing out yellow-rumped warblers and chickadees? I want to find the shallow reed bed where Jonathan, grown into a toddler, waded after minnows; before we could convince him to leave the water, his legs were streaked with leeches. I wanted to find the place where Erin wove tule reeds into a little cubbyhole, crawled in, and read Dr. Seuss, tracking the words with her finger. Could it be here, in this empty space, that Frank and I drank wine at a picnic table, talking about our kids gone off to college, until stars popped out spangling in the pines like lights on a Christmas tree?

One year this ground was covered with toads. Another year, it was baby garter snakes and buttercups. Now, the ground is covered with black stubble burned right to the water. I stand beside the cove where Frank and I rode the canoe back to shore on a windy day. I remember the cool wind, the bucking canoe, the exhilaration, the wheeling eagles, but all I can see is the lake calmly reflecting the devastation of this place, just sitting there, as if all that life—all those precious, irreplaceable times—hadn't roared into flames and vanished forever.

I ask Gary if we can go to the headwaters of Ranger Creek, where I remember a spring that flowed out of the mountainside and made its way through flowered meadows to Davis Lake. He's reluctant to go there, not sure if the place has been secured. But he circles the truck around the yellow tape and brings us slowly through the ashes to what was once a willow flat at a bend in the creek.

I'm surprised by what I see. Stumps are still smoldering, two weeks after the fire. But already, new grass has grown four inches high, green as frogs. The willow thickets have burned down to blackened stubs that reach up like a hand extending from the ground—the black fingers as short as my own. But inside each hand, as if spiraling from a wound in the palm, is new growth, the coiled leaves unfurling. There are birds here, osprey, soaring over the water, watching for trout.

The springs surge from the barren ground into a burst of green, shimmering and miraculous in that field of grey. Trees have fallen over the creek and burned in from both ends, but between the banks, the tree trunks are intact, shading the water, shaded themselves by tall green rushes. Wherever water reaches into the ashes, plants grow—rosy spirea, cinquefoil yellow as buttercups, and sweet bracken fern.

What is this world, that it has all these things—the dead and dying forest, the charred bones of young owls, and water pouring from the earth, ancient snow finally emerging from darkness and flowing into the great expanse of blue? What is this world, that life and death can merge so perfectly that even though I search at the edge of water, I can't find the place where death ends and life begins?

I am standing here, in all my color, the blue veins in my elbows, the reddened skin on my knuckles, my fireman's yellow suit; standing here in all my noise, the breath in and out, the wind flapping my collar. But some day my children will bring my ashes, grey and silent, to be caught up in a dirt-devil that makes no noise at all. And where will the color be then, and the sound of a person breathing? This silence, so hard to understand.

In Heraclitus's world of constant change, don't we all yearn for some pause in the river, an eddy, where the water slows and circles back upstream for a long, calm time before it rejoins the flow? This is what Davis Lake was for me—a quiet circle of the seasons, a place where the world seemed to come to rest. A place my family could return, year after year, as the cranes returned, as the water returned, and the yellow blooms of the bitterbrush. The constancy of the lake had reassured me, the reliable circle of life.

But in this greening place of ashes and springs, I begin to understand that time cannot move in a circle, coming again to where it was before. Time sweeps in a spiral, going round and round again—the cycles of the seasons, the flow of the cold springs, the growth of a forest or a child, but never returns to the same place.

And shouldn't I be grateful for this? That birds will nest in the Davis Lake basin, even though that particular pair of owlets will never fly again. Trees will grow beside the creek, as my grandchildren will grow on the green-banked stream. Willow thickets will tremble with morning ice, the songs of red-winged blackbirds, the slow unfolding of next year's dragonfly's wings. And we who love this world will tremble with the beauty of the spiral that has brought us here and the mystery of the spiral that will carry us away. ▣

CONTRIBUTORS

BRUCE BABBITT served as attorney general of Arizona, governor of Arizona, and secretary of the Department of the Interior. As governor, he steered to passage the Arizona Groundwater Management Act of 1980, which remains the most comprehensive water regulatory system in the nation, and created the Arizona Department of Water Resources, the Arizona Department of Environmental Quality, and a major expansion of the state park system. As secretary of the Interior, he led in the creation of the Pacific Northwest forest plan, the restoration of the Florida Everglades, the passage of the California Desert Protection Act, and legislation for the National Wildlife Refuge system. He pioneered the use of habitat conservation plans under the Endangered Species Act and worked to create 22 national monuments. Babbitt is the author of *Cities in the Wilderness* and is perhaps best remembered by American schoolchildren as the person who brought the wolves back to Yellowstone National Park. He now works on conservation issues in the Amazon Basin as a fellow of the Blue Moon Fund.

RICHARD P. BENNER spent twelve years as a staff attorney for 1000 Friends of Oregon, working primarily on coastal and resource issues. In 1987, as the first executive director of the Columbia River Gorge Commission, he directed the commission's preparation and adoption of a management plan for the National Scenic Area. From 1991 to 2001, he served as director of the Oregon Department of Land Conservation and Development and is currently the senior attorney for Metro, the nation's only popularly elected regional government.

LINDA BESANT is a writer and dance aficionada who left nonprofit administration to begin writing in 1993. In addition to *Open Spaces*, her work has appeared in *Wilderness Magazine, Fireweed*, and *Manzanita Quarterly*. The love for dance that led her to take a ballet class as an adult beginner has evolved into an "encore career" as dance historian and lecturer at the Oregon Ballet Theatre in Portland.

EMORY BUNDY was director of public affairs for King Broadcasting Company and director of the Bullitt Foundation. He has won national and international awards for his public service documentaries that promote understanding of environmental and economic issues. A bicycle commuter since 1973, he is co-chair of Citizens for Mobility and a board member of Sane Transit.

JOHN DANIEL, born in South Carolina and raised in the suburbs of Washington, D.C., has lived in the West since attending Reed College in Portland, Oregon. He worked as a logger, railroad inspector, rock-climbing instructor, and hod carrier before beginning to write poetry and prose in the 1970s while living on a ranch in south-central Oregon. In 1982, Daniel received a Wallace Stegner Fellowship in Poetry at Stanford University. He is the author of two poetry collections, *Common Ground* and *All Things Touched by Wind*, and several works of nonfiction, including *The Trail Home, Rogue River Journal: A Winter Alone*, and *Looking After: A Son's Memoir*, about caring for his mother as she declined with Alzheimer's. His latest book is *The Far Corner: Northwestern Views on Land, Life, and Literature*. Daniel won two Oregon Book Awards for Literary Nonfiction, the Pacific Northwest Booksellers Award, and a fellowship from the National Endowment for the Arts. He is the chair of PEN Northwest and on the board of Literary Arts. He lives with his wife Marilyn in the Coast Range foothills west of Eugene, Oregon.

BOB DAVISON and JEFF CURTIS have been involved with conservation issues and the Endangered Species Act for over 30 years. Davison, who holds a Ph.D. in wildlife science, was deputy assistant secretary for Fish and Wildlife and Parks in the Department of the Interior, staffed the U.S. Senate Environment and Public Works Committee, and worked for several national wildlife conservation organizations. He now lives in Corvallis, Oregon, where he teaches in the Department of Fisheries and Wildlife at Oregon State University. Curtis served as counsel to the U.S. House of Representatives Subcommittee on Fisheries, Wildlife and the Environment; deputy director of the Oregon Department of Fish and Wildlife; and director of WaterWatch of Oregon. He is the western conservation director for Trout Unlimited.

SANDRA DORR lives in canyon country near Grand Junction, Colorado, where she directs the Western Colorado Writers' Forum, a community writing center. Her latest book is *Desert Water*, a collection of poetry. She is writing a novel set on the Oregon coast in August, high berry season.

ANGUS DUNCAN is the founding president of the Bonneville Environmental Foundation, a nonprofit business venture that supports watershed restoration in the Pacific Northwest and generates revenues from renewable energy projects and retail sales of carbon-offsetting Green Tags. Duncan represented three Oregon governors on the four-state Northwest Power Planning Council from 1989 to 1995 and chaired the council in 1995. He has also worked in private-sector renewable energy project development and was the director of energy policy for the U.S. Department of Transportation. In 2004, Duncan chaired the committee that wrote Oregon's Climate Change Strategy; and in 2006, he chaired the governor's committee that designed an Oregon carbon emissions cap-and-trade mechanism. He is chair of Oregon's Global Warming Commission and a member of the Governor's State Energy Policy Council.

DAVID JAMES DUNCAN is the author of *The River Why, The Brothers K,* and several works of nonfiction. His work won a Lannan Fellowship, a Western States Book Award for Nonfiction, and the American Library Association's Award (with Wendell Berry) for the Preservation of Intellectual Freedom. Duncan is a contributing editor to *Orion* magazine, and his writing appears in three volumes of *Best American Spiritual Writing*. He lives with his wife, sculptor Adrian Arleo, and their family on a western Montana trout stream.

TOM GRANT, a widely known jazz pianist from Portland, has toured with jazz greats such as saxophonist Joe Henderson and drummer Tony Williams. In the 1980s, his records were a staple of Smooth Jazz, and many of his records were jazz radio hits. Grant has toured the world with his band and continues to record and play to enthusiastic audiences.

STEPHEN L. HARRIS, a professor emeritus at California State University, Sacramento, has published a dozen books, including *Classical Mythology: Images and Insight*, *The New Testament: A Student's Introduction*, *Understanding the Bible*, and *Fire Mountains of the West*. He is a graduate of the University of Puget Sound in Tacoma and received his Ph.D. from Cornell University.

DENIS HAYES is a practical visionary who has devoted his career to promoting environmental values through politics, law, and the written word. At the age of 25, he was the national coordinator for the first Earth Day. He directed the National Renewable Energy Laboratory and was a visiting scholar at the Woodrow Wilson Center, a senior fellow at the Worldwatch Institute, adjunct professor of engineering at Stanford University, and a Silicon Valley lawyer. He is the recipient of awards from the Natural Resources Council of America, the Global Environmental Facility of the World Bank, the interfaith Center for Corporate Responsibility, and the Commonwealth Club. Hayes has served on dozens of governing boards, including those of Stanford University, the World Resources Institute, the Energy Foundation, and the Federation of American Scientists. As director of the Bullitt Foundation, he "intends to make the Pacific Northwest a global model for sustainable development."

ROY HEMMINGWAY was Oregon Governor Vic Atiyeh's appointee to the Northwest Power Planning Council and Governor John Kitzhaber's policy advisor for salmon and energy. He also served as chair of the Public Utility Commission of Oregon. He is a private consultant on energy matters.

THOMAS F. HORNBEIN, a mountaineer and physician, is professor emeritus of anesthesiology, physiology, and biophysics at the University of Washington School of Medicine. He lives in Estes Park, Colorado, where he first met mountains. In 1963, as a member of the first American expedition to climb Mount Everest, he and Willi Unsoeld reached the summit by way of the previously unclimbed West Ridge, then descended via the South Col route to complete the first traverse of a major Himalayan peak. He is the author of *Everest, the West Ridge*.

WILLIAM KITTREDGE grew up on his family's ranch in southeastern Oregon and worked there until he left to study at the Iowa Writers' Workshop. He then wrote and taught at the University of Montana, where he was Regents Professor of English and Creative Writing. Considered one of the most important voices on the American West, Kittredge held a Stegner Fellowship at Stanford and received two fellowships from the National Endowment for the Arts. He has published essays and articles in the *Atlantic Monthly, Harper's, Esquire, Time, Newsweek*, the *Washington Post*, and the *New York Times*. He has written two collections of short fiction, *The Van Gogh Fields* and *We Are Not In This Together*; two collections of essays, *Owning It All* and *Who Owns the West*; a memoir, *Hole in the Sky*; and a novel, *The Willow Field*. He is co-editor with Annick Smith of *The Last Best Place: A Montana Anthology*.

JANE LUBCHENCO is the under secretary of commerce for Oceans and Atmosphere and National Oceanic and Atmospheric Administration (NOAA). Before taking that position, she wrote "Lessons from the Land for Protection of the Sea," with Renee Davis-Born and Brooke Simler. The article was updated for this anthology by Dr. Kirsten Grorud-Colvert, a member of the Department of Zoology at Oregon State University. Grorud-Colvert is also the marine reserve science coordinator for the Partnership for Interdisciplinary Studies of Coastal Oceans and the Communication Partnership for Science and the Sea.

KATHLEEN DEAN MOORE is the author of several award-winning books, including *Riverwalking, Holdfast, The Pine Island Paradox*, and *Wild Comfort: the Solace of Nature*. She is distinguished professor of philosophy at Oregon State University, where she directs the Spring Creek Project for Ideas, Nature, and the Written Word. Her most recent book is *Moral Ground: Ethical Action for a Planet in Peril*.

LEE C. NEFF writes about plants and people in a two-year-old garden in Kingston, Washington. Her deadheading opportunities are rather modest, for she only has 17 clumps of daylilies. But her garden is growing.

JAMES OPIE has an enduring interest in indigenous weavings from nomadic tribes, an interest that matured throughout the 1970s when the pre-revolution atmospheres of Iran and Afghanistan permitted unrestricted travel to carpet-making centers. His first book, *Tribal Rugs of Southern Persia*, was followed by *Tribal Rugs* and numerous articles and lectures, many of which have been translated into Farsi.

DIARMUID F. O'SCANNLAIN is a federal appeals judge with the U.S. Court of Appeals for the Ninth Circuit. He served from 1969 to 1974 as deputy attorney general of Oregon, public utility commissioner of Oregon, and director of the Oregon Department of Environmental Quality. He retired from the Judge Advocate General's Corps of the U.S. Army Reserve in 1978 after 23 years of Reserve and National Guard service. His professional interests include judicial administration and legal education.

JAROLD RAMSEY grew up in Madras, Oregon, and taught at the University of Rochester in New York before moving back to the family ranch in 2000. He is the author of four volumes of poetry, many essays on Shakespeare and modern poetry, and several books on American Indian literature, including *Coyote Was Going There* and *Reading the Fire*. "An Impromptu on Owning Land" is from *New Era: Reflections on the Human and Natural History of Central Oregon*.

RICHARD RAPPORT is a clinical professor of neurological surgery at Harborview Medical Center in Seattle. He has written two books of nonfiction, *Physician: The Life of Paul Beeson* and *Nerve Endings: The Discovery of the Synapse*, and numerous essays, one noted in the Best American Essays series and another published in *The American Scholar*.

ERIC REDMAN, the president of Summit Power, works closely with the Clean Air Task Force and other environmental groups on climate matters and leads Summit's participation in carbon sequestration partnerships and development of coal gasification abroad. He is a frequent speaker and author on coal gasification, carbon management, and climate matters. Redman began his career as a legislative assistant to U.S. Senator Warren G. Magnuson. He is the author of *The Dance of Legislation*, a best-selling account of congressional enactment of the National Health Service Corps.

WILLIAM RUCKELSHAUS was the first administrator of the U.S. Environmental Protection Agency (EPA), acting director of the Federal Bureau of Investigation, deputy attorney general of the U.S. Department of Justice, and again administrator of the EPA. He also was senior vice president for law and corporate affairs for the Weyerhaeuser Company. He served on the National Oceanic and Atmospheric Administration Science Advisory Board in 2003 and a year later was appointed chair of the William D. Ruckelshaus Center, a collaborative problem-solving institution of the University of Washington and Washington State University. In 2005, Washington Governor Christine Gregoire appointed him as co-chair of the cleanup of Puget Sound.

ROBERT SACK is professor emeritus in the Department of Psychiatry at the Oregon Health and Science University in Portland. He is a specialist in sleep disorders medicine and has done research on circadian rhythms and melatonin. Sack is a contributor to *The New England Journal of Medicine.*

EDWARD W. SHEETS, an independent consultant who was the facilitator for the Klamath Basin and Snake River settlements, has worked on energy and environmental issues for 36 years. He was the executive director of the Northwest Power and Conservation Council, the director of the Washington State Energy Office, and special assistant to U.S. Senator Warren Magnuson. He has a master's degree from the University of Washington and a bachelor's degree from Brown University.

SCOT SIEGEL is the author of *Some Weather* and two poetry chapbooks, *Untitled Country* and *Skeleton Says.* He is on the board of Friends of William Stafford and edits the online poetry journal *Untitled Country Review.* Siegel lives in Lake Oswego, Oregon, with his wife and two daughters and works as an urban planning consultant to small towns and cities.

KIM STAFFORD is a poet, essayist, and short story writer who has written a dozen books, including *Having Everything Right: Essays of Place, The Muses Among Us: Eloquent Listening and Other Pleasures of the Writer's Craft,* and *Early Morning: Remembering My Father, William Stafford.* A shorter version of the essay in this anthology was given as a speech to the Oregon Historical Society. He is the founding director of the Northwest Writing Institute at Lewis & Clark College in Portland.

JOHN STRULOEFF's poems and stories have been published in many journals and magazines, including the *Atlantic Monthly*, the *Literary Review*, *Prairie Schooner*, and *ZYZZYVA*. He was a Stegner Fellow and National Endowment for the Arts Literature Fellow. He grew up on the north Oregon Coast and now lives with his wife and son in the foothills of the Santa Monica Mountains, where he directs the Creative Writing program at Pepperdine University.

ANN WARE is a poet from Bellingham, Washington. A native of Amity, Oregon, she spent her summers on the McKenzie River and has a deep knowledge of the flora, fauna, geology, and archeology of the Pacific Northwest.

CHARLES WILKINSON is a distinguished professor and the Moses Lasky Professor of Law at the University of Colorado School of Law. He has written fourteen books on law, public land law, and Indian law, including *The Eagle Bird, Crossing the Next Meridian, Messages from Frank's Landing, Blood Struggle: The Rise of Modern Indian Nations*, and *The People Are Dancing Again: The History of the Siletz Tribe of Western Oregon*. His awards for teaching, conservation work, and collaborations with tribes include the National Conservation Award from the National Wildlife Society and university awards from Colorado, Oregon, and Michigan.

ADDITIONAL RESOURCES

LAND USE PLANNING

Committee on the Oregon Planning Experience (COPE). "An Evaluation of Planning in Oregon, 1973-2001: A Report to the Oregon Chapter of the American Planning Assoc." November 2001. http://www.oregonapa.org/tools-planners.

Hunnicutt, David. "Oregon Land-Use Regulation and Ballot Measure 37: Newton's Third Law at Work." *Environmental Law* 36, no. 1 (2006): 26-52.

Sullivan, Edward, and Ronald Eber. "The Long and Winding Road: Farmland Protection in Oregon 1961-2009." *San Joaquin Agricultural Law Review* 18, no. 1 (2008-2009): 1-69.

Sullivan, Edward. 2006. "Year Zero: The Aftermath of Measure 37." *Environmental Law* 36 (2006): 131-63.

WATER IN THE WEST

American Friends Service Committee. *Uncommon Controversy: Fishing Rights of the Muckleshoot, Puyallup, and Nisqually Indians.* Edited by Mary B. Isely and William Hanson. Seattle: University of Washington Press, 1970.

Brown, Bruce. *Mountain in the Clouds: A Search for the Wild Salmon.* New York: Simon and Schuster, 1982.

Getches, David H. *Water Law in a Nutshell.* 3d ed. St. Paul, MN: West Publishing, 1997.

———. "Colorado River Governance: Sharing Federal Authority as an Incentive to Create a New Institution." *University of Colorado Law Review* 68 (Summer 1997): 573-658.

Leopold, Aldo. *A Sand County Almanac.* London: Oxford University Press, 1949.

Martin, Russell. *A Story that Stands Like a Dam: Glen Canyon and the Struggle for the Soul of the West.* New York: Henry Holt, 1989.

Natural Resources Law Center. *The Watershed Source Book: Watershed-Based Solutions to Natural Resource Problems.* Boulder: University of Colorado School of Law, Natural Resources Law Center, 1996.

Petersen, Keith C. *River of Life, Channel of Death: Fish and Dams on the Lower Snake.* Lewiston, ID: Confluence Press, 1995.

Postel, Sandra. *Last Oasis: Facing Water Scarcity.* New York: W.W. Norton, 1997.

Reisner, Marc. *Cadillac Desert: The American West and Its Disappearing Water.* New York: Viking Press, 1986.

Stegner, Wallace. *Beyond the Hundredth Meridian: John Wesley Powell and the Second Opening of the West.* Lincoln: University of Nebraska Press, 1954.

———. *The Sound of Mountain Water.* Garden City, NJ: Doubleday, 1969.

Tarlock, A. Dan, James N. Corbridge, and David H. Getches. *Water Resources Management: A Casebook in Law and Public Policy.* 4th ed. Westbury, NY: The Foundation Press, 1993.

Teale, Edwin Way. *The Wilderness World of John Muir.* Boston: Houghton Mifflin, 1954.

White, Richard. *"It's Your Misfortune and None of My Own": A New History of the American West.* Norman: University of Oklahoma Press, 1991.

Wilkinson, Charles. *Messages from Frank's Landing: A Story of Salmon, Treaties, and the Indian Way.* Seattle: University of Washington Press, 2000.

———. *Crossing the Next Meridian: Land, Water, and the Future of the West.* Washington, D.C.: Island Press, 1992.

———. *The Eagle Bird: Mapping a New West.* Rev. ed. Boulder, CO: Johnson Books, 1999.

Wilson, Edward O. *The Diversity of Life.* New York: W.W. Norton, 1992.

VOLCANOES AND SUPERQUAKES

Atwater, Brian. *The Orphan Tsunami of 1700: Japanese Clues to a Parent Earthquake in North America.* Seattle: University of Washington Press, 2005.

Clark, Ella. *Indian Legends of the Pacific Northwest.* Berkeley: University of California Press, 1966.

Harris, Stephen L. *Fire Mountains of the West: The Cascade and Mono Lake Volcanoes.* Missoula, MT: The Mountain Press, 2005.

Hildreth, Wes. *Quaternary Magmatism in the Cascades: Geologic Perspectives.* U.S. Geological Professional Paper 1744. Reston, VA: U.S. Geological Survey, 2007.

THE ENDANGERED SPECIES ACT

Baur, Donald C., and William Robert Irvin, eds. *Endangered Species Act: Law, Policy, and Perspectives.* Chicago, IL: American Bar Association, Section of Environment, Energy, and Resources, 2010.

Goble, Dale D., J. Michael Scott, and Frank W. Davis, eds. *The Endangered Species Act at Thirty* Vol. 1, *Renewing the Conservation Promise.* Washington, D.C.: Island Press, 2006.

U.S. Fish and Wildlife Service. "Endangered Species Glossary." Last modified, December 29, 2010. http://www.fws.gov/endangered/about/glossary.html.

————. *Endangered Species Program.* http://www.fws.gov/endangered.

NIGHT LIGHTS

Angier, Natalie. "Modern Life Suppresses an Ancient Body Rhythm." *New York Times*, March 14, 1995.

Brody, Jane E. "Getting a Grip on the Winter Blues," *New York Times*, December 5, 2006.

International Dark-Sky Association. *Light Pollution and Wildlife.* 2008. http://www.darksky.org/mc/page.do?sitePageId=90127&orgId=idsa.

THE POWER OF WIND, SUN, AND FALLING WATER

CleanEdge Reports. http://www.cleanedge.com.

McKinsey Company/McKinsey Global Institute. http://www.mckinsey.com/mgi.

Pew Center for Climate. http://www.pewclimate.org.

Rocky Mountain Institute: http://www.rmi.org.

Sightline Institute. http://sightline.org.

Worldwatch Institute. http://www.worldwatch.org.

LESSONS FROM THE LAND FOR PROTECTION IN THE SEA

National Center for Ecological Analysis and Synthesis. http://www.nceas.ucsb.edu

National Marine Sanctuary Program: http://www.sanctuaries.noaa.gov/.

National Park Service: http://www.nps.gov/.

Oregon Ocean Information: A Resource for Planning in the Territorial Sea, including updated status of Oregon's marine reserves process: http://www.oregonocean.info.

Oregon Ocean-Coastal Management Program. http://www.oregon.gov/LCD/OCMP.

Pacific Fishery Management Council. http://www.pcouncil.org.

Partnership for Interdisciplinary Studies of Coastal Oceans: http://www.piscoweb.org. including a brochure entitled *The Science of Marine Reserves*.

White House Interagency Ocean Policy Task Force. http://www.whitehouse.gov/administration/eop/ceq/initiatives/oceans/.

KLAMATH BASIN AGREEMENT

Ed Sheets Consulting. *Klamath Hydroelectric Settlement Agreement* and *Klamath Basin Agreements*. http://www.edsheets.com/Klamathdocs.html.